# MAN & HORSE

## THE LONG RIDE ACROSS AMERICA

## JOHN EGENES

DELTA VEE TRADE PAPERBACK
2017

www.facebook.com/johnandgizmo/

To Gizmo, who traveled the long trail with me.
And to Megan and Julia, who showed me a new one.

# CONTENTS

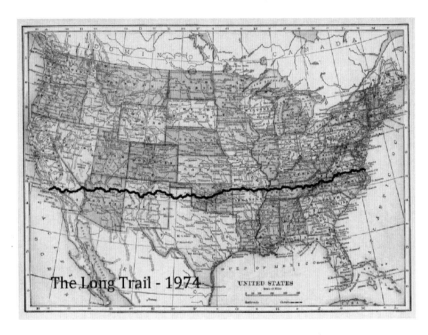

The Long Trail: April–November, 1974

# PROLOGUE: THE DUST FROM THE TRAIL

The young horse stands in the pale light of a gibbous moon, his hindquarters positioned so they block the cold northwest wind. Spring has remained cool and dry here in the high desert of the southwest, and the nightly winds have steadily robbed the place of its water. A heavy toll has been taken this year on the plants and animals who live here, and the horse can sense the corpse of one of his kind close by, though the man who travels with him is unaware of it.

The moon is bright, but not quite bright enough, and the man labors to read a beat-up paperback novel. He wishes the moon was full, and as it moves lower across the sky, the man finally gives up his struggle and stuffs the book into his saddlebags. He gets to his feet, walks over to the horse, and scratches the animal's ears, one by one. The horse enjoys this. The man says goodnight and retires to his sleeping bag, leaving the horse to gaze at the night sky.

Coyotes bark their high, shrill cries as the moon begins to set behind the mountains to the west. Finally, the horse turns into the wind and walks the short distance to where the man is sleeping. The horse allows his legs to buckle and slowly settles to the ground next to the man. He tucks his legs beneath him and closes his eyes to dream the dreams that horses dream.

# DAY ONE

The third of April, 1974, our first night on the trail. Gizmo and I are camped behind an old one-room schoolhouse, a dilapidated wood frame building with a severely pitched wood shingle roof that no longer keeps the rain out. A derelict bell tower clings to the roof's ridgeline at a slight tilt, fighting a losing battle with the elements. The building is of no use to us, except to conceal us from the passersby on the two lane highway we have followed out of Ventura, California this morning. The sky is clear, and there is a waxing half moon rising over the hills to the east as we settle in for the night.

We started from the Pacific Ocean this morning. We left very early so we could get a jump on the traffic. Gizmo and I waded in the ocean before setting off through town. After several blocks I decided against riding on the slippery pavement. I got off and led him all the way through Ventura, about 6 miles, then stepped back up on him and rode out of town along the empty road.

This morning I had a hundred dollars in my pocket. It was all the money I had to my name. I have no idea how I will make it last for seven months, but I have a blind faith that it will. We stopped at a roadside stand today, where I broke a twenty for a hamburger and bought a Snickers bar for Gizmo. And now, as we settle in for the night, I have $98.45 left, which is stuffed down into one of my saddlebags.

The trail ahead stretches out more than 4,000 miles in front of us, but in some ways the one I have already traveled to get here was longer. In a week I will turn twenty-four. This dream of riding a horse across the North American Continent started several years ago, back when I was sixteen and it has grown steadily since. Today I have begun to live it.

*LOGBOOK:*
*First night on the trail. Made it to an old one room schoolhouse that isn't used anymore. We're camped behind it, off the road and out of sight.*

# FOLLOW YOUR OWN DREAM

Yant ou ride your own trail, and I ride mine.

When it comes to following a dream sometimes you get lucky, but most times you make your own luck. I was certainly young and stupid when I dragged Gizmo out of an innocent adolescence and onto that long trail across the North American continent. I don't think of myself as a wise person, but I know I'm wiser today than I was back then. I think I'm a bit wiser than I was yesterday. I hope that tomorrow I'm wiser still.

They say that wisdom is a marriage of experience and compassion. Dreams are born of compassion and realized through experience. And I've always believed that a dream isn't worth much if it's easily attainable.

I had thought about making a long ride for quite some time—probably years, if I'm honest. I didn't think about the details, only the *idea* of a ride— or more generally, of being on a horse and riding to remote places. It was hardly an original idea, but I was very young, and I hadn't yet managed to accrue any significant amount of wisdom. The idea of being a lonesome cowboy was a bit banal and overused, but it appealed to my nonconformist tendencies. And besides, even if the *idea* of a ride was a common thing, the *doing of it* wasn't.

By the time I began to think of the ride as a real possibility, I had already spent thousands of hours hitchhiking and riding freight trains, so I was well schooled in the real-life experience of being alone for long periods of time in the not-so-romantic reality of life on the open road. I wasn't a believer in greener pastures, but I always loved seeing what was on the other side of the hill. Curiosity has driven me all my life.

While I was in high school, a single serendipitous event occurred that would change everything for me. I stumbled across an old book in the school library. I checked it out, read it cover to cover three or four times, and never returned it. I still have it today. I owe thousands in fines by now, but that book profoundly changed my ideas on what is possible, and it strengthened my resolve as a nonconformist (not that I needed more encouragement). The book, *Tschiffely's Ride*, was written in 1933 by Aimé Félix Tschiffely. He wrote an account of his travels on horseback from the tip of Argentina to New York City, a ride that covered ten thousand miles and took three years to complete, from 1925 to 1928.

Thirty-three years after he wrote it, I read this book, and I couldn't get enough of it. It would bore most people to death, but my first time through, I was completely won over by Tschiffely's odd writing style and his matter-of-fact descriptions of incredible and unbelievable adventures. I devoured the pages. The story took me away to other lands, other worlds. There was a small section of black and white photos—badly printed and out of focus, but captivating nonetheless. I spent hours looking at those pictures, trying to figure out what gear he had used, what kinds of fittings were on the saddle and packsaddle, and generally obsessing over the smallest details. Most of my questions went unanswered, but it didn't discourage me.

And so my dream started. I began to study maps. I mean, really looking at them, and I did this for several years. I scrutinized the route from Mexico to Canada through California, Oregon, and Washington. A new trail, called the Pacific Crest Trail, was dedicated in 1968, but hadn't been built yet. It was just about the time I began to think about the ride in earnest. The Pacific Crest Trail wasn't even a line on the map then. It was only an idea, but that idea—that there might be a *trail*, an actual route to follow—inspired me. I couldn't find any source of information about long-distance travel except for the odd book on hiking. I was on my own and would have to make it up as I went along.

I didn't think about the ride constantly. Other things were going on in my life, so the dream came and went often over the span of several years, into the early 1970s. During that time, I graduated from high school, did a stint in the Navy, and found myself involved in other activities. I played in bands (which I still do today) and bummed around by hitchhiking and riding freight trains (which I no longer do). But the ride never seemed to completely fade away, and I found myself looking at those maps every so often.

It started with gas station maps, the kind you used to get free at service stations. They had the oil company logo on the top, names like *Flying-A, Texaco, Richfield,* and *Whiting Bros.*, along with mileage charts that let you figure out how far it was from one place to another. I scoured state maps and soon found more detailed area maps in the atlases at the library. I copied the main roads with tracing paper and a pencil (no photocopiers back then). It was slow and tedious work, but it felt like I was *doing something*—working toward a goal—when I was copying those maps. It took hours and hours of painstaking drawing. Of course, the maps I copied weren't very accurate, but I didn't know that, nor did I care.

A map is a magical thing for a wanderer like me. More than any thing I can think of, maps drive imagination and fuel dreams. To this day, I would rather look at a map of a faraway place than at a photo or video. The invention of maps allowed us to reinvent humanity's place in the universe. They profoundly changed the way we think about the world around us. Think about a world without maps, a world in which you knew where a place was and knew how to get there but only by the landmarks along the way and their relationships to each other:

> *To get to that village, you ride through the*
> *pass in the mountains, go past a waterfall on your*
> *right, and then over a shallow spot in the river.*
> *You pass beneath a towering mountain peak,*
> *follow the river valley onto a wide plain where there*
> *are two small hills in the distance. The village sits*
> *between those hills. The journey takes two days.*

Before the invention of maps, you might imagine your journey as if you were on the ground. You would need to visualize yourself moving past the various landmarks along the way. You measured the journey in *time*, and not in *distance*. When maps came along, we could visualize that journey with a god's eye point of view. We could see the entire journey, as if from outer space, and place ourselves within it, both in location and in scale. The map allowed us to measure distances in length instead of time.

I pored over maps, all sorts of maps: topographic maps, road maps, population maps, hand drawn maps, weather maps. I found them in various atlases and encyclopedias, in books about the old west, and in the local natural history museum. They helped me to form pictures in my head.

I calculated distances and timeframes. I had considered riding from Mexico to Canada but found that it wasn't far enough. I wanted to make it hard on myself. I discarded the north-south idea and studied the route from ocean to ocean across the North American continent. The more I considered it, the clearer it became.

I learned that the United States Geological Survey had topographic maps of the country for sale. I headed downtown to the Federal Building in the old city center of Los Angeles, where the USGS offices were located. They didn't sell maps there, but I could order a master map that listed all the topographic maps in the continental United States. There were several scales to choose from, and after looking at various examples there, I settled upon 1:250,000, which meant that one inch on the map equaled a little less than four miles. The individual maps were about eighteen inches tall and thirty inches wide, so a little over seventy miles tall and about 120 miles wide. It was the width I was concerned about, since that was my direction of travel. I ordered the master map.

It was huge. It came in two sections, split down center of America. I glued the two sections together and pinned it to the wall. It was six feet tall, nearly ten feet wide, and covered an entire wall of the tiny one-room shack I was living in. The continental United States were overlaid with a grid made of approximately six hundred rectangles. Each one comprised a 1:250,000 scale map with a name in the center.

The minute I pinned that map to my wall, the ride became real. I sat and stared at it hour after hour. Once I figured out my route, I would order the maps that it passed through. I plotted routes in my head, measured distances with a ruler, and generally obsessed over it for months. I used push pins with string to rough out sections of the ride as I created my route. I made marks on the map at places I wanted to visit. Most of them were simply too hard to get to on horseback, so I scratched them off my list. I kept to a southerly route, steering clear of the higher elevations in the Rocky Mountains in Colorado, because I knew it would be too hard on my horse. I needed to think of the horse before I thought of myself. It was not only common sense; it was the right thing to do.

A line evolved on the big map. It was made up of many shorter ones that represented segments of the ride. These were drawn with different colored pens and pencils at various times and eventually connected to form the entire route. Finally, I used a black marker to trace over them and created a single, fluid conduit that started at Ventura, California and passed through Nevada, Arizona, New Mexico, Texas, Oklahoma, Arkansas, Missouri, Tennessee, and North Carolina to finish at Virginia Beach, Virginia. I had to order thirty-two maps in all. As the crow flies, they represented a little over 3,800 miles, west to east. But since a horse and rider hardly travel the same path as a crow, we would cover almost 4,400 miles by the end of the ride.

During that time, I saw a series of magazine articles in *Horse & Rider* by a man named Jefferson Spivey, who, in 1968, had ridden a horse across America. I studied his articles, picking up every detail I could. I wasn't discouraged that someone had beaten me to it. In fact, I felt just the opposite—I was thrilled it could be done. It was a relief to know I wasn't a complete idiot for thinking I could do it. If nothing else, his articles cemented my belief (however blind and naïve it might have been) that I could make a ride like that. I wrote to Spivey and, after pestering him with several cards and letters, finally got a letter of encouragement from him. We have since become good friends, and many years later, when I had become a saddlemaker in New Mexico, I built a series of cross-country saddles for Jeff that he had designed. Life flows in funny circles.

A lot of water flowed under the bridge between the time I figured out my route and the day Gizmo and I took our first steps eastward. The day I found a beat up World War II German cavalry saddle in a tack shop for forty-five dollars and brought it home, I knew I was going to go through with the ride. I had experience traveling, and experience with horses. When that experience was married to the dream, I was ready to go. Or so I thought. I found out that even years of prior experience didn't equip me for a journey like that. Gizmo and I were still babes in the woods and would have to figure it out as we went. And we did.

# EARLY DAYS

**M**y old man split when I was seven. Just up and left his 34 year old wife and four kids, got himself a new young wife, and started another family somewhere else. I didn't see him again for almost 18 years, and then only very briefly. We exchanged a few words, a few niceties, and then he left and I never saw him again. He lived into his eighties, but I never again had contact with him. And the funny thing is, it didn't take long for his absence to feel normal. I got used to the loss, or so I thought. My grandmother used to say that you can get used to anything. You can get used to hanging if you hang long enough.

My old man's departure deflated my family's financial resources just like a West Texas tornado sucks all the furniture out of a house. It didn't take long for the bank to foreclose on the modest tract home we lived in. Most of our belongings went with the house. We hadn't been rich, just nineteen fifties middle class comfortable, but that comfort came to a screeching halt.

Folks tell you that money can't really buy happiness, so you figure you'll be fine. Just keep a positive attitude. What you're basically saying is, you don't need a new car or fancy clothes or a big screen TV. You can be happy doing without. That's all well and good, but it just naturally assumes that you still have enough money to pay the rent and the electric bill, and you have enough left over to buy some food for the kids. It assumes that money for day to day needs is always there. But what does a seven year old kid know about all that? He thinks somehow it's his fault that his father is no longer around. He spends a lot of time racking his brain about what he could do to make his old man come home again. He spends several years, in fact, until he finally realizes it's a futile waste of time.

Money can't buy happiness. Try to believe that the next time you're evicted for not being able to pay the rent, or the next time they shut off your phone or electricity. Try convincing yourself that having the money for medication or to fix your kid's teeth isn't going to make you any happier. The truth is, money can buy quite a bit of happiness, depending upon which side of the poverty line you're sitting on. When our financial situation imploded, my mother went from having to decide between taking a vacation or buying a new washing machine, to choosing whether she should pay the rent or the phone bill.

I wasn't a victim, and I never saw myself as one. Still, being ripped out of a typical middle class family—a comfortable life where the biggest worry was whether I'd make the Little League team—well, one day it's there and the next it's gone. One day you're living on Easy Street, with a working father and a stay at home mother. The next you're on the hard road. One day your mother is wearing an apron and having coffee with the other wives on the block. The next she's working fourteen hours a day at an unskilled job, bringing home fifty-six bucks a week to feed four kids. One day you're a seven year old boy, playing ball in the street, and the next you're living in that street. We got evicted from enough places that no place ever felt like home, and our string of temporary domiciles made the street more familiar to me than any of them were.

My mother was ill equipped to deal with the struggles of supporting four kids on her own. The minimum wage was a buck an hour back then. It goes without saying that her employers didn't pay her that much. She was a lone woman, a divorced mother of four. Today she'd be on welfare, and we'd comment about her lack of marketable job skills. But back then welfare was not an option, and it often came down to either paying the rent or eating—take your choice—and the rent always lost out. Toast for breakfast, peanut butter sandwiches (no jam) for lunch, pancakes for dinner. I learned to drink coffee by the time I was eight and I've never stopped.

There were times when I saw my mother frantic with fear, times when we were about to be put out of our home because she was behind on the rent again. I can still see her looking through the phone book, trying to locate my old man. I can still feel the desperation, cowered in my bedroom as I listened to her in the other room, pleading over that old wall phone with him on those rare times when she did find him, trying to get him to send at least one week of the overdue child support that he would ultimately never pay. And I remember that back then it was $37.50 for four kids. I did the math and figured I was worth less than ten bucks. I had no idea what normal families lived on, or what normal kids were worth.

It seems amazing now that I didn't think of myself as poor. My brother and sisters and I didn't view ourselves that way. Mostly, we just buried the idea and didn't talk about it. Deep down, though, I knew that my life was a world apart and vastly different from the lives of my middle class classmates. They had access to things that I didn't have and probably never would. They had two parents. They had real homes and nice cars and good clothes. The idea that their basic necessities—food, housing, utilities, school supplies—might someday go unpaid for lack of money would have been unthinkable to them. It wasn't even a consideration, and would have never entered their minds. It would simply never have occurred to them.

I saw their lives as carefree. I couldn't have put words to how I felt about that because I viewed my world in black and white. Things that cost money were out of reach. It's interesting, the way poor folks are shown on television. Poor families in sitcoms live in decent looking homes and never seem to have their electricity shut off. They stay in the same house for years and always seem to be happy. They make jokes about their finances, but they never seem to run out of food or gasoline for their car. They're able to laugh at their situation.

For me, it was the little things. My friends could borrow their parents' car and ten bucks, so they could take a girl on a date. If their clothes got a little ragged or out of style, no worries. They could buy new ones. If they needed a few bucks for gas to get to work, to a job they didn't really need, no problem. These things profoundly shaped my formative years. They were the stuff that middle class America was made of back then, and I was forced to make alternative choices, choices that shaped the things that would become important to me; choices that became the roads I would ultimately follow. You wouldn't think 10 bucks could make much of a difference. Money can't buy happiness, but it allows you to be somewhat comfortable while searching for that happiness.

I certainly wasn't forlorn. I never felt sorry for myself. I saw our situation as just the way the world was. It was the hand I was dealt, and there was no choice but to play it. Sometimes it was frustrating, and sometimes I regretted it, but overall, I was reasonably happy, even without the security of a middle class home.

There were times when I thought I should be mad at something or someone, that I ought to blame my father or my mother, or God or Mother Nature, or whatever caused my family's prosperity to evaporate. I figured I should be angry but the truth is, I never was. I never carried a grudge or felt resentment toward my old man, or at our reversal of fortune. Maybe I was afraid of becoming bitter, scared of having that ruinous event become the definition of my life from then on. Or maybe it was because it was all so overwhelming, so preposterous and unbelievable, that the reality of it seemed as though it was happening to someone else, and by the time the full impact had settled I was still young enough to accept my lot. I didn't learn to resent my old man until much later, until I had children of my own.

Looking back, I realize now that my mother was a saint. She was still young and pretty when she was thrust into her role as a single mother. I was too young to understand that she gave up any hope of future romance by working long hours and seeing to the raising of her kids. Once in a while she would go out with someone, but as soon as they got a look at her home life and four kids, they were gone. She never said anything, so I didn't think about it at the time. When I was very young I didn't have any idea what went on in her personal life, and frankly, I was much too self absorbed and self protective to give it much thought. But it's true, I reckon she did give up at some point, though she never let on how lonely she must have felt at times. And being the introvert I was, I certainly wasn't about to talk to her about it, even as I got older.

It didn't help matters much that I was hitchhiking all over the place. I can't help but wonder what my mother must have felt when her teenage son left for days or weeks at a time without so much as a phone call or letter. I'd phone her every once in awhile to let her know I was okay, but those calls were few and far between. When I was seventeen I called from a jail in Louisiana where I was spending six days for vagrancy. In those days there were no parenting helplines to call, no government guidebooks handed out to single mothers, and my mother was simply doing the best she could to cope. Kids back then had a lot more freedom to do stupid things, without their parents being showered with the righteous indignation of others. In those days child abuse was when you hit your child—not spanking them, but hitting them hard enough to break something—and child neglect meant leaving your child without food until they were starving, or leaving them at the bus station and never coming back. Times are so much better now. We know what to look for in a broken kid.

It's easy to look back in horror at how callous things were then. My mother was anything but callous. I reckon I'm glad she wasn't governed by today's rules. She absolutely adored her children, and she was doing the best she could—a helluva lot more, I would later learn, than many mothers of friends who I thought were part of "normal" families. I'm grateful I was allowed those wonderful times of freedom and could squeeze between the cracks in so many ways. The world was a far different place back then, and I can't help but think that if I were faced with today's rules while growing up, it would have put an early end to me.

I came of age in a time before people talked about such things, before poverty and race and single motherhood were discussed much, except in derogatory terms. There was no help available for women like my mother, or for families like mine, who had fallen through the cracks and ended up on hard times. The only way open to us was to suck it up and do the best we could, to move forward and pretend that everything was fine. And so that's what we did. And eventually it worked in its own fashion, and we were slowly able to dig ourselves out.

When your formative years are spent with this skewed view of the world you see yourself living in a space apart from everyone else. When you grow up not realizing there can be hope for something better, and when you can't imagine living what most people think of as a normal life, you end up bitter and disillusioned, or you do the best you can and try to remain positive. My family leaned toward the latter and it rubbed off on me. I'm a glass-half-full kind of person, taking things as they come and not trying to figure out why. Not exactly a Pollyanna, but not resentful, either.

I was the third of four children and the first one to graduate from high school. No one in my family had ever gone to university, so it was never a real consideration. I came from working class roots where there was no pressure to go to college. And though I now hold a Doctorate degree, I never considered myself a candidate for higher education back then. Instead, I saw myself as something my classmates could never be. While I felt blocked from many of the activities they took part in, there were still a lot of things that were open to me, things that they would never explore. Because while I was limited by what I thought was available to me, so were they.

I was stuck on the road less traveled, and I convinced myself that it was the best path to take, even though it hasn't always proved to be true. In traveling this road, I lost myself inside my own head much of the time. I read books, wrote stories, and started writing songs. I learned to hitchhike, learned to ride freight trains, and learned to travel the country with only myself for company. I didn't *have* a lot, but I figured I could *know* a lot. I could learn things, and no one could ever take them away from me. And I knew they wouldn't abandon me.

# THE START DOWN THE TRAIL

A long time ago, a fellow named Lao Tsu said, "The longest journey begins with a single step." I know what he means, but I'm not sure I agree with him. I don't think the journey truly begins until you're well into it, until you start to feel the miles and the hours, until all the days and weeks and months start to bear down on you. After your feet have swelled and blistered, and swelled and blistered again. When you're sick and tired of it all and wonder why you started in the first place, and all you want to do is quit and go home, but you suck it up and keep going. And those miles and hours, days and weeks and months begin to build you up again, without your even knowing it, and you get a second wind and you fall into the discipline of the road you're traveling. I reckon that's when the real journey begins.

For me, the journey began somewhat early on, out in the Mojave Desert, when we'd been on the trail a few weeks. Maybe it's because things got tough in a hurry. Even though you start out from the California coast with populated areas to travel through, most of the southern part of the state sits smack dab in the middle of a great big desert. But you don't notice it because of all the roads and houses and street lights and water pipes and such. And once you get to the edge of the city, where the paved road turns to dirt and the wires that power the lights come to an end, you find yourself thrown into desert tortoise country, winding your way through the small hills and gullies filled with cactus and Joshua trees, sagebrush and wildflowers, and more kinds of critters than you'd ever imagined could live out there.

And no water. Or at least, water being so scarce that you have to rely on Geological Survey maps that have names like "Needles" or "Kingman" or "Williams" that say, "scale = 1:250,000, contours at 200 feet, produced by the US Army, 1957." A map like that shows all sorts of important things that become critical if you want to stay alive. Things like water wells, old mineshafts, abandoned shacks, and so on. Of course, being almost two decades out of date, it lacks such things as major highways and small paved roads, military installations, and entire settlements that were built since the late 1950s. But even so, those USGS maps were invaluable, and they saved our lives more than once. It wasn't until twenty-five years later that they invented all these gadgets we have so that we always know where we are. The GPS and all that fancy tech gear was barely a dream back in 1974.

It was left to me to use dead reckoning. To dead reckon your way along, you use landmarks and milestones you pass to figure out those ahead. And you use your line of sight to work out where you are by looking at what's around you. It's simple enough, and I've used it all my life, even after all the satellite gadgetry came along.

When you're riding in a boxcar on a freight train across the country, there are no road signs to tell you where you are, so you have to figure it out by looking at what's rolling by. You can dead reckon your way around a city by looking at the tallest buildings or at hills and mountains in the distance. Same goes for hitchhiking, and for riding a horse across the continent. I'd see a hill or small peak in the distance and try to compare it with what I saw on my map. If I looked in another direction and saw something else, I'd try to find that on my map as well. If I could locate two landmarks, I could tell where I was. It sounds easy, but the desert has ways of fooling you when you're looking at a map. Those hills and valleys and peaks all start to look the same. I'd often think we were in one place when we were in another. If I think about it now, that part hasn't changed all that much over the years. It's become a metaphor for my life.

On April 3, 1974 Gizmo and I left the Pacific Ocean at Ventura. We had spent the previous night in a horse stall at the county fairgrounds there, where the ride almost came to a premature end when I barely escaped being squashed as my young horse tried to lie down on top of me to sleep. It was a portent of things to come because he often did this at night, throughout the entire ride. There were lots of news media folks there the day before, with all manner of commotion and goings-on, but that morning dawned clear and still, and we set off early before anyone was up and around. I chose to leave in the middle of the week, on a Wednesday, so I wouldn't be bothered by weekend tourists for the first couple days.

It took a couple weeks to become fully embedded in the desert, away from city lights and traffic, to a place where the natural sounds of wind, plants, and critters were the only contributors to the soundscape. By the time we reached the isolated areas of the desert, Gizmo and I were sleeping beneath a moonless sky that revealed a blanket of stars extending all the way to the horizon. I could look straight out and see stars. To keep us company, bands of coyotes would come so close to camp that it felt as though I could reach out and pet them. They sang us to sleep with their high choruses, and the young pups hit high notes that would make an opera singer jealous.

Gizmo got away from me one day. We were still on the outer edges of the inhabited desert, but it was desert nonetheless, and I was constantly on the lookout for water. We hadn't managed to find any the night before, so I had to make a dry camp and forgo dinner because I couldn't cook the dried food I carried. We broke camp very early and started down the trail toward a homesteader's shack that was marked on my map. I was relieved when it came into sight over the hill, and we rode straight up to it.

The shack was in reasonably good shape, as far as desert shacks go, with a serviceable roof, windows, and doors, a power line connecting it to the grid, and a water tank on a small tower out back. As we approached, I called out (as is the custom in remote places), but no one answered. There was no vehicle there, and nothing to indicate the place was occupied. I stepped off Gizmo and led him to a faucet near the front door. I knocked on the door and called out again, with no results, then bent to turn the faucet on. I allowed Gizmo to drink his fill before I filled my canteen.

The shack's front door burst open, the doorway suddenly filled by a large bearded man who came out shouting and waving his hands like a lunatic, hollering for me to stop. Before I had a chance to collect myself, he came charging at Gizmo, who was so shocked and frightened that he pulled back and dragged me along with him. As my horse raced backward away from the man, I was pulled off my feet and fell. The man kept shouting and waving his arms, until Gizmo finally broke free, turned, and took off. In a few seconds, he was over the mounds of sand and out of sight, and I sat there in the dirt, stunned. I got to my feet, thought about pulling my gun then thought better of it and simply glared at the man. I turned to follow my horse and started walking.

When your horse gets away from you, you're obviously left afoot. It's interesting to watch people in this situation, after they get bucked off or when their horse pulls back at the hitching rail and breaks his lead rope. Many people will run after the horse, shouting, "Whoa, WHOA!" or some such. Caught in the frenzy and chaos of losing their mount, they're afraid of losing control of the situation, and so they try desperately to maintain it. Problem is, they've already lost it. It's one thing to be on top of a horse that is bucking and trying to unload you. With a little skill or luck you might succeed in regaining control. But once the horse breaks free and runs off, your influence suddenly diminishes to pretty much zero. He's gone, and he can run a whole lot faster than you can. Shouting "Whoa!" rarely has any effect.

And so it was that I began what turned out to be a thirty-mile journey—westbound across the desert, far to the northeast of Victorville, in what was then a sparsely populated area of the Mojave. Gizmo was smart enough to find a powerline road and follow it. Luckily for me there was no wind or rain that day, and I could follow his tracks. And through luck and a bit of good fortune, I didn't have to walk the entire thirty miles. As fate would have it, late in the day after I had walked over twelve miles, some powerline workers drove up in a pickup truck and gave me a ride to the nearest settlement, a switching station about ten miles farther up the road. I telephoned the local police, who had possession of my wandering horse. They had found him saddled and riderless, and they were glad to hear from me. I hitched a ride several more miles to where they had him tied to a fence post.

When I jumped out of the truck, my prodigal son whinnied loudly and was glad to see me. I felt weary from the day's travel, beat up and sunburnt, with blisters on both feet, and stiff and sore from the miles I'd covered. Gizmo didn't seem the least bit tired from his escapade, and he acted somewhat proud of himself. I told him at camp that night that we'd have to cover those thirty miles again, since he had headed west instead of east. Though I wasn't sure if he had understood me, from then on he always seemed to want to head eastward. I'm pretty sure that for the rest of the ride, at night he even *grazed* east.

# THE MOJAVE

T he trail across America takes us through the deserts in the American Southwest. I haven't given much thought to the fact that, because we are traveling west to east and crossing great deserts first, we will become hardened to the trail, rough and feral, and adopt the attitude "it's us against the world." It's a perspective that puts our own survival first and foremost. This point of view will become somewhat distorted and obsessive within a very short time, and although I don't seem to notice it, others do.

The fact that we are crossing the open country of the desert first, and will eventually get to the more settled and civilized parts later, is important. For many years afterward I will think about what might have happened had we started from the east coast and ridden in the other direction. The eastern part of America is fenced and tame. There is no open country, no place to spend days and weeks by yourself.

If Gizmo and I had started on the east coast I might have remained a bit more sane and normal. We would have started out spending our nights with people in their homes, and not in cemeteries and abandoned buildings as we did when we finally reached the east. Had the ride begun on the east coast we would have conditioned ourselves to a different set of circumstances and environments. We would have developed a far different style on our journey down the trail. Our trail habits would have been altered, and both Gizmo and I would have emerged as different beings if things had happened the other way around.

In 1974 we are able to take shelter in some of the primitive shacks built by homesteaders in the 1940s and '50s. Those shacks would be gone within two decades. They would eventually give way to the pressures created by the coming roads, bulldozed and paved, that would connect them to nearby highways and to the civilization beyond. They would all be remodeled or replaced by modern dwellings, and used by weekenders from the city, repurposed as vacation hideaways to serve as holiday retreats. Eventually, the city itself would expand to meet the desert, and the homes would become full-time residences.

As we travel through this wild country Gizmo and I listen to the stories shared by the original homesteaders who we meet out here. In two more decades these people will have disappeared and the area will look nothing like the way my horse and I see it now. Gravel will replace dirt, and pavement will eventually replace the gravel. The hearty homesteaders will abandon and sell off their rough lives as they are forced to move away, to be absorbed into much easier, more modern lifestyles, replaced by city folk.

> *LOGBOOK:*
> *Came upon an odd man, a hermit out here in the desert, miles from anyone. Said his name is Wally. He lives in a shack with a huge pack of dogs. He says there are 66 of them. There are horses and goats and chickens and pigs running all over the place. He has the only water for miles, so I guess that's what keeps them there. Didn't want to spend the night there so we rode on. A couple of the horses wanted to follow us and I tried to shoo them away. I finally had to fire a shot over their heads to scare them off.*

Now, as we ride through it, the Mojave is still a very remote and uncultivated place. People in Southern California—whether they are transplants or natives—turn naturally toward the west to face the Pacific Ocean. They are seduced by Los Angeles and Orange County, Ventura and Santa Barbara. They flock to Hollywood and the beaches of Santa Monica, to Disneyland and the Hollywood Bowl, to the Sunset Strip and Universal Studios. They come to find homes in the great housing projects that spread like prairie fires across the southland, from the central coast all the way down to San Diego. The Mojave Desert is not a consideration if you are looking to live and play in Southern California in 1974.

To most people, the desert is empty. As they drive through it on the highway they see nothing out here. A few diehards venture out to see the explosion of wildflowers that occurs early in the spring, but it is the tall, green, wooded mountains that people think of when someone mentions the word *wilderness.* The Mojave is a place you are forced to travel *through,* to get to someplace else. It is not a destination in 1974, just an inconvenience. But this outlook will undergo a drastic change in the next twenty years, and the desert will eventually become not only tolerable, but alluring to those living within the confines of the city.

I check my topographic map, printed by the United States Geological

Survey in 1957. It has a scale of 1:250,000. Gizmo will carry me across this map in about a week, depending on how many days of rest we take. The desert nights put on a spectacular display of celestial objects. April brings with it the constellation Leo, with the red star Regulus at his heart. Leo is joined by the Gemini Twins, Castor and Pollux, and Sirius, the brightest star in the heavens. Orion still makes his appearance in the night sky, and the Pleiades looks like a tiny dipper overhead.

The Mojave is still cool at night in mid-April, and I enjoy making large campfires sometimes. I gather dead cholla cactus, greasewood, and creosote bush to make the fire and pile the wood on in great heaps so I can watch the flames rise higher than my head. I know that a small fire is best when camping, that it's harder to spot from a distance, but I indulge myself once in a while. I know that I won't be able to light a big fire once Gizmo and I get beyond the high deserts of Arizona and into New Mexico.

Coyotes come out after the darkness settles. They move in very near to us and sometimes I catch glimpses of their eyes in the firelight as it dances out upon the surrounding terrain. When the moon has waxed I can make out their silhouettes against the horizon. They set up a grand commotion most nights, with many joining in the chorus. I can pick out the voices of the youngsters, higher pitched and filled with youthful exuberance. Gizmo isn't bothered by the coyotes, and neither am I. I keep my old single action Colt loaded at night, though I neither want nor expect to use it. I'm not worried about the predators that surround us. They mind their own business. We mind ours. Live and let live—that's our dictum.

> *LOGBOOK:*
> *I don't understand how you can sit in front of a campfire with the wind at your back and the smoke still blows in your face*

The days pass in cycles that become rhythmic. The search for water is constant, and I scrutinize each water well I see on the map for details. I learn to spot likely signs of water from far away. Cottonwood trees growing in bunched stands at the base of a draw. Green plants that are conspicuous against the browns and tans of the desert foliage. Hard rock breaking the surface of a small gully. The shaded bend of a dry streambed. These indicate that water lies near the surface, and I am learning how to identify them. Water becomes the primary concern while crossing the deadly Mojave. Later, keeping track of the miles traveled each day will be of great importance, but here in the desert, it is water that occupies my thoughts.

When the wind dies, it leaves an austere silence behind. Sometimes I hear ringing in my head when I sit and read, when nothing is moving. Seemingly quiet, the desert is filled with small sounds that require concentration to hear them. I am intrigued by the abundance of subtle sounds, and I know that their presence accompanies the invisible wildlife I have learned to spot all around us. Far from being empty of animal life, the desert is filled with it. It is delicate and elusive, as are the sounds I am learning to hear. The soundscape contains as much information and life as does the desert itself.

*LOGBOOK:*
*Got up before the sun. Gizmo is teething and he's been chewing up all my rope and leather. Has a loose incisor that I'll try to take out. The views as we walk along are beautiful. I stop sometimes just to listen to the desert. It feels like it's talking to us.*

It is an exceptional year for wildflowers, and both of us profit from them. Gizmo, from the nourishment they give him when he dips his head down to bite off a bunch, never missing a stride as he does. And me, from the sense of amazement I get when looking out over a vast landscape of them, their colors redefining what the desert has meant to me, lending a sense of balance to a world I had previously thought to be drab and monotonous. I realize that very few people in the world are lucky enough to see the sights we are seeing, and I am grateful for that. I know I'll never forget it.

We have our fair share of difficulties in passing through the Mojave Desert. The lay of the land makes it difficult to reconcile the map with the topology around us, and I get lost. We run out of water and face death itself, but it is staved off by blind good luck when we manage to find a working windmill on our third day without water. We follow underground riverbeds, plodding through deep sand, and the going is slow and exhausting for my horse. Sometimes we follow high tension power lines that make paths straight across the barren land, though most do not go in our direction. Scorpions found in clothing and sleeping equipment become somewhat routine, and I check for them every morning and evening. I accidentally brush against a cholla cactus, and I have to use pliers to pull the needles out of my leg. It is very painful and becomes swollen and later infected. I live with it for almost a month before it finally subsides. Both of us are steadily losing weight, something we cannot afford if we are to face the high deserts of Arizona and New Mexico. I am bitten by a black widow spider the day before we cross the Colorado River, as the Mojave Desert sends us a parting farewell. We have been transformed.

# THE VIEW FROM BETWEEN THE EARS

When you ride a horse, you spend a lot of time looking at the back of his head. You view the trail ahead through the poll, the crown of his head, the part that sits between his ears. You notice how those ears move independently, each one turning toward a sound of interest, warning him of danger, announcing another horse's arrival, or signaling a human with a bucket of grain. Those ears can rotate almost 180 degrees—a half circle—and when riding out in wide-open spaces like the desert, he can point one of them forward and the other to the rear at the same time. He's also hearing a lot more than you are because his ears are bigger and shaped better for capturing sound. Plus, he can hear frequencies that are way beyond what you can hear, such as the rustling of a mouse in the bushes or a bat flying around at night.

Sometimes those ears are both pointed back in your direction. That means either he's paying attention to you or there's something behind you that you should be paying attention to. If the ears are pointed backward but lying flat against his head, he's either angry or, more likely, resentful. If you're riding a horse who has his ears pinned back in anger, either a direct threat is approaching or you're doing something wrong. Most likely, it's you who is causing it.

Anyone who has ridden horses knows what I'm saying when I talk about seeing the trail ahead through the horse's ears. It's just a natural thing. A rider in the show ring judges how she'll make the next jump by measuring the distance between her and those ears and then the distance from the ears to the jump. It's all done in a split second, and the rider doesn't even know she's doing it. It's a way of putting things into perspective. I got so used to seeing the world from his back that Gizmo's ears are still imprinted upon images I see today.

As the days and weeks passed, he became more and more trail-hardened and used to all the new sights and sounds he was exposed to. This was normal, and I had expected it. He was becoming trail broke, as any good four-year-old would in those circumstances. And while he eventually quit spooking at things, he still maintained his aural vigilance, and his ears were continually seeking out and identifying the elements of the soundscapes we traveled through. I learned not to focus so much on his body language or on his eyes, but to concentrate mostly on his ears. They were the early warning alarms that counted.

The perspective seen from atop an equine is a unique one. The horse's ears, like the windshield of the car you're driving, remain at a fixed distance from you as you travel along. Much like the windshield, you tend to look past the ears without seeing them, but they provide a measure of perception about what's in front of you. How big, how far away. As Gizmo's ears spun around, back and forth, they taught me to shut up and listen—to keep an ear out—for that which normally would have gone unheard and unnoticed.

Any good hand with horses will tell you that you need only get the horse's head to go somewhere and the rest of him will follow. This is true, and it's worth remembering, especially when you're trying to get the horse into a trailer. It's such a simple concept that it seems it should be a simple matter to get a horse to go just about anywhere. But it's not so. Those ears are too big. They get in the way. They hear ghosts and goblins, dragons and monsters, and they tell the head to turn the other way and engage the body, and the head wants the body to run like hell. Where the head turns, the body follows. And where the body goes, you and your lead rope go too—until you let go. You don't ever want to wrap that lead rope around your hand.

I think I finally learned to hear out there in the deserts of the southwest. I first learned to listen—mostly by watching Gizmo's ears and imitating him—and then I learned to hear. Since I couldn't twist my ears as cleverly as he could, I cupped my hands behind them to make them bigger, and I turned my head in the direction his were pointing. I stayed very still and often could hear the kinds of small sounds that even my breathing would have masked. I didn't just pay attention to things he was intent upon. I sat still in camp for long periods of time, playing this listening game with him, making it a sort of competition (which he always won, of course), and setting a goal for myself that I would try to hear *something* that was inaudible. I got better and better at it as the days and miles passed behind us.

The fact is, the desert was full of things that made sounds, and I saw it as my job to hear them, recognize them, and arrange them into what they meant at the time. The important thing was that I could hear them at all. The *most* important thing was that I was able to suspend my actions, and those of the world around me, for the short time it took to actually *hear* those sounds.

Gizmo was a constant presence in my life then, as I was in his. The view between his ears was the way forward. To look back, I had to twist myself around in the saddle so I could see the way we had come. It was far more difficult to view the past than it was to see the future.

# BY ROAD OR BY RAIL

I doubt there is anything more pitiful than a pre-teen boy. I struggled through my adolescence, but I didn't have it as bad as my brother, who was ten at the time our father left. He was suddenly the man of the family, a terrible burden for a boy that age. A huge pile of responsibility landed squarely on his shoulders, and he tried his best to bear that burden without tipping over. I managed, in my own introverted way, to escape a lot of it. I wasn't required to be the man of the family, but I didn't have one to look up to, either. No father, no mentor. I looked up to my brother. I always have. But he was three years older than me (almost half my entire life back then), and I didn't fit into his circle of friends, who were so much older and more worldly than I was. Besides, he was hardly in a position to become my mentor because he didn't have one, either. So, being left to my own resources to learn how my life was supposed to work and what I was meant to be doing with it, I never really did figure it out.

I crawled into myself and became a classic introvert. Jokes and smiles on the outside, but playing my personal cards pretty close to the vest. A psychiatrist would say I had abandonment issues that caused me to mistrust everyone and to rely only upon myself, and that shrink would be right. I viewed my problems as my own and no one else's. I hated asking for help. I didn't want to depend upon anyone else, so I spent the rest of my boyhood stumbling around, making mistake after mistake, wall-eyed and clueless. Things that other kids learned and took for granted, I hadn't a clue about. I wandered through life in the dark, blinded like a deer in the headlights. It was profoundly embarrassing to be a kid without a dad in those days, and I never talked about it or confided in anyone. You just didn't do that back then, and truth be told, for the most part, I haven't since.

Eventually, I learned how to play music, and I learned about horses, and I read science fiction and philosophy and started bumming around. Like every adolescent boy in America back then I fell instantly in love with Hayley Mills when *The Parent Trap* came out. I learned about women by making mistakes (at the time, I didn't realize that every young man learns about women using this method).

I loved to play pinball and sometimes I saw myself as that chrome ball, shooting straight out toward some imagined goal, only to be bounced, shocked, and throttled back by life's unexpected bumpers. I was headed nowhere in particular and sometimes I envisioned myself battered and beaten and eventually falling through the cracks between the flippers, into darkness and oblivion.

I learned things the hard way, through trial and error (mostly error), and the most important thing I learned was how to observe. I discovered this early on. I knew instinctively how to sit quietly and just watch, how to take it all in. I started playing guitar, but never took lessons (usually because we couldn't afford them). I was given an old Stella guitar when I was nine and taught myself by listening to records by Johnny Cash, Little Jimmy Dickens, Ferlin Husky—and later, Flatt and Scruggs, Merle Haggard, and the Beatles. By the time I was ten or eleven I was fingerpicking along with recordings of folk music and playing songs whose meanings were beyond my ken, but which I played and sang along with anyway. Music was something I could grasp, and it saw me through those days of youthful oblivion. It gave me an identity and a purpose, even though I couldn't have known it at the time.

My brother worked at a local riding stable, taking people out on horseback rides, feeding the horses and cleaning stalls, and doing all the stuff one does when working with livestock. He became one of the crew there, a young skinny redneck kid who smoked Camel cigarettes at fourteen and always had a pack rolled up in the sleeve of his t-shirt, way up on his shoulder. Later on he ended up going into the Navy for a few years, which probably saved him from being a lifelong redneck, though it didn't stop him from smoking. I never did take up smoking, but I tried it a few times, because I always thought my brother and his friends looked cool, smoking and drinking Cokes in the aisle of that old barn, silhouetted against the hot summer sun, with their cowboy hats and their Acme Ruffout boots, and their cigarette packs rolled up in their t-shirt sleeves. I still think smoking looks cool.

I didn't really fit in with the crowd at the stable, but I loved the horses. I would spend hours in the tie stalls at the back of the old barn, a place that was dark and dreary, and where few ventured. No one knew that a skinny ten year old kid was hiding back there, and I think that that's where I really learned to be alone. It felt comfortable, talking to the horses and imagining their replies. I loved to read, back there in the darkness, smuggling books in so no one could see them. Sometimes I would read an entire book at a sitting, with no intrusion or distraction from the outside world. Science fiction was my genre of choice, though I occasionally made forays into westerns, murder mysteries, and spy novels.

I can look back on that time and see the links I was building. The ability to entertain myself, through books, without feeling alone. The lure of the frontier, instilled in me from science fiction and westerns. And the common denominator that tied everything together: those horses standing in their tie stalls. I loved everything about them; their patience and stoicism, their strength and honesty, their intelligence. In their own ways, they taught me those qualities, though I would never begin to attain them in measure those horses had.

And I loved the smell of them, and the sounds they made back there in those stalls. The alfalfa hay in the mangers, the smell of urine and horse shit on the straw they stood on. The dank odor of the hundred year old weathered barn wood that drew its breath from countless equines of years gone by. The sound of incisors tearing at the hay, and of molars grinding it. Of horses swallowing and licking and snorting and sighing. If I needed a place to hide, to be alone, there was no place better.

I had lots of casual friends, but not a single close friend. No true confidants, only those I could share jokes and stories with on a somewhat superficial level. There were those who affected me greatly, who I admired and looked up to, but I kept those sorts of feelings to myself and never let on. And as I entered my teens I entered a world of hitchhiking, traveling, and bumming around.

I had skipped half the second grade, and all of the fifth, because I was what the teachers called "intellectually advanced", which meant that they thought I was too smart for the grade I was in. Turns out they were wrong. In any event, I ended up being the youngest in my class by the time I reached junior high school. When you're eleven or twelve or thirteen years old, a year makes a big difference. And when all the girls in your class are a year, or a year and a half older than you, it makes life even tougher on an adolescent introvert already saddled with no sense of who he is.

And I know that a kid that age has a pretty warped sense of their own place in the scheme of things because looking back, I can see now that no one but me really cared about my age. No one ever said anything about me being younger, but I felt it anyway. Most adolescent boys are in awe and scared to death of girls. For me, being a year younger made it worse. It was terror and torture at the same time. It drove me deeper into my own reclusive reality. Without a father or mentor I had to fumble my way through the process of learning about girls. I couldn't ask my brother because he already had plenty of troubles of his own. We lived on the wrong side of the tracks, so I wasn't going to score any points with girls there and I didn't bother to try. I couldn't afford to be a fancy dresser or drive a flashy car so I was, by default, not one of the *in* crowd. And as it turned out, I wasn't really one of the *out* crowd, either.

I was a non-conformist partly because of my circumstances and partly by nature. I didn't fit in. After a while it got to where I didn't really want to fit in. By the time I was in my teens I had made it a point not to go along with the crowd—though more often than not it left me wishing I could be involved in what others were doing. Instead, I figured I'd just blaze my own trail through it all. I was dumb enough to trust in blind luck and the funny part is, it seemed to work. In time I came to savor the uncertainty of it all. I thrived on venturing blindly out into the unknown.

I mentioned earlier that music was a savior to me. Listening to music—especially those Sun recordings of Johnny Cash, and then the Beatles and other British bands when they came along—introduced me to songwriting as an outlet for my angst-ridden inner self. By then, I could play the guitar reasonably well and could strum along with records. I spent countless hours alone, listening to various forms of country-western music, folk and bluegrass, and to the new influx of British Invasion music. But it was *playing* music that was the real escape for me. Playing music introduced me to like minded souls, other musicians who seemed to be like me, lost in their search for meaning within the chords of a song.

Back then, at the start of the sixties, there weren't many who played guitar or were in a band. That didn't come until later. Those of us who were in a band in my school could be counted on your fingers… and probably on one hand (musicians in the school marching band and orchestra were nerds and didn't count). Back then, if you were a musician you were an oddity. There were only a few of us.

Today, it seems as if everyone is in a band and has their own recording studio on their laptop, and their own artist website. Back then, this wasn't so. Being a musician back then would be like to being an astronaut today. Astronauts are members of a very small club. What they do isn't mainstream and most of us look at astronauting as something *someone else* does. That's the way people looked at pop musicians in those days. Pop music had not yet completely taken over our culture.

Kids in the school band and orchestra studied music as an academic pursuit, while we pursued it as a social activity. They followed the rules, we broke them. They conformed to tradition, we rebelled. They were geeks, we were cool. At least, that's the way we saw it back then. Turns out it was mostly the other way around.

I discovered hitchhiking then. I was twelve or thirteen, and I would hitchhike home from junior high school on days when I wasn't going to the local record shop after school. I thought it was cool to stand on a corner and extend my arm, fist closed, thumb out, waiting for a car to pick me up and take me up the street, dropping me off a half block from our apartment. In fact, I thought it was so cool that I often stood on the corner waiting for a ride far longer than it would have taken to walk home. I tested various positions and looks, trying to see which was coolest and would affect drivers so much that they'd just have to pull over.

I tried holding my arm up, elbow bent, so that my hand was level with my shoulder, but quickly discarded that pose because it wasn't cool. I eventually adopted a posture in which my arm was extended out and down, elbow straight, with my hand about waist high, my thumb pointing upward. Sometimes I altered this basic stance so that my arm hung downward, with my hand next to my leg and my thumb pointing straight out away from my body. I thought this posture was the coolest of all because it was subtle. Unfortunately, it seemed to be lost on the passing drivers.

I didn't care though, because it was the *hitchhiking* that mattered and not the ride home. A few years later I would connect with Kerouac's writing in a big way, because according to him it was the journey that mattered, and not the destination. And looking back I can see that, along with my discovery of playing music, these short adventures in thumbing rides shaped my life in ways to come. Both my guitar and my thumb took me to places I would never have ventured. And it was always the journey that was important. The destinations always seemed to be incidental. It was the trip itself that mattered.

By the time I was fourteen I was thumbing rides around Los Angeles. I hitchhiked to coffeehouses in Hollywood and the San Fernando Valley, or all the way to the beaches of Santa Monica, Redondo, or Huntington. I hitchhiked to the Hollywood Bowl in 1965 and snuck in by climbing over the fence so that I could see the Beatles. After the show, I hitchhiked home. It was an adventure that might have been the highlight of my classmates' lives, something to brag about from then on. I was thrilled to see the Beatles, but I barely mentioned it to anyone. As long as *I* knew what I had done, I didn't much care if anyone else did.

I usually had my guitar with me wherever I went. I sat and played while waiting at freeway onramps, stopping to stick out my thumb at passing cars. Within a short time I had expanded my hitchhiking area to include trips north, out of Los Angeles, following Highway 101 to Ventura and on up to Santa Barbara. At first these were short overnight sojourns, sometimes extended a day or two. Gradually they became longer and longer until soon they would take me to the beaches above Santa Barbara for weeks at a time. It wasn't long before I was regularly thumbing my way to San Francisco, so I could experience the new hippie scene that was blossoming there.

To facilitate these overnight trips I bought an old US Marine Corps mummy bag, a down-filled sleeping bag so compact that you could not turn around inside it. It cost a dollar at an Army surplus store and it was my ticket to freedom. It allowed me to disconnect from any house we were living in and, looking back, I see that it was a logical step away from a life of moving from house to apartment every time we got behind in the rent. That mummy bag set me free from worry over where my next bed would be, though I didn't really see it that way. I carried a guitar case, with my clothes and belongings rolled up in a mummy bag thrown over my shoulder, and I was mobile and free to travel anywhere, not dependent upon anyone else for my subsistence. And that felt good back in those ramblin' days.

I learned how to ride freight trains. I learned to keep low in a train yard, out of sight of the railroad bulls, the night watchmen who roamed the yards with flashlights and handcuffs. I learned to find an empty boxcar, to wedge the side doors open so they wouldn't slide shut during the ride and lock me inside. I learned to make a small cooking fire inside the car, using the oil-filled rag taken from the "hotbox" on the end of a train car's axle. I gathered scraps of cardboard to use as my bed, to soften the constant bouncing and jarring recoils of the empty cars as they rolled along at ninety miles an hour. I learned that the closer your car was to the train's engine, the smoother the ride would be, and the farther it would take you, because they dropped cars off on railroad sidings as the train moved along, starting with those at the back. If you fell asleep during the night in a boxcar near the back of the train, you were likely to wake up stranded on a siding, in the middle of nowhere. I learned to read the information printed on the side of the boxcar, names that gave clues as to where the car was headed. And I learned to always carry water, because once you're in a boxcar you never know when you'll stop, or where you'll end up.

# AN OLD HORSE TRADER

John Becker was born in 1889 and had led an incredibly varied life. He lived with his wife, Ruth, in a small house they had homesteaded in the fifties, far out in the Mojave Desert. They invited us to stay the night, and I was glad I had accepted. I sat transfixed as he described living in logging camps in the Pacific Northwest in the early part of the century. He told stories of driving a horse drawn milk wagon in Los Angeles in the 1920s and running a Hollywood agency for actors and models during the Depression. But I was most enthralled with the tales of his life with horses.

He poured each of us a shot of whiskey as we sat in the living room, surrounded by saddles and bridles, spurs and lariats, and other horse gear on saddle stands and hanging on the walls. There were old photos of the couple in Los Angeles when they were young. One showed them standing next to a tall, lanky show horse, John holding the lead rope in one hand and a riding crop in the other. He was wearing Jodhpur riding pants with a long coat and white gloves. He stared sternly at the camera with a somewhat military look about him.

"Our last horse left us just about a year ago," he said. "I don't think we'll be gettin' any more now. Tie you down more than kids do, I expect." He paused, then added, "You can always get a babysitter for the kids, but not for a horse."

He got up to take a look out the back window and check on Gizmo. There was a gleam in his eye, and I knew that we had stirred some old memories in him. Satisfied with how the horse was doing, he sat down again then returned to his storytelling.

"There was this one time, oh, musta been just before the war. We brought in twenty or twenty-five head of unbroke horses from Nevada. Every one of 'em was right off the range and wild as all get-out." He stopped, chuckled to himself, and continued. "I was in the business of buyin' and sellin' horses back then. We was livin' out near San Bernardino, and we'd sometimes run 'em through the horse and mule auction down in LA, but the market was real bad right about then. So, I figured I'd try to sell 'em one at a time."

He stopped to think about it for a while then turned to Ruth, "Say, was we livin' in San Bernardino, or was it at the place down in Hemet?"

"Hemet, I think," Ruth replied.

"Yep, I think it was Hemet," he agreed. "You see, there wasn't much out there in those days. Just a cow-calf operation or two and a few folks tryin' to make a livin' offa land that wasn't fit for much of anything. We turned those horses out on two or three hundred acres, but there wasn't much for 'em to eat, so we had to feed 'em. Of course, hay was a lot cheaper back then, and you could get a bale of good alfalfa for next to nothin'.'"

He took a sip of the whiskey, paused as if lost in thought again, and then continued.

"Well, we brought those horses down and turned them out into the pasture. Had to rope 'em to catch 'em. Ain't a one of 'em would come up to you, so you had to run 'em into a corner and toss a rope on 'em. Like I said, they was wild, right off the range.

"I put an ad in the local paper with the idea that I could sell 'em, one at a time. I said in the ad that they was unbroke. I think I was wanting to get sixty-five dollars apiece for 'em, or thereabouts. But there wasn't any takers. I got a couple of calls about 'em, but I damn sure couldn't sell 'em.

"It was comin' winter, and I was getting' to the age where I didn't want to take on a bunch of rough stock like that. Didn't want to be breakin' all those critters to ride. Hell, it probably woulda killed me. Anyway, I kept trying to run ads and let folks know I had 'em for sale. I sold a few, but still had most of 'em left. They was pretty nice horses, all up, and I hated to see 'em just goin' to the killers for dog food.

"But then, I had this bright idea. I figured I'd change that ad, and so I did. In big bold letters on the top of the ad I put, 'WILD HORSES FOR SALE,' and I ran that ad for a couple of weeks.

"Well sir, them folks couldn't get there fast enough. Seemed like everyone wanted to have their own wild horse. Sold 'em all in two weeks."

Throughout the story, I noticed Ruth, nodding and smiling as John related it. When he was finished, she nodded a bit more emphatically and said, "Yeah, that's right."

"Why do you suppose those folks would buy wild horses and not unbroke ones?" I asked.

"Well now, that's the funny part about that," he replied. "Most of them folks wasn't horse trainers or anything like that. Hell, most of 'em didn't know one end of a horse from the other. But ya see, I think that maybe livin' down there in Los Angeles and bein' tied down and all that … well, maybe they just wanted a part of something wild and free. Maybe they figured those wild horses would rub off on 'em a little."

He took another sip, and I did the same. He got up again to go to the window to check on my horse, and I watched him watching Gizmo. He was seeing a wild horse, and there was a light on inside him that would never go out.

# GIZMO

Gizmo was young and full of himself when we set off from the county fairgrounds at Ventura. Born on February 1, 1970, he was just four years old, still pretty green and inexperienced, but honest and dependable. We had already forged a strong bond and knew each other well by the time we started down the trail. I had raised Gizmo from a six-month-old weanling, and we had spent several months prior to the ride training hard, building ourselves up to the time when we would leave the Pacific Ocean and head out toward the sunrise on a journey that would last seven months and cover over four thousand miles.

He was still young enough to be losing his baby teeth. Incisors and premolars were still being replaced by his permanent teeth, and I had followed the old Spanish method of using a hackamore bridle on him instead of a bit. Hackamores have a rawhide noseband (bosal), in place of a snaffle or curb bit, to free a horse's mouth while his adult teeth grow in. Once we were on the trail for a few weeks, I sent the hackamore home and simply rode him with his halter using a long lead rope for my reins. Gizmo never had a bit in his mouth his entire life.

He was a registered American Quarter Horse with a diverse family tree. He stood fifteen-one, with a slender build and a handsome, refined head. He was a sorrel—called *chestnut* by some—with a blaze that ran down from his forehead and widened to cover the entire front of his nose and upper lip. A white stocking ran up almost to the knee of his left front leg. Long pasterns with strong slopes down to the hoof enabled him to float freely at the walk and trot. He had a long overstep behind, which meant that each hind foot stepped far in front of the print left by the front foot, and this enabled him to cover ground quickly and smoothly. His front feet were striped with a mixture of dark and light, and his hind ones were all dark. They were small and fit his overall frame. He wore a double ought shoe.

A horse's eye is the first thing I notice when I look at him. It says a lot about his intelligence and signals the amount of trust he carries within himself. Gizmo's were intelligent and kind. They were soft enough to be reassuring, yet had enough white showing to display a sense of curiosity. His head usually turned to follow his eyes, and that indicated an awareness of his surroundings and an inquisitive mind.

His dam was a Quarter Horse mare named *My Wayward Lady*. We called her *Wayward*. She was chestnut with a flaxen mane and tail and stood fourteen-three. Wayward was a fine example of the classic "bulldog" Quarter Horse—short, stocky, quick, and smart. She was bred in Texas from King Ranch stock, but raised in Oklahoma. Her lineage traced back to the famous *P-234*, or *King* as he was called, who was one of the foundation sires of the American Quarter Horse breed.

Gizmo's sire was a well-known West Coast racehorse by the name of *Palleo's Note*. As his name suggests, his family tree traced back to the famous *Leo,* another of the breed's foundation sires. Like most racing Quarter Horses back then, Palleo's Note had a lot of Thoroughbred breeding in his background. He was a big, long-legged stocky stallion who earned his Racing Register of Merit by the time he was a two-year-old.

Gizmo was destined to follow neither his mother's ranching heritage nor his father's racing history. Instead, he became a free spirit, and he never hesitated to express that essence.

He weighed just under a thousand pounds when we left Ventura in April. It was a good working weight for him. He was neither overly fat nor thin. He had been worked hard for four or five months prior to the ride and was well muscled and fit. During the rough trek across the western deserts, he lost a bit more than two hundred pounds, but between the plains of the Texas Panhandle and the Mississippi River, we found good grass and he gained more than half of that back. By the end of the ride he was thin, but hard as a rock.

He was a tough little horse who never quit and was as game a critter as you could find. Horses can be compared with people sometimes. There are those who soldier on by sheer force of will, and there are those, like Gizmo, who seem to push forward through the inertia of their own curiosity. A strong will is tough, but curiosity is resilient, and I reckon curiosity is the stronger force.

He quickly learned that whatever I ate, he could eat. This included everything from Snickers bars (his favorite) to hamburgers, apple pie, ham sandwiches, cookies, green chile enchiladas, ice cream, biscuits and gravy, chocolate cake, hotdogs, cotton candy, beef stew, and a whole smorgasbord of other delicacies. He would drink water from a gas station's radiator filler hose without spilling a drop, and always demanded that I share any sodas, beer, iced tea, or other drinks I had. These included coffee (cold), root beer floats, and chocolate shakes as well, though I drew the line at whiskey shots. I did watch what he ate, and I wouldn't let him have anything that might hurt him, such as bananas, celery, oleander, and other equine food hazards. And I never fed him too much of any of the food I ate. He usually only wanted a bite or two, just to be included, but he was known to eat an entire pie or chocolate cake once in a while.

He taught me more than a few things during the ride. I learned not only to listen and observe, but also to *hear* and to *see.* I recognized the way he tore grass from the ground as he grazed. He made a *chop-cha-CHOP* sound, a three-beat cadence that repeated itself several times until he had to take another step forward to find a new bunch a few feet away. *Chop-cha-CHOP, Chop-cha-CHOP, Chop-cha-CHOP,* then a few silent bars while he shifted, and then back to *Chop-cha-CHOP.* It was a constant for me, a reassurance that all was well with him.

Gizmo was a sound sleeper much of the time, though not always. I staked him out at night on a thirty-foot rope that was fastened to his front foot by a hobble. I would buckle the leather hobble onto his pastern and clip the rope to it. This allowed the rope to stay flat on the ground, so he wouldn't get it wrapped around his hind legs and cause rope burns. He could easily lie down with this rig, and could even have a nice roll if he wanted to. When he was finished eating and checking out his surroundings, he would generally wander as close to me as he could get then lie down. I learned early on that I needed to give him enough room, or he would end up sleeping on top of me.

> *FROM THE LOG:*
> *When I'm leading Gizmo through town, every time he sees himself in a store window he whinnies. What a goofball.*

He knew he was something special and that we were doing something extraordinary. He took our celebrity in stride, posing for cameras and enjoying the attention he received along the trail. He was never barn sour or herd bound in his entire life, and I think the ride helped to cement that disposition in him. Horses are herd animals, gregarious by nature. Gizmo was certainly gregarious with people, and he enjoyed being with his own kind as well, but he didn't mind leaving them behind in the corral whenever I took him out on a ride. He maintained that attitude for the rest of his life.

He was a precocious colt, inquisitive sometimes to the point of being annoying. He was always into everything. If you left a bucket on the ground nearby, or a halter hanging from a fencepost, he had his nose in them immediately. He'd drag my coat away from my gear and drop it on the ground beneath him. He was like a magpie that way. He didn't actually *want* my stuff for anything specific. He never chewed on or destroyed any of it. He seemed to like the idea of having unlimited access to my things, and he wanted to make sure I knew it. He'd come over to listen to the radio if one was playing. Music seemed to be a sort of tonic for him, and oftentimes I wished I had a way to play a radio while we were riding along on the trail.

Since then, I have spent a great deal of time composing music for dressage freestyles. They are a bit like ice skating freestyles, where Olympic skaters go through their required movements set to music. Many claim the horses can feel the music and have a sense of rhythm. They maintain that the dressage horse in a freestyle can sense the music and will move to it, accordingly.

I reckon a horse has no real concept of music as beats and rhythm—at least, not something he can relate to. Musical rhythm is a wholly human notion. It is the concept of sound measured against time, and horses don't care about time. I don't think a horse can sense rhythm as we know it any more than we can sense the frequencies of light or sound except by color or pitch. They affect us, but we can't dance in time to them because we can't hear or see their rhythm. But even so, I'm pretty sure that music has a profound effect upon horses, and on other animals as well. As I mentioned, Gizmo loved listening to music, and he sure responded to it. But he didn't try to dance to it.

# DESERT DWELLERS AND ROSICRUCIANS

Wherever you find remote, isolated, and inhospitable country, you'll find a few people who choose to make their lives there. For whatever reason, these folks have chosen the road less traveled and entered negotiations of a sort with the land by adapting themselves to it while doing their best to modify it to suit their own needs. This negotiation usually involves leaving a lifestyle behind, often at great expense, to adopt another that may mean losing their families, their friends, and even their lives.

Not all of them will stick it out. Some will return to their prior lives or to something familiar. Reality can be cruel, and sometimes the dream doesn't live up to the hope that gave birth to it. Their stories have one thing in common: the desire for solitude. To choose isolation is to choose the *hard way*. And certain people choose it not only *knowing* that life will be hard, but *because* it will be hard. The people we met in the desert had chosen that hard road.

I was glad we had started the trip in early spring. There were two things that decided this for me: First, the Mojave Desert is no place for a horse by the time May rolls around. Second, I had figured on a seven-month journey and didn't want to ride in the snow at the end of it.

The weather was behaving reasonably well as we made our way into the California desert. The wind wreaked havoc sometimes and caused me several days of worry over whether Gizmo might get spooked and run off. But he seemed to bear up well for a four-year-old and settled into the routine in his own easygoing manner.

A horse seems to embody the traits you share with him. He manifests a bit of your own character after a while, especially when you're the only constant in a landscape that changes every day. They say that horsemanship is the embodiment of technique through love. I don't know how much of my technique rubbed off on Gizmo. It was mostly climbing on and off the saddle and talking to him a lot in between. But I know the love was there, alongside a sizable helping of respect, and I like to think maybe Gizmo felt a bit of that too, in his own equine way.

The sun was shadowed by the desert's high, wispy clouds, and the air just cool and windy enough for me to need my jacket. We were south of Dunn, which had turned out to be nothing more than a couple of abandoned buildings in the middle of nowhere. A few miles outside of "town," I found what looked to be an empty community building of some sort, possibly the headquarters of an old riding club. I had no idea what it had been used for, but there was a working windmill with a small corral for Gizmo, and the building would provide me shelter from the cold spring winds that came up during the night. Gizmo would have to make do with the ragweed that grew around the water trough, there being nothing else for him to eat.

I unsaddled and turned him out into the corral then stepped onto the porch of the building and opened the door. Inside I found a few pieces of furniture—a large wooden table and several unmatched chairs, a wooden bench, and two small army cots that were nothing more than thin mattresses on top of spring mesh. It was rustic and rough, but I looked forward to sleeping on a real bed for a change and made myself at home. I could see Gizmo through the window and felt better, knowing I could keep an eye on him in case coyotes came to visit during the night. I had a couple hours left until sunset, so I opened my small Sterno stove and cooked an early meal of dried macaroni without sauce. There was no electricity but I found some candles in the cupboard to use later. I settled in a chair with a paperback novel for company.

Shortly after dark, I saw headlights approaching and heard tires coming up the primitive dirt road, which was nothing more than two ruts across the desert sand. The lights bounced up and down, back and forth, as the vehicles negotiated the rough terrain. I checked to see that the Colt was loaded, then stepped into the doorway, holding the pistol hidden behind the door jamb.

It turned out to be a small group that held meetings in this place. They weren't intruding upon us, rather, it turned out that Gizmo and I were the trespassers. The group consisted of eight people, which included three women and five men. The eldest, a tall thin rake of a man in his sixties or seventies (I couldn't tell ... he seemed ageless), informed me that they met here weekly and that I was welcome to stay and partake in the evening's events. I didn't see any harm in staying—and besides, I didn't relish the idea of sleeping in the corral with Gizmo—so I accepted.

I introduced myself and Gizmo, though none of them offered their names in return. I thought it a bit odd at first, but let it pass. The elder (he looked like old paintings of Erasmus, or maybe Archimedes, but for some reason I immediately thought of him as "Jerry") led the proceedings by commencing with five minutes of silence, during which time I studied my visitors as they closed their eyes and bowed their heads. Five minutes doesn't seem like such a long time until you sit through it in silence with a bunch of strangers, and then it seems like you're in the event horizon of a black hole where time stands still. Regardless, I managed to occupy the interval by imagining the lives of the people in the room.

Two of the women looked like sisters (I later learned they were mother and daughter); the older one wore her age well and looked twenty years younger than she probably was, while the younger's premature wrinkles and weathered face bore the signs of physical work outdoors in the desert sun and wind. The younger woman was in her mid-twenties, but their ages seemed to meet in the middle somewhere. Each was beautiful in her own way, and their countenance and manners exposed what I figured was a previous life of patrician aristocracy. When they spoke, it was not in the language of desert people, but in the manner of those from East Coast affluence. In my mind, I saw them as Philomena (the mother) and Charlene (daughter).

The third woman, whom I christened Betty, was a short, mousy person. I pegged her as a peacekeeper, the sort who will do anything to avoid confrontation. She busied herself making sure everyone was comfortable and happy, to the exclusion of herself, and generally kept up a cheery exterior. One of the men was Betty's husband, and another was his brother, though I never did figure out which was which. They were both short, stocky spark plugs (as was she), who wore plaid flannel shirts and ball caps with tractor insignias on them (International Harvester and John Deere). I named them Mutt and Jeff, and since I didn't distinguish one from the other, the names were interchangeable.

There was a young man in his early twenties who spoke barely a word. His dark skin and black hair, and his quiet manner suggested he was an immigrant who didn't speak English. When he finally did speak, his thick accent (Georgia, I later learned) exposed him as a transplanted southerner whose skin was dark from years spent outdoors in the sun. I named him Marlboro because he was the quiet type, and he kept a pack of cigarettes in his shirt pocket.

The last man—and possibly the most incongruous to me—was in his late fifties or early sixties. I called him Lord Loam (after the liberal aristocrat from the play *The Admirable Crichton*). At first glance, his dress matched that of the others, but I then noticed that his jeans and shirt were starched and pressed, not a thread out of place. His hair appeared as an informal grey blanket on his head, but was in fact styled and manicured, and I wondered if it was real. He carried himself in a self-assured way, sharing his perspective on various subjects and topics of discussion. He asserted his views while deferring to others in what seemed to be an attempt to better understand their views, but were in fact nothing more than patronizing doubletalk. It all seemed very egalitarian, but I suspected his involvement in the group was more than what appeared on the surface, and I spent a good part of the evening trying to discover what it was.

The night's discussion began with Jerry informing me that the group belonged to a certain Order of Rosicrucians (I didn't get the name of the specific fraternity), which was based largely upon a modern version called the Archeosophical Society. I had no idea what he was talking about, though I had heard of Rosicrucians before. The term *natural philosophy* was bandied about. They discussed alchemy along with the concepts of esoteric wisdom and something called the *threefold body*. Most of this was beyond my ken, but I sat and listened and offered a question or two now and then.

Jerry led the discussion with Lord Loam acting at times as both his second and his foil. The two got into animated discussions about various esoteric functions of so-called "helpers," mysterious beings who belong to an "invisible college" and make themselves known to us only by secretly lending a helping hand here and there when we need one. When I mentioned that they seemed like angels on our shoulders, I was emphatically corrected (by both Jerry and Lord Loam, who agreed on this point) that no, they most certainly were *not* the same as angels, which set them off on a long discussion about different sorts of helpers—those that sat on your shoulder and those that didn't. Afterward, I simply thought of the helpers as ghosts.

Charlene (whom I was starting to take a shine to) mentioned that Jerry lived with his ninety-six-year-old mother (he was obviously older than I thought) in a remote section of the Mojave (as if the place we occupied was a booming population center), and that he had been hand digging a water well for six years. I asked her how deep it was.

"Eleven feet," she replied.

"Eleven feet in six years," I said dryly. "How far down is the water?" She turned to Jerry and relayed my question.

"My mother is a water witch. She witched the well," he said. "The water lies at eighty-nine feet."

"So, only seventy-eight feet to go," I answered, jokingly.

"No," he replied seriously, "we'll require at least ten to fifteen feet of standing water, so I will need to dig another eighty-eight to ninety-three feet."

I did the math in my head (he was averaging a couple feet per year) and decided not to say anything. I let the subject drop. About this time, we heard a hissing sound coming from the front porch.

"Rattler," Charlene said and was quickly on her feet and out the front door. I heard her stomping her boot on the porch floorboards, after which she stepped through the doorway holding a dead rattlesnake by its tail. It was about two and a half feet long.

"Just a baby," she said and tossed it back onto the porch. "I'll take it home to feed the chickens."

Now, around the folks I grew up with, this event would have instantly become legendary. A young woman nonchalantly steps out and crushes a live rattlesnake with her boot then picks it up to show everyone. And the thing was, she didn't show it to us for bragging rights. She was simply letting us know that it was dead and no longer a threat. No one seemed excited or in the least bit impressed (except for me, of course). The discussion continued without another mention of it. The shine I had taken to her was starting to become a bit of an infatuation.

All the while I kept an eye on Lord Loam, who seemed to be in a friendly contest with Jerry to be leader of the group. I could see the constant game of one-upmanship going on between them. Jerry was undoubtedly the more knowledgeable about the Rosicrucian path and retained an astounding command of seemingly random details regarding its history and the various philosophies surrounding it. Added to that was his commanding presence—tall and gaunt, with a powerful low voice that was reminiscent of John Carradine. He spoke with calm, authoritative measure and made a compelling picture. Lord Loam, on the other hand, was quick witted and sharp. I suspected he was, or had been, a corporate lawyer or a highly educated car salesman. He was obviously at home in the debating arena and enjoyed the constant parleys he shared with Jerry.

During the course of the evening, I noticed that Jerry and Lord Loam would defer to Philomena, often in patronizing ways. They sat transfixed whenever she offered a comment or opinion, no matter how banal or cliché it was. I had a sudden epiphany and imagined that these meetings weren't about a contest over leadership at all, that the group was merely an excuse for the two men to compete for the affections of the lovely Philomena. I made up stories in my head about their battles to win her over, Jerry attempting to impress her with his deep-voiced, measured, reflective philosophy and Lord Loam trying to win her affections with smooth compliments and flattery. Talk of Rosicrucians and helpers and angels faded into the background as the true significance of these weekly meetings became clear. Of course, it wasn't clear to anyone else, but I was convinced I was on the right track. I talked about it quite a bit in the days that followed, but Gizmo was never really interested.

I sat and listened to tales of angels and helpers, natural pathways to enlightenment, and Esoteric Christian and Para-Masonic teachings. I couldn't help thinking that people drag their spiritual belongings with them no matter where they go. I didn't exclude myself from that either.

The night ended late (I have no idea what time) with the group—Jerry, Philomena, Charlene, Betty, Mutt and Jeff, Marlboro, and Lord Loam— piling into the vehicles and heading down the dirt road, their bobbing headlights exposing the eyes of coyotes and rabbits, leaving Gizmo and I to watch the dark sky blanketed by stars in the moonless night.

Bright and early the next morning—it couldn't have been more than a few hours after the group left—an old Chevy pickup truck came bouncing up the road. I had just gotten up and dressed and was pulling on my boots when Charlene climbed out of the truck and onto the porch. She poked her head in the door.

"Good morning," she said cheerfully. "Glad you're up. I was hoping you had time for breakfast. There's a cafe down the road a ways. How 'bout some coffee before you head out?"

"That's about the best offer I've had in a long time," I answered. "But I might have to take a raincheck. I'm a bit worried about Gizmo. I'm hoping I can find a little feed for him up the trail."

"No problem. I brought a bale of grass hay along. That should keep him occupied while we go have breakfast."

"Well, if you put it that way … I reckon I can't deny him a good meal then, can I?" I smiled.

I finished pulling on my boots and got up to help her with the hay. I knew that Gizmo wouldn't be able to carry any of it later, so I threw the whole bale into the corral, where he began tearing it apart, grabbing at the leafiest pieces.

We climbed into the cab of the pickup, and before we pulled away she looked at me and smiled. "You don't even know my name, do you?" she asked in a mocking accusation.

I blushed.

"It's Karen," she said and held out her hand.

I took it and answered, "And I'm John. Nice to meet you."

"I know," she replied.

# OUT THE CLUB CAR WINDOW

We're taking the day off today. It's a lovely spring day in the Mojave. We have passed through seas of wildflowers, and the locals say it is a rare year for them. They light up the desert in yellows and reds, blues and purples. We ride along through the dry sage and buckbrush, and suddenly, we top a small rise where we encounter a valley full. We cross through them, and Gizmo snips them off with his incisors as he trots along, never missing a beat. When we reach the other side of the swale, we climb over a small hill, and they're gone, just like that. Back to the dull browns and pale desert greens.

We started down the trail this morning, but within a couple of hours, we came to this place, and I decided to knock off early. A local had told me about it a few days ago, so I have been keeping an eye out for it. We're in a very remote canyon, having followed the Union Pacific railroad tracks to here. I haven't seen many trains on them in a couple of days, so I think maybe they don't use this line much anymore.

Just as the man had described, there is an underground river flowing across the desert here. It's hard to believe because everything is so dry and there's no trace of water anywhere, but this spot we're camped in is proof. The river hits bedrock and rushes to the surface. We find several pools of moving water. It's odd that the water runs but seems to come from nowhere. It appears suddenly, flows across a small area, then disappears just as suddenly.

I stake Gizmo out so he can get to the water, and he immediately starts splashing around in it with his nose. He takes long drinks and pauses to clean his nostrils by snorting. He rolls in the sand a few times, jumps to his feet, and shakes the sand off. He repeats this routine several times. He grabs a few mouthfuls of the pale green grass that grows here then eventually lies down near the water's edge and goes to sleep.

The water is a bit salty tasting, but it serves our needs. I boil some and pour a bit into my canteen along with some sand. I swish it around and then rinse the container out to keep the mold away. I boil more water and let it sit a while to cool then fill the canteen again. It feels good to know we have water to drink. I make some tea and sit down to read my paperback,

*The Gods Themselves* by Isaac Asimov.

I've decided to wash my clothes, so I'll take a bath while I'm at it. I pull my extra pair of jeans out of my pack, along with two t-shirts, some underwear and socks, and my other western shirt. I strip off the clothes I'm wearing and grab the small bar of hand soap. Before I start for the river, I realize there is cholla cactus around, and I don't want to step on any. I pull my boots back on without socks. The sun is getting hot, so I pop my cowboy hat onto my head and carry my belongings to the water's edge.

Ever the curious type, Gizmo wanders over to see what I'm up to. I have to keep taking things away from him as he picks up socks, shirts, and underwear and tosses them around. I lay my rain slicker out as a ground cloth, a place to put my clothes to dry after I've washed them. It's a painstaking task, but I'm proud of myself for taking the time to do it. I pull my boots off and step into the water to bathe and find that it is surprisingly cold. I realize that the river must travel far beneath the surface before it returns to the light of day. It feels good to scrub myself, and I take my time, enjoying it. Gizmo takes my lead and goes back to splashing in the water with his muzzle. He lets his lower lip flap as he does this, and it's a comical sight. He can be a bit of a clown sometimes.

I do not carry a towel. It's one of those things I do without to keep the weight down for Gizmo. Since my clothes are all wet, I am forced to drip-dry. I don't mind because the day is warm and pleasant, so I pull my boots back on and step back to the edge of the water to let the sun dry me. Gizmo comes over to have his ears scratched.

There's something about standing naked in the world, stripped bare and exposed to the elements. I'm definitely not an exhibitionist. I've gone skinny dipping and don't mind exposing myself around others if I have to. Still, I lean toward being a bit prudish about those sorts of things. But when you're in such a remote place, you get a feeling of unreserved freedom, you're exposed yet unconcerned about others. I enjoy standing here, naked except for boots and hat, listening to the sounds: my horse and the gentle rustle of the bush, quail warbling, the chatter of a couple of pinion jays, the soft buzz of flying insects and the faraway whistle of a train.

A train. It occurs to me that the train I'm hearing will be passing right through our hidden retreat. For a moment I feel anxious and instinctively look around to take stock of my situation. I consider throwing some clothes on, but they are still wet. I resign myself to hunkering down and waiting it out. The whistle does not blow again, but the rumble of the boxcars grows and grows, gradually, until I know the freight train will show itself at the end of the canyon any second. And it does.

Except, it's not a freight train. These are not clunky diesel engines, coupled together to increase their might, pulling a two-mile-long string of boxcars with a caboose attached to the end. No, instead I see a smooth silver rocket, a streamlined engine pulling a collection of aluminum rail cars that seem fused together as one, a sleek and shiny habitat that glides across the desert floor, the great domed windows of its club cars stretching high above its roofline.

The train's windows—and its windows are *everywhere*—are filled with the faces of travelers, pilgrims from Chicago on their way to experience the great American Southwest. There are parents and grandparents, children and grandchildren, aunts and uncles, sisters and brothers. And in their first face-to-face encounter with the west, they see a cowboy and his horse, and it's not like they thought it would be.

Gizmo and I stand side by side as they pass. The engineer blasts the train whistle. Passengers point to us and wave. Parents shield the eyes of their children. Gizmo turns to look at them, and I smile, tip my hat, and wave. I look down at my naked self and think, do I look stupid in these boots?

# EYE TO EYE

It was in the Great Desert of the Southwest, out in the Mojave, where Gizmo and I accidentally intruded upon an unusual conversation. I was walking, Gizmo's reins looped over my arm as we made our way slowly along the south side of a long, narrow gully. Lately I had gotten into the habit of stopping every so often for a short pause, to simply be still and listen to the voice of the desert around us. Gizmo usually made some noise by stretching his head down to see what he could grab in his teeth, but I learned early on to filter his sounds out from those around us. It was interesting and instructive to listen to the soundscape of an environment that you aren't familiar with. Especially a hostile one, or one that you've always thought of as hostile.

A few minutes' stop to listen to the Mojave always rendered a diverse palette of noises. Day sounds differed from night sounds, especially those made by the wildlife. During the day, I heard the whistle of sage and creosote bush in the wind; the hum of a truck on a highway many miles away in the distance, the soft warbles of a covey of quail or the squawk of a pinion jay, the buzz of a dragonfly or the chirp of a cricket, the insistent chatter of a cicada, the warning hiss of a rattlesnake's tail. I became attuned to the smallest of sounds, the kind made by a jackrabbit sifting for morsels in the bush or by the scratch of a lizard scurrying across a large rock.

During the night, the sounds shifted. The late afternoon brought the gentle whispers of king birds and flycatchers to snap up gnats and mosquitos out of the evening sky. Nocturnal creatures came forth: rabbits, coyotes, bobcats, desert foxes. And some of the birds could be heard as well: canyon wrens, herons, whippoorwills, nighthawks. All these sounds made up a sort of harmony with the small campfires that marked our camps at night. Coyotes were the most vocal, but the others performed their own special parts in the chorus.

It was during one of these short pauses that we stumbled upon two desert tortoises. I had been listening, eyes closed and mind relaxed, when I sensed something else there. I hadn't noticed them when we stopped, so I was a bit surprised to look down to find the two creatures, noses just inches apart, facing each other and staring into one another's eyes. They were obviously having a conversation of the sort tortoises no doubt have, and I felt a bit bad about interrupting it. They were standing stock-still, not moving at all. At some point, I decided I would stand there and watch them, remaining utterly still, until one of them moved (Gizmo did not see fit to take part in this little exercise). I remained a statue, barely blinking, for what must have been several minutes. It seemed like hours. I began to think they weren't even alive, but I resisted the urge to reach down and poke one of them to find out. I finally gave up, pulled Gizmo to one side, and stepped around them. They gave no acknowledgement that they had seen us and remained unmoving as we walked past and left them to their dialog.

To this day, I have no idea what those dryland terrapins were talking about. But I'm guessing their gossip will find its way back around to me eventually.

# A SPITEFUL WOMAN

The throbbing in my head drove me to consciousness, and I awoke with a start. The headache forced out all thoughts of anything else as the pain washed over me like a tsunami. I forced my eyes open to the dark quiet of the desert night, but could see only red and orange flashes and heard nothing but the pounding pulse inside my skull, so I quickly shut them again. As I gained a tentative awareness of where I was, I levered myself to a sitting position and tried to make sense of what was happening.

My face was hot against the cool night air, and I was sweating. My back and shoulders were clenched tight, locked in a fierce battle against the terrible pain. It took some groping around before I found my flashlight, turned it on, and looked for the plastic aspirin bottle in my saddlebag. Reaching for it, I saw that my right arm had swelled up. As I reached up to feel my face, I shined the light on my body and discovered that my entire right side was badly swollen. Barely managing to pull myself out of my bedroll, I made a feeble attempt at standing up, but failed. I was suddenly very dizzy and nearly fainted when the blood rushed from my pounding head.

I took stock. Gizmo and I were on the eastern edge of the Mojave Desert, several miles north of Needles and close to the Colorado River, still on the California side. Because of mosquitos near the water, I had pitched camp a good way away, in a dry camp. I was sick—sick enough that it scared me—and I didn't know why, but I figured it was either something I had eaten or some virus or infection I'd picked up somewhere. It didn't matter because at this point I was feeling about as sick as I'd ever been.

My stomach began to clench and I knew that the small bowl of macaroni I'd eaten a few hours before wasn't going to stay down, so I crawled as far as I could from my sleeping bag before throwing up. The vomiting wouldn't stop, and I ended up in dry heaves that lasted an eternity. Somehow I managed to swallow a few gulps of water from my canteen, and it came back up a few seconds later. The exertion made my head pound even harder, and I figured I might be having a stroke. I thought about calling out for help, but I knew that no one would hear my cries, so I kept quiet and conserved what little energy I had left.

An interval of time passed in which I alternately sat with my head in my hands, and lay down. It felt as if I existed in a space between the barest consciousness and passing out. I used my flashlight to make a closer inspection of myself, wondering why my body had swelled up so badly—my face and neck, my shoulder and right arm, the right side of my body, and my right leg, all the way down to my foot—bloated and sore. As I shone the light, I happened to catch a glimpse of something in my sleeping bag. Small and black, it was a spider—dead—that had no doubt crawled in with me at some point. Looking closer, I saw the distinctive red hourglass on its belly and knew it was a black widow.

I've subsequently read about black widow spiders, and I'm glad I didn't know what I was in for at the time. The female is the one who bites, but it's a wives' tale to think that she kills the male after mating. It's one of those stories we tell to make her sound more sinister. Believe me, she doesn't need her formidable exploits embellished, and you don't want to mess with her. Take it from me. Her venom is ten times stronger than a rattlesnake's and goes about its job in a more insidious manner. The rattler's venom affects a person's motor nervous system, but a black widow's attacks your central nervous system. The snake's is meant to paralyze the muscle it enters, in a localized manner, and to partially cripple its prey. The spider's is meant to stun its victim's entire body, through the nervous system, to paralyze it and send it into a coma. I have no firsthand experience with rattlesnake bites, but I can tell you that the black widow is very good at her job.

I had rolled over onto her and killed her, but not before she had left her mark. I picked the dead spider up and wrapped it in some tissue, then stuffed it down in a saddlebag. I wasn't sure why I did this, but I suppose I wanted to make sure later, in the light of day, that I wasn't imagining it.

The first inkling of daylight was beginning to show in the east. I knew I couldn't stay where I was, so I dressed hastily, forcing my feet into boots that were now a size too small. I packed up the gear and saddled Gizmo then headed off toward the Colorado River. We crossed uneventfully into Nevada, over an old wooden pedestrian bridge near the Aztec Road. We were at the very tip of the state's southern triangle and would spend only a few hours inside Nevada's boundary before crossing into Arizona. Three states in one day—on horseback. Beat that, John Wayne.

I felt somewhat better once we had crossed the river and turned southeast toward the mountains in the distance. The ghost town of Oatman showed on my map, and I figured I could make it there in a couple of days. We followed a section of the old Government Road, one of the main wagon roads used by settlers and miners from the gold rush days of the 1850s. The century old ruts made by miners and immigrants still existed in many places in 1974, though much of it has since been obliterated by motorcycles and four-wheel drive vehicles that have left their own legacy of a much faster and more invasive brand of travel.

As Gizmo and I slowly made our way up the folds in the long slope of desert floor that lay at the foot of the Black Mountains, I could see parts of a road that had been well used during the mid-nineteenth century, whose travelers had left behind countless artifacts to bake in the hot desert sun: wagon parts, bits of old shovels, chain, glass bottles that had turned blue in the sun (and would later become prime targets for collectors), and all manner of other paraphernalia and keepsakes that had been long abandoned by their owners and left untouched for more than a hundred years.

I was glad Gizmo had drunk his fill and that I'd had the presence of mind to fill the canteen at the river because the country was forbidding with no large trees in sight and not a hint of water anywhere. After an hour or so, I began to ache again, my back tightening into constant spasms and convulsions, and I slipped off Gizmo to walk alongside him. Our pace gradually slowed until, by midday, we were moving at a crawl, probably less than two miles per hour. I had taken all the aspirin in the bottle—I had no idea how many—and I was still in tremendous pain. I became somewhat delirious and found myself hallucinating and talking gibberish. I know this only because I also became alert and lucid at times and could take stock of my surroundings. These intervals of awareness lasted for short periods, and then I fell back into a pain-induced stupor and continued, stumbling along as before.

In one of my clearheaded moments I had the good sense to tie Gizmo's rein to my wrist. This probably saved our lives because I would have dropped it eventually, and after that it would have been a slippery slope. I'm sure I'd have fallen by the wayside, and with me piled in a clump by the side of the trail, he would have wandered off, fully saddled, looking for water. It's easy enough to predict what would have happened to him.

The girth would eventually come loose, but the saddle wouldn't fall off. Sooner or later Gizmo would have stepped through the reins and become tangled. After a while, the saddle and its gear would slip, roll under his belly, and he would be caught in the cinch and other fastenings, left to stumble around for hours, and unable to find food or water. Night would finally come, and he'd be stuck, unable to get free, and the coyotes (most likely) or a mountain lion or other predator (possibly) would have gotten him.

Or miraculously, he might have made it back down the long trail to the river, to be found by someone, and maybe have lived happily ever after. They would have sent searchers for me, and might even have found me, but by that time, it wouldn't have mattered. The likelihood is that my own belongings, and those tied to Gizmo, would have simply joined those of our predecessors from a hundred years before, discarded and bleached white by the dry desert sun. In a hundred years, they too might become treasures, sought after by collectors and plunderers.

As it was, Gizmo's constant tugging at that rein kept me focused just enough to keep walking up the slope of the mountain in the distance to a destination that never seemed to get any closer.

Our journey ceased to matter, and I had no idea what time of day it was, or even whether it was day or night. I pictured myself starring in an old B western movie in which I had taken on the role of Randolph Scott or Joel McCrea. I was sure that my sidekick, Smiley Burnette or Gabby Hayes, would come save us at the last minute. I was simply putting one foot in front of the other, step by step, and focusing on staying upright. The pain consumed me for so long I was oblivious to everything except the tread of each boot, falling with a crunch against the desert sand. I rarely lifted my head to see where we were going, but we managed to advance in more or less a straight line toward Oatman.

At one point, I attempted to climb up on Gizmo, knowing we could make better time if I rode. I tried as hard as I could, but just couldn't lift my foot high enough to reach the stirrup. I *willed* myself into the saddle, but failed. I spent what seemed like an eternity—but probably only a few minutes—forcing myself again and again without success.

"Damn, Gizmo. I wish I had trained you to kneel down like those fancy trick horses." He snorted a dry cough, and we stumbled ahead again, still tied together.

I had calculated the distance from the last night's camp to Oatman at about thirty miles. It was ten miles farther than a normal day's ride, and I had meant to cover it in two days, but by late afternoon all sense of time and direction were lost to me, and I only knew that we needed to keep heading for the mountains. Stopping was pointless. There was no water. There were no trees. There was nothing substantial to tie Gizmo to for the night. If we stopped, we would die. If I sat down—if I paused to rest—I would not get up again, and we would die. My face and neck were badly swollen, and my entire body felt as if it had been squeezed in a press. I fought through the pain and thought about nothing except getting to Oatman, though part of me had long since given up getting there. Late in the day as the shadows grew long, I noticed a pair of King birds flitting about, catching insects, unconcerned about anything but the task they had set for themselves.

I turned to look back at where we had been. We were high up in the dry embrace of the Black Mountains of western Arizona. I gazed out over the vast expanse of desert that lay to the west below, the desert wind blowing across the sage and cactus that stretched across the long slope back to the river and beyond. I could see the headlights of cars, barely visible in the fading daylight. I imagined the people down there, driving along, headed to the river for a bit of swimming and fishing. I thought of them in their cars, carefree and happy. I thought about the Desert Water Bags that hung from their front bumpers and the cool night wind the motorists would be savoring as it came through wind wing windows and enveloped them as they sat on the mohair seats and drove alongside the great river, silently below.

I looked at Gizmo, "Damn, I don't know if we're gonna make it, bud," I said finally.

He grunted, continued his slow gait, sleepy eyed with his head slumped in defeat, while his feet clicked against the rocks on the trail. I draped my arm over his neck and sort of hung there and let him drag me. It stretched my back and felt good for a few short moments, but I couldn't keep it up and finally had let go to regain my feet. I stumbled and nearly fell in the process. The thought of dying within sight of people crossed my mind, and the irony of it stung almost as much as the black widow's bite.

And then suddenly we crossed a gravel road. Momentarily revitalized, I hoped it would take us to Oatman. We turned to follow it uphill. I still saw no sign of a town or people anywhere, and I began to wonder if anyone actually lived in this place. The sun was just setting over the Sacramento Mountains, far back to the west of the river below, when we came around a bend in the road into a small swale and found ourselves facing several ramshackle buildings that made up the town of Oatman. We trudged into town—Gizmo weary from the long day's slow journey, and me staggering like a drunk man—and stopped in the street, a bit overwhelmed. After a few minutes, people came out to greet us. Along with a few others, including three young girls, were Cleon and Theila Anderson, a retired couple who would end up saving our lives.

> LOGBOOK:
> Yesterday was hell. A black widow made herself at home in my sleeping bag last night and I thought I'd die. She bit me several times on the right arm and I was sick and swollen, but I felt good enough to travel. So like a dumb ass I hit the trail. Barely made it here to Oatman. God it hurts. Every time my heart beats it pumps fire.

What happened for the rest of the night—and for most of the next few days—is still mostly a blur to me. Theila, a retired nurse, immediately recognized that I was sick and instructed the girls to take Gizmo while she led me to their home across the road. She began to treat my symptoms: high fever, headache, nausea, and general ill health. At first, I was only concerned with Gizmo's well-being, but Theila put my fears to rest when she reported that the girls had unsaddled and fed him and were brushing him. I mentioned that I thought I'd been bitten by a spider.

Upon hearing this, she turned to Cleon and declared, "We've got to get him to the doctor, first thing in the morning."

She wasn't kidding because first thing in the morning turned out to be just after first light. Although the sun rises late in Oatman—being on the western slope of the mountains—the morning twilight breaks the darkness of the desert night very early, long before the sun shows itself.

We climbed into Cleon's old pickup truck and drove all the way down to Needles, traveling along the old Oatman-Topock Highway, the original Route 66 from Needles to Kingman. It wasn't much of a highway—in fact, it was a small, two-lane road, its original pavement long ago replaced by piles of debris and reclaimed by the desert sand. It had thousands of potholes and the odd wild burro we had to dodge along its path. It hadn't seen much use since World War II when the government closed the Oatman mines, and had finally been completely abandoned when they cut the new highway and bypassed the town. The new road ran around the south side of the mountains, coming through Topock from the east. The old Oatman-Topack highway was a ghost road used as a lifeline by only a handful of tough desert people.

It took us an hour and a half to get to Needles (today it takes a quarter of that time), where the doctor pronounced me "okay," although he did say I was lucky to survive, since there were eight or nine bites on the back of my shoulder blade. I had brought along the spider to show him, but he said it was too late to administer a shot of antivenom. Instead, he prescribed aspirin and bedrest. He offered a tetanus shot, which I declined. After Cleon and Theila picked up some supplies in Needles, we drove back up the mountain to Oatman.

I like to think I'm tough—not in a fighting or adversarial way, rather in more of a survival sense—but I must say, that little black spider put me down for the count. I had severe muscle cramps all over my body—at least, that's what it felt like. It was nothing but excruciating pain for the first few days. I tried taking hot baths, thinking it would relax the cramped muscles, but baths did nothing to assuage the pain. The poison attacked my nervous system and fooled me into thinking it was my muscles that hurt when in fact it was the nerve endings all over my body. Hot baths didn't touch it. Theila gave me a bottle of codeine, cautioning me that the pills were very powerful, and I started taking them. They didn't lessen the pain, but they knocked me out for periods of time, and that allowed me to get through a couple of days of misery with a bit less discomfort.

While I was in misery, Gizmo was having the time of his life. The three young girls—Jessica, Sharon, and Midge, ages eight to eleven—took over his care and feeding with a vengeance. They were up before dawn to bring him water, hay, and grain (which they kept for their pet goats and rabbits) before climbing aboard the small van that took them to school in Topock. When the van dropped them off each day in the late afternoon, they wasted no time in going to him. The girls spent the rest of the afternoon brushing and feeding him, talking to him, and generally gushing about horses, horse shows, and horsey things in general, as young girls do.

The girls had turned Gizmo out into the front yard of an abandoned house in town, which was nothing more than a dirt patch surrounded by a dilapidated picket fence that stood about two and a half feet tall. Gizmo could have easily stepped over it to freedom, but for some reason saw fit to stay within its confines. He seemed perfectly content to be waited on and fussed over, and saw no reason to look for greener pastures. I had moved myself onto the house's front porch, where I could do little more than sit in an old broken chair and watch him, or lie on my bedroll spread out on the porch. I managed to take short walks a few times, but always felt debilitated by the time I finished. Except for his welcoming whinnies when I returned from my walks, Gizmo mostly ignored me and seemed happy to have a few days' rest, shading himself beneath the eaves of the dilapidated structure.

In this manner, we spent the next three days, resting and waiting for the effects of the spider bite to subside. I saw it as a chance to spend some time reading, but couldn't sit with a book long enough to accomplish that, so I gave up and simply set myself against the clock, waiting for the hours and days to pass. They say a watched pot never boils. Those three days were the longest of my life, although a good part of them was spent in a codeine-induced haze through which many hours slipped by unnoticed.

I decided on the fifth day to saddle up and hit the trail. I felt somewhat better, and figured I was strong enough to ride. The girls were sad to see Gizmo leave, but I promised them they could write to him and that he would stay in touch (we kept that promise). After a quick breakfast and some hearty goodbyes, Gizmo and I headed out to the northeast along the old Oatman Highway, a continuation of the abandoned road we had driven to Needles.

The stretch east from Oatman, called "Bloody 66," had long been considered one of the most treacherous stretches of road in America. Gizmo and I walked along what was truly a ghost road, a highway abandoned more than twenty-five years before when Route 66 was rerouted along the southern edge of the Black Mountains. The old road wound around the northern end of the mountain range by navigating a series of terrifying turns and switchbacks—without guardrails—past many old mine shafts and quarries. These were still filled with remnants of their glory days. Broken-down wagons and old rusted horse-drawn machinery rested where they had died and served as monuments to the time when the mines had brought prosperity to the area. Traveling along the old road was a step back in time, even in 1974, and I savored it as we walked slowly through it all. This was but one of several abandoned sections of old Route 66 we would travel and was the most remote and ghost-like of any of them.

That night, after picking our way down the backside of the mountain and entering the wide expanse of the Sacramento Valley, Gizmo and I made camp at a small spring next to some holding pens. It had hurt to travel, but it hurt to sit still, too, and I was glad to be moving again. And for the first time, I felt as if we had crossed a threshold. We had left California and the Mojave Desert behind and had crossed the Colorado River. We had faced some hardships and come through them in good shape, all things considered. We had settled into a daily groove and had found our rhythm. The past was behind us, to the west. And now, our eyes looked toward the east.

While I was gathering wood for the fire a small scorpion fell from a piece I was carrying. It raised its stinger in defiance, and I stepped on it, crushed it, and vowed to double-check my boots every morning from then on.

# THE MYSTERY OF WOMEN

There's nothing more formidable than a sixteen-year-old girl. She is already a woman (though she may not yet realize it), and has in fact been headed toward becoming one since half that age. Boys, on the other hand, haven't begun to mature above the neck, and won't for some years to come, if ever. At sixteen, a girl (I call them "girls" because I'm viewing them through the eyes of a teenage boy) is already able to intuit most of the answers to life (again, though she hardly yet recognizes it), whereas her male counterpart hasn't a clue. A boy will try to impress a young woman with acts of bravado and coolness. And though she is completely unimpressed, the young woman *acts* as if he is the most wonderful thing on earth. I know this now because I have since raised two daughters and was able to get an insider's view of this process. I watched them and their friends discussing how stupid and pitiful the boys were, even though in their view, those boys were hunks. Girls have long conversations and collaborate with each other when it comes to boys. Boys don't discuss girls in any meaningful way, except to compare notes in a competition to score points in a never-ending game of one-upmanship. This game continues throughout our lives.

Sometimes I think back about girls and how much I feared them. Girls knew things I would never know. They were beautiful and smart, confident and sure of themselves. They wore trendy clothes and hung out together in groups. They went to parties and dances and movies, and took part in activities that seemed far out of my reach. And though they weren't the girls' equals, the boys at my school mirrored them in personality and appearance. I was on the outside, looking in. Those girls were exciting and worldly—everything I was not or ever would be. And oh how I loved them, though I made sure it was always from a distance, silent and unrequited. Which meant they never returned my adoration, and that's pretty much how it went throughout my teenage years. I wasn't one for having a girlfriend or going on dates, though I did have each for a short time or two.

As I was saying, a sixteen-year-old girl is the most daunting thing in the world. And back then, to a fifteen-year-old boy like me, those sixteen-year-old girls represented both an ultimate revelation and my worst nightmare. I mixed with them easily in a group, as a charming, witty (or so I thought), and somewhat handsome (for a scrawny kid who was a year younger than they were) boy who could entertain with funny jokes and clever ripostes, not to mention the fact that I played guitar and wrote my own songs. I was also into horses in a peripheral way back then, which lent me a sort of rustic, rural charm within a group. I saw myself as a well-rounded person, a Renaissance man, genuinely interested in much more than just the simple hedonistic pleasures of popular culture that kept my classmates preoccupied. Looking back, I think I *was* well rounded in an unsophisticated sort of way, and it led to my somewhat alteritous view of life that included compassion for those with whom I have little or nothing in common. And "little in common" was what I had with my female classmates back then.

I didn't go to my high school prom. I didn't go to any high school social functions, for that matter, except the times when I played in the band. Dressing up in a conventional manner was out of the question by the time I was a high school freshman, my bent toward thrift store clothes having been firmly established by then. I knew I didn't have the social graces necessary to hold my own, so a Friday or Saturday night might find me rolled up in my mummy bag and camped in a pasture or inside a drainage culvert beneath a highway somewhere many miles from home.

In any event, it was decades later at a high school reunion that I learned some truths about my views of myself and my family and about comparisons to my classmates. As adults at the reunion, some of my classmates described their home lives while growing up. Many accounts seemed to include an alcoholic stay-at-home mother who was beaten by an abusive father. All manner of tales contained physical harm and violence, including emotional and sexual abuse.

I sat and said nothing as my classmates compared notes and mentioned others who grew up in similar circumstances. These stories were old news, common knowledge to them, but were revelations to me. Many of my long-held notions about those perfect middle class families—families I had wished to belong to—were shattered, and by the end of the evening I felt as though my own broken family was the only normal one of the bunch. Despite being poor, at least we had grown up caring about one another, and we weren't victims in the ways many others were. I came away from that reunion feeling lucky.

Another thing was revealed to me during that high school gathering. I visited with some of the women in my class, popular women who had been cheerleaders, student council members, and who were well placed in the hierarchy of the school's *in* crowd. I had been in awe of them during high school, of course, but rarely spoke to them and certainly didn't socialize with their circle of friends, which included the jocks and sports heroes in the class. But in discussing the good old days at school, one of them confessed to me, "You know, we all had the *biggest* crush on you back then."

I must clarify here that I did indeed go to dances during my youth. I went mainly to see the musicians play, but I learned to dance after a fashion and how to enjoy myself at those sorts of functions. In fact, those times when I would lean against the wall and watch all those pretty girls dancing, well … I was like a puppy in a room full of rubber balls.

They were big dances held on Friday nights in Pasadena away from my own hometown and my classmates. I was a stranger there, and I liked it that way. My classic clothes, with pinstriped shirts and button-on celluloid collars, seemed to fit in. Ties were required, so my collection of old silk thrift store ties served me well. Two thousand kids would jam into the Civic Auditorium to dance to various bands who came through town on tour. The house band was called the *Diaboliques,* and they laid down a steady stream of rhythm and blues, soul, and pop covers. I was in awe of those musicians and held spellbound by their matching sequined suits and flashy Fender guitars.

Nature puts non-predatory animals into herds to confuse their predators. A flock of birds or a herd of elk becomes one big blur, and the predator has difficulty focusing on one member. Now, this is a very weak analogy, but boys at a dance could be viewed as predators in some ways, even if you see them only as harmless fools. The fact is, we're still out to catch a girl, on some level.

There were so many girls there during the first couple of weeks that I just stood in the corner paralyzed, as if my feet were nailed to the floor, my mind racing. My eyes couldn't believe what they were seeing. It was overwhelming. I hadn't a clue about where I fit into that scene of mass hysteria, with the kids dancing and singing and shouting, sneaking outside together, doing god knows what. But it was compelling—more than compelling—and I finally figured out that, just as nature intended, I should probably concentrate on only one girl at a time. Cut her out of the herd. Ask her to dance and try to enjoy it.

By the third Friday night dance, I had worked up my courage and asked a girl to dance. She turned me down flat, mumbling something about "I have to go and … blah blah …" and off she went with her girlfriend. I was crushed, of course. And naturally, my first instinct was to go home right then, grab my gear, hitchhike to some remote place, and disappear like a solo blast over the centerfield bleachers. But my better sense prevailed, and I stuck it out. Eventually, I summoned the nerve to try again, and the next girl said yes. I danced with so many girls that I lost count, and I was happily tired by the end of the evening. That night was probably one of the highlights of my life back then. In some ways, it still is.

Besides giving me the opportunity to see real professional musicians performing and learning how to dance (which basically I achieved from watching others), those Friday night dances gave me my first real insights on how to deal with women, at least on a superficial level. It was a beginning of sorts.

When dancing, I could speak to the girl or not, which usually depended upon her general countenance and how much intelligence I saw in her eyes. The music was loud, and we couldn't hear each other anyway, so a sentence or two made up the conversation during a three-minute song. If I felt brave, I might ask for a second dance (rarely a third—that seemed like a long-term commitment), and I could talk to her for a minute or so between songs. Occasionally I saw girls from my own school, but I never asked any to dance. I kept this scene separate from my hometown social life. In some ways, it was like reading books in those tie stalls at the back of the horse barn, back when I was a kid. It was a place I could call my own.

I never knew what girls talked about when they went off in pairs or small groups. Come to think of it, I still don't. I just assumed they were talking about boys, and I reasoned that I didn't figure into any of those conversations. Call it low self-esteem, but back then I figured I wasn't anything special to girls. But I didn't care, and the idea of being a non-person didn't bother me at all. I accepted it, and it was mildly comforting in a way. I was the guy that girls looked straight past when they turned to look at the hunky guy who had just entered the room. But I was on a solo trail, and I was already marching to my own drum. I knew that we didn't hear the same song and that the path I was on was eventually going to lead me away from those girls. I loved them anyway. I saw greatness in them, in their beautiful smiles and easy grace and the way they glided across that dance floor, the night breezes playing in their hair, and the great, spinning mirror ball casting pirouettes of light across their eyes as they moved. The magic of those nights stayed with me all through high school and throughout my long sojourn with Gizmo. In a sense, that magic helped me forge a connection with all people, even as I sought back then to live a life of solitude. That magic stays with me still.

# THE ARIZONA HIGH DESERT

The Colorado River marks more than just the boundary between California and Nevada or Arizona. It is a graphic indication of where the Mojave ends and the great Sonoran Desert of Northern Arizona begins. Through the region, the river forms the bottomland in the watersheds between the gentler slopes of the Mojave's Piute Mountains in the west and Arizona's Black Mountains to the east. It is where nature has put an end to the Mojave, and we enter the northwestern corner of the Sonoran. This is a new kind of desert, one that will be more forgiving in some ways, more demanding in others.

After a few days in Oatman I recover enough from the black widow spider bite to continue, and we ride down the trail along the eastern slope of the Black Mountains, following an abandoned leg of old Route 66 that was bypassed many years before and has been completely forgotten now. The road winds down into the Sacramento Valley and crosses what will someday become Interstate 40, near Kingman, the last real civilization we will see for a while as we make our way into Hualapai country. The Hualapai Indian Reservation borders on large tracts of government land administered by the Forest Service and the Bureau of Land Management, so there are few private ranches in the area. Most ranches here consist of smaller holdings attached to large tracts of government-leased land.

We climb steadily into high desert country, to altitudes over a mile high. Because the terrain is still very desert-like, only the appearance of large pine trees gives away its elevation. The country is rugged with buttes and mesas that blend with taller peaks that have names like *Cottonwood, Tin, Cross, Peacock, Snowy, Aubrey, Aquarius,* and *Yampai*. It is slow going, and I lose the trail many times, having to backtrack because of washed out gullies and dead end canyons.

There were very few fences back in the Mojave Desert, but there are more here, though they are still few and far between. When a fence interrupts our trail, we travel along it until I can find a wire gate. If none is to be found, I find a corner post and untie the barbed wire, take down the fence, pull Gizmo through, and repair the fence behind us. If no corner post can be found, I cut the fence with my fence tool, then repair it after we cross. I can find a gate most of the time, even if it is far out of our way.

*LOGBOOK:*
*Camped at a windmill here, with a bit of grass growing*
*around the cattle tank. A calf wandered up, looking for its*
*mother. Since Gizmo was the right color it decided he would*
*do, and it tried to nurse. Gizmo didn't know what to do. Just*
*turned his head around to see what was going on back there,*
*and snorted a lot. I laughed for the first time in days. It felt*
*good.*

Windmills and cattle tanks are easier to come by in this country because a lot of the land had been settled by cattlemen in the past. They have left their mark upon the land, fencing, drilling wells, and creating berms and dams for collecting water. The harsh sandy desert of the Mojave has given way to sandstone cliffs and red dirt with larger plants and more available water. Piñon and juniper trees are plentiful here, and they constitute a primary difference between the Mojave and the Sonoran Deserts. There is good grass through here for Gizmo, and camps are easy to find. The going is rough for him, however, because the trails are steeper and harder on his hooves. He still has the set of shoes he started with. The hard borium patches that were welded to their soles have lengthened their lifespan, but now they are beginning to wear faster from the stones and hard ground he is forced to cover every day.

I am concerned for my horse's back. Gizmo has lost weight, and his backbone is beginning to show just slightly. I'm not overly worried, but I know that the saddle will begin to fit incorrectly over time as his physiology changes. I know I will need to keep a close eye on it so that he doesn't get cinch galls or saddle sores. I walk and lead my horse much of the time through this high desert, especially when we're traveling downhill.

The sweetgrass that grows in bunches throughout this country offers sustenance to me, in the form of tea I make from it, and nourishment for Gizmo. It often grows alongside the locoweed in a dance of give and take. I am vigilant about making sure none of the weed lies near where Gizmo grazes at night. I often cut tall grass with my knife and bring it to him when there is none growing around the campsite.

Gizmo seems to be holding his own through this country. We have traveled over five hundred miles and he has been transformed from a green, inexperienced four-year-old colt into a well-seasoned veteran of the trail. He rarely spooks at anything now and has learned to keep his eyes and ears sharp for sounds around us, something I now rely on to signal possible danger.

We emerge from the rugged country of the high desert into a broad grassland, and the mountains of the Kaibab National Forest appear in the distance. I locate Bill Williams Mountain and Mount Sitgreaves on my map. They lie far to the east, each one rising nearly ten thousand feet above sea level. We stay a couple of days in Seligman, where I sleep in a bed for the first time in several weeks. I give Gizmo an alcohol rubdown each of the two nights we stay, and it seems to brace and revitalize him. Gizmo is rock solid now, and so am I. We have each lost twenty percent of our body weight, and neither of us has an ounce of excess fat. It has given way to lean, hard muscle, though not the kind a body builder would exhibit. Each of us seems to mirror the other; Gizmo and I both gaunt and tough, though not yet what you would call skinny.

From Seligman we begin our long climb into the forests of the Kaibab, passing places with names like *Partridge Creek, Sereno, 15 Mile Tank, Corva,* and *Welch*. We follow an abandoned rail line that takes us deep into the mountains, longer, but an easier route because railways do not climb steep hills, but instead go around them with gentle grades. The trail is over seven thousand feet up. I don't push my horse hard knowing that this is his first time at this altitude. I want both of us to acclimatize to it gradually.

It is beautiful country that will someday become a hiking trail for outdoor enthusiasts who will be able to drive to its trailheads for a leisurely day's hike. For now though, we ride through extremely isolated country that has not seen travelers for decades. The route takes us nearly to Williams and continues in patchy sections all the way to Flagstaff. I am grateful for the secluded passage through the rough mountains. From Flagstaff, we leave the San Francisco Mountains and enter the Painted Desert of the Navajo Reservation, an area that covers almost eight thousand square miles.

# THE GIRL AT THE WATER TANK

Today, after all these years, I look back upon the wildness of the great Mojave Desert that Gizmo and I experienced and realize that it is all gone now, destroyed by the pressures of the expanding urban population and landscape. The same is true for much of the rest of the great southwestern deserts in the United States, which exist in the states of California, Arizona, New Mexico, Nevada, Utah, and small parts of Colorado and Texas. There are some places you still can't drive to in your comfortable sports utility vehicle, but those that aren't on Indian reservations or protected lands have pretty much disappeared. Things were different in 1974.

What the mountains to the northeast of Kingman, Arizona lacked in height, they made up for in sheer ruggedness. An unforgiving land for both man and beast. The interstate highway has since plowed straight through the center of it all, granting easy access to anyone driving by and destroying the solitude and stillness the land had once possessed. Gizmo and I were lucky enough to cross this area when it was still largely untouched. We rode through the Hualapai reservation and onto government land that was administered by the Bureau of Land Management. Scattered throughout we found a number of ranches inhabited by people who, I can only conclude, must have been among the toughest people on earth.

We followed an underground gas pipeline for miles during this time because those pipelines tended to follow a straight line, their builders having ignored both mountains and canyons to follow a compass heading and laying the pipe over and under any natural obstacles. Some sections of pipeline were so remote they had to be patrolled by light aircraft, and Gizmo and I waved to several pilots over the weeks of our desert trek as they came over very low to check that everything was intact. Sometimes the climb became too steep, and I resorted to studying my map to find a way around. There were occasions when I simply had to turn Gizmo back the way we had come and pick our trail as we went, looking for an alternate route.

It was during one such diversion from the main pipeline road that I followed a cow trail around the bottom of a large mesa, hoping we would catch back up with the road on the far side. This took us many miles out of our way, and the cow path disappeared by the time we got halfway around. I was accustomed to navigating by dead reckoning, and my USGS map kept me abreast of where we were. It showed a small icon with the word "Ranch" next to it on top of the mesa. I had no idea how the rancher got home because I could see no ranch road nor any sort of horseback trail. I figured we would probably end up passing around below it.

After a couple of days of wandering through this inhospitable country, we came to a windmill on my map that I had drawn a circle around. Oftentimes, wells on the map didn't exist anymore, having long since been taken down or, if they were wooden, collapsed from the onslaught of the weather. This one, a ten-foot Aermotor on a thirty-foot tower, looked to be in fine working condition, complete with an attendant cattle trough from which its clear water overflowed. This was a rare find for me, and I aimed to make the best of it.

You can find two basic kinds of cattle tanks in the West. One is what you might imagine, a metal (or wooden) trough that cows drink from. But any cowboy knows that most tanks are simply dammed-up indentions in the ground that collect the natural flow of rain water. A rancher will bulldoze an earthen dam across a low area so that water collects and creates a small pond. I preferred to stay away from these. The water was usually hard to get to and we had to walk through a lot of mud to reach it. Gizmo often became bogged down before he could get to the water to drink. And that drying mud and seepage drew all manner of deer flies, mosquitos, and other biting critters. So, while we did drink our fill at earthen water tanks, the metal ones were much more to our taste.

This particular windmill and tank lay nestled in a small grove of cottonwood trees. The trees had huge leafy canopies that provided shelter from the hot sun and would even keep most of the rain off in a storm. Gizmo needed a break, so I decided to spend a couple of days. There was plenty of firewood nearby—cottonwood makes terrible firewood, but I found mesquite and some dead cedar—and I had a couple of books to read. Green grass grew around the water tank and along the path the water had taken when it overflowed down into the arroyo, so Gizmo had food for a couple of days or more. It was a tranquil, idyllic setting, exactly what I'd had in mind when I first envisioned the ride. In a place like this, I could be a lone cowboy, miles from anyone or anywhere, just me and my horse on the lone prairie. I settled in to enjoy the solitude.

It was late in the afternoon when I made camp. I went through my daily routine of seeing to Gizmo's needs first. I brushed him down and made sure he was watered and fed. I staked him out to eat, using one half of a pair of hobbles and buckling it to one front foot before clipping the picket rope to it and tying it to something close to the ground—in this case, one of the legs of the windmill tower. I had learned the hard way many years before that a horse can run off even when hobbled. And if you stake a horse by his halter, when he raises his head the rope comes up with it and will eventually tangle around a hind foot. It often causes a bad rope burn, or worse. Staking a horse by his front foot sets his head free and allows the rope to travel along the ground, which keeps him from tangling his hind feet. It also allows him to lie down if he chooses, which Gizmo did every night.

I had taught Gizmo to be tied by his front foot when he was a yearling. First I tied him to a heavy log using a soft cotton rope and a single hobble. This setup allowed him to drag the log around a bit. Tying him hard and fast to a post might have broken his leg had he spooked and tried to run off. I kept the rope short so he could not run far enough to gain speed and hurt himself before the rope pulled taut. He adapted to the log within a few minutes. I did this over a period of days until he had fully accepted it and could be tied by his foot with a thirty-foot rope to a post.

Once I had tended to Gizmo, I put the camp in order. I spread my rain slicker out as a ground cloth with my saddle blanket on top for a bed. I put my saddle at one end, for a pillow and set my saddlebags to the side so I could get to my utensils and reading material. I made a small cook fire and settled in, listening to the rhythm of Gizmo tearing off grass then chewing, sighing, chewing some more, and tearing off another mouthful. Once darkness came, Gizmo wandered near me and lay down as close to me as he could. I reached over to scratch his ears.

The next morning, I stumbled upon a rattlesnake in camp. Mornings and evenings are when snakes come out to sun themselves, before and after the heat of the day. I almost stepped on him as I started to walk away from camp to pee. I reached back and grabbed my single action Colt, thumbed the cylinder until the snake cartridge was lined up, and I shot him. I kept a single .410 shotgun cartridge in one of the chambers for just this purpose. I had cut its length down so it would fit, and it was perfect for snakes. Long ago I adopted a live-and-let-live attitude, but when a rattlesnake takes up residence in your house, you should probably dispose of it somehow. I wasn't about to take a chance on its biting Gizmo, so I dispatched it. I didn't feel good about killing it, but the upside was that it would make a good breakfast for me. I managed to cook it over the fire, and with some salt and pepper liberally applied, it didn't taste too bad. It didn't taste at all like chicken, any more than chicken tastes like rattlesnake, but it was good to have some meat for a change, and I hung a few pieces out to dry for the trail ahead.

I took a much-needed bath after breakfast. I stripped down, climbed into the cold water in the tank, and brought my clothes with me so I could wash them as well. There's nothing quite like taking a bath in a cattle trough, especially when you're in the middle of nowhere. It's cold enough that you want to get it over with in a hurry, but it's such a wonderful experience that you end up lingering for as long as you can stand it. This is what I was feeling as I first scrubbed my clothes and then myself. And this is the point I mentioned earlier—the point when fate came knocking.

As I was scrubbing myself, whistling, and singing, Gizmo had come over to the tank and had his nose in the trough, pushing the water around. He wasn't drinking, just playing around in the water. Suddenly his ears went up, his head jerked around, and he stared off into the distance. I looked in that direction and couldn't see anything, but I knew something was there.

When you're out in open country, a horse is the best watchdog on the planet. I decided to get out of the bath, just in case.

Before I could climb out of the water tank, a horse and rider came up over a small mound and into camp. Gizmo whinnied several times in greeting. I didn't share his enthusiasm, caught with my pants down like I was. I stood in the tank, my shirt and pants hanging over the side. The low morning sun was at the rider's back, so I couldn't make out much more than a cowboy hat and boots and the glint of spurs on a bay horse.

"Howdy," said a voice that didn't match the picture I was seeing, "Everything okay?"

*Oh crap,* I thought.

It was a woman's voice.

She stepped down off her horse and walked into the shade of the cottonwood.

*Oh my god, she's beautiful.*

I had no idea how I must have appeared, but it couldn't have made a good first impression. I caught myself gawking, my mouth open, slack jawed.

"Oh …" I mumbled, "uh, sorry … I'm, uh—"

"Looks like you're havin' a bath," she said with a note of droll sarcasm.

"Well, yep, I am," I stammered. "Didn't know anybody was around." I crouched down in the waist-high water and began to shiver a little.

"Where you headed?" she asked.

"East coast," I answered, "Virginia."

"You're riding all the way to Virginia? Wow!"

"Yeah, just call me crazy … or stupid, either one."

She looked to be about my age, and the first thing I noticed was her hair, blossoming in auburn currents from beneath a grey Resistol that had a stampede string hanging down behind. She wore a snap down western shirt that was tucked into a pair of Wranglers, with a carved belt and a silver trophy buckle that looked as big as a dinner plate. Her jeans were partially covered by a pair of handmade chinks—chaps that fell just below the knees—festooned with tooled leather and fringe. Her boots had high bulldogging heels—the kind that working cowboys use—with a pair of well-worn spurs strapped on them. I could tell she had seen a lot of miles from between a horse's ears.

It dawned on me that I should get out of the water, but I was too embarrassed to say anything. She read my mind.

"Do you want me to look away while you get out?" she asked, with a grin.

"Uh, yeah, that'd be good," I answered, awkwardly.

She wasn't the least bit embarrassed and simply turned around and kept talking. My teeth had begun to chatter, and my fingertips were wrinkled and shriveled by the time I hoisted myself over the side of the tank. While I was slipping and sliding and grasping the edge of the water tank in my failed attempt to exit gracefully, she was saying that Gizmo and I were on her family's ranch, and how she'd been raised there. I tried to listen politely, but my attention was focused on covering my naked self. I pulled my wet pants on as fast as I could while trying to participate in the conversation.

I turned my backside to her, as was only proper, but the wet jeans just wouldn't slide up my legs, and this caused me to hop around on one foot while trying to force the other through the pants leg opening. I flopped around like a trout on a riverbank and almost fell back into the tank. I wished I hadn't thrown my extra pair of jeans away, and silently cussed Gizmo for my having lightened the load on his behalf.

The woman was trying to maintain the illusion that she wasn't looking, but her occasional giggles gave her away, and it only made matters worse. By this time, I was mortified.

"I'm sorry," I said, gasping as I hopped around, jerking at a pant leg, "I thought this was BLM land. That's what it says on my map," I explained.

"Oh, this part is," she said. "We have a lease on it, but that doesn't matter. You're more than welcome to ride anywhere on the ranch. It's okay."

I managed to get my pants buttoned up and pulled a dry t-shirt out of a saddlebag.

"Okay, you can turn around now," I said. "I'm sorry, but my clothes are wet, and I probably look like an idiot."

She looked at me as if for the first time and began to giggle again, which only made me feel more like the fool I was. But I also felt an instant connection, an incredibly strong chemistry between us. Of course, in hindsight I realize it was only wishful thinking on my part, but it made no difference to me at the time because I was staring at a goddess sent straight from heaven. Gizmo couldn't have cared less and by this time he was used to the company and had gone back to picking at the grass, ignoring the bay gelding the woman had ridden in on.

"I'm John," I said, "and this is Gizmo."

"Well, hello John. And hello there, Gizmo," she said cheerfully. She walked up to him and started scratching his ear. Gizmo stopped what he was doing and welcomed the sudden attention, leaning his face into her fingers.

"Very nice to meet you. My name is Elizabeth … call me Liz … and this is my horse, Cotton," she said, gesturing with the bridle reins she held in her other hand.

"Elizabeth, Cotton … I don't suppose you play left-handed guitar, do you?" I asked, referencing the folk singer, a feeble attempt at humor.

She didn't seem to hear me, and at this point was directing her conversation toward Gizmo. I wasn't sure if she was talking to me at all. I just stood there like a fool and said nothing. She didn't seem to mind, though, and kept petting Gizmo who glanced at me with a knowing look that said, "This is how it's done, moron."

Finally, she turned to look at me and smiled. We stood there silently for a moment. I was a statue, frozen in place, completely under her spell. And looking back, I know that *she* knew I was helpless from the minute she saw me. Women are born with this wisdom. And men are both oblivious and completely vulnerable to it.

"You're welcome to unsaddle and sit awhile if you want," I said. "I don't have much, but I can boil us up some tea, and there's some rattlesnake I cooked up earlier."

Stupid, stupid, stupid! Offer her rattlesnake? What the hell are you thinking?

"You eat rattlesnake?" she asked.

"Well, it was here in camp this morning, so I shot it. Didn't want it to go to waste, so—"

"Ah, that must have been the gunshot I heard. Was that you?" She seemed impressed, which caused my manly instincts to kick in.

"Not sure. Could've been. About an hour after sunup," I said.

"Did it try to bite you? Are you okay?" she asked.

Her apparent worry about my safety was only a patronizing gesture of mock concern meant to allow me to recoup some of the "man points" and dignity I had lost earlier while putting on my pants. I didn't realize this at the time, though it should have been painfully obvious.

"Didn't try to bite me, but it was close enough that I was afraid Gizmo might end up on the wrong end of it," I replied.

I could feel my confidence returning, given the opportunity to talk about man-stuff. I wanted her to stay, but didn't want to appear pushy or forward. At first I didn't repeat my offer, but then I thought about those Friday night teenage dances I'd gone to and about the first time I'd summoned the nerve to ask a girl to dance. And I thought, *what the heck … nothing ventured, nothing gained.*

"So, how 'bout it?" I prompted. "You're welcome to hang out awhile, and Gizmo and me'd enjoy the company." I could feel my face growing hot and red and there wasn't a damned thing I could do about it.

"Sure, I'd love to," she replied.

It took a moment for her answer to sink in, and then I couldn't quite believe it.

"Ah, well, great! Just throw your gear down anywhere, and I'll see if I can dig up something to drink out of," I said, a little too eagerly. I fumbled through my saddlebags for another cup, and it dawned on me that I had only one.

And so it was that we spent the day together, talking and laughing, sharing stories and secrets, telling each other our memories and dreams, drinking from the same cup. She talked about horses and barrel racing and how she'd sometimes find an injured animal to take in and save—everything from birds to baby bobcats—and how she was thinking about going to vet school. I didn't have the nerve to ask if she had a boyfriend. She never mentioned one, but she didn't say she *didn't* have one either.

I babbled on about life on the trail, how I had raised Gizmo, and the sort of useless information that women have a knack for drawing out of men. But I think, on one level, she was genuinely interested. I suppose it isn't every day that a man comes through on horseback, riding from ocean to ocean, and I was hoping that maybe Gizmo and I had made an impression on her. I especially hoped that *I* had (I didn't much care what she thought of Gizmo). Again, wishful thinking, but it's part of what keeps a man alive sometimes.

I pulled my boots on, and we went for a walk. She talked about her life growing up on the ranch. My wet jeans made a squishing sound with every stride, which I found annoying, though she didn't seem to notice. She mentioned the kinds of feed that were good for horses and cattle, and I made mental notes to remember for Gizmo's sake. She identified more varieties of grasses than I could ever remember, with names like buffalo, fescue, dropseed, wheatgrass, cottontop, squirreltail, and brome, along with several types of bunch grass, and others that are lost to me now. She talked about plants and flowers, too, and pointed out some of the ones I already knew, like purple sage, manzanita, and creosote bush, and others I was unfamiliar with, such as deer brush, desert broom, and Mexican cliffrose.

I watched her face as she spoke. Her eyes were blue-green, the color of the turquoise earrings revealed every now and then when the breeze ruffled her hair. There were freckles on her nose and cheeks, and her face seemed to form a permanent smile that naturally put me at ease. Though she tended to ramble on, she carried a gentle cadence in her accent, and her sentences were broken by pauses and short silences that told me she was a listener as well as a talker. It was lovely to hear another's voice like this, relaxed and fresh, in a private conversation that wasn't focused upon Gizmo or me or our ride. I mostly listened and spoke sparingly. Her voice was music to my ears, and I hummed its tune in my head as we walked along.

My Wranglers dried as we went, and I felt a lot more comfortable by the time we returned to camp. I suggested we have some tea. I boiled up some water, and she grabbed a handful of sweetgrass that grew in the damp shade of the water tank. She cut the roots and dirt off, ripped the grass into small pieces, and then dropped it into the water to steep. It made good tea—a lot better than the stale dried brown stuff I had been drinking—and I vowed to switch to it right then. For the most part, I was able to make the sweetgrass tea for a good many weeks, all the way to Texas, until I could no longer find it.

We talked long into the afternoon. She asked me about my reasons for choosing such a foolish undertaking (my words), and I talked a bit about dreams and the sorts of things that motivate people like me. I asked her about her own dreams, and what she wanted to do, besides being a veterinarian.

"I want to see places," she responded.

"What sorts of places?"

"Wild places. Old places. Out-of-the-way places. You know, places where people don't go. Places with lots of old people, wise people. Just interesting places, I guess." She paused. "I know it sounds corny, but I want to see the world. I want to know what's out there."

"It seems to me you live in one of those places, but I know what you mean," I mentioned. "I suppose that's the reason I dragged Gizmo out here."

"He seems to enjoy it, doesn't he?" she said.

"Well, he's used to it now, and I reckon he's enjoying the company right now," I said.

It was a clumsy way of flirting with her, and I felt the heat rise in my face again. I looked away so she wouldn't see me blush, but I was pretty sure she saw me anyway.

We sat close, facing the mesa—not facing each other, but side by side—our elbows an inch apart. She took off her hat and tossed it over on top of mine, where it rested on my saddle. As her hair billowed out in waves of red, some of it settled on my shoulder, and I was suddenly aware that this was the first time I had actually touched her.

Oh crap, now what do I do? I thought. C'mon, Gizmo … help me out here.

I tried to pretend I hadn't noticed and concentrated on acting cool and casual. But I kept rambling on about what a great horse Gizmo was, how I'd modified the saddle for the ride and added borium to the bottoms of his shoes to make them last longer, and how a horse loses weight off his back at first when traveling across country. She responded by abruptly changing the subject.

"Mmm," she sighed. "What a lovely day this is." She leaned into me and rested her head on my shoulder.

At that point, I was panic-stricken and became welded in place. I managed to slide my arm around her, but I was a petrified log, the appendage nothing but a lifeless, broken branch. I held my breath and didn't say a word. I couldn't have even if I had wanted to.

"Owls come at night sometimes and steal our baby kittens," she said.

Huh? What's she talking about?

"Um, yeah," I replied, after a pause. "They're quiet. They don't make noise when they fly."

My throat was dry. I had no idea what to say or do. I didn't know where the conversation was headed.

"They do it when no one is looking," she said. "Like people. They steal your dreams when you don't expect it."

"So, you think an owl is sort of a dream stealer?"

"Well, I don't know if owls are dream stealers, but I think maybe people can steal dreams, and they act like owls when they do," she responded. "They steal 'em in silence when you're not looking."

"Well, maybe so," I said. "But don't you think that people steal your dreams only if you let 'em? Kittens aren't like people," I continued. "They don't have much choice when it comes to owls, I think."

"Hmm … yeah, maybe you're right," she said, "but when you lose your dream it feels like you lost a kitten."

I felt that one. It hit home. "Did an owl steal your dream?" I asked.

"I think maybe it did …" She paused a long time before continuing. "Or maybe it's trying to." She sighed.

She didn't offer more, and I wasn't going to pry, so I left it there. We sat leaning against each other for a long time, neither saying a word, just listening to the horses and the sounds of the countryside. She finally broke the silence and spoke as if there had been no break in the conversation.

"It's just that, well … I see someone like you, who had this dream to ride your horse, and you just went and did it, and well … you didn't ask permission, and you didn't care what anyone thought. You just went and did it. I love that."

That caught me off guard. It was true, I hadn't given a single thought to how this ride affected anyone else. I was doing it for selfish reasons, and she was right. I had started the ride because it was my own dream, and I hadn't considered what others thought, or how it might affect them. It had never occurred to me that anything I did might somehow have an effect on others.

"It wasn't quite as cut and dried as all that," I replied. "I didn't just decide one day to jump on my horse and head east. It was more like—"

"No, but you're doing it, aren't you?" she said. "I wouldn't have thought to do something like this,"—she gestured toward Gizmo and my gear— "and even if I had, I would have let them talk me out of it."

I wondered who *them* was. "Depends on how bad you wanted it," I said. "Is there something you want as bad as this?

"Yeah, I think maybe there is," she answered.

And with that, she turned toward me, reached up to my face, and kissed me. It was a very sweet kiss, and it lasted a long time, or it seemed like a long time to me. And through it all, I was both excited and afraid.

A young man dreams of meeting a woman like this. And he dreams of being a lonesome cowboy hero, John Wayne riding in off the range to rescue her and take her away. It can be any man's fantasy. And for me it came with the fear of commitment and abandonment that a confirmed loner has. I was a man with "no ties to nuthin'," as the cowboys say. All of a sudden, a beautiful woman had fallen for me, and I had no idea how to deal with the situation. I tried to think of a way to let her down gently.

When the kiss ended, she jumped to her feet, walked over the gelding, and began to saddle him.

"I have to go," she said, turning to untie her horse.

She was going to ride back to the ranch, pack a bag, and return so that she could ride off with Gizmo and me. I watched in silence as she bent to pick up her hat and pulled it down over her hair. I stood there, ready to explain that, while I thought she was a lovely person, I needed to ride this trail alone.

She led Cotton over to me. As I opened my mouth to speak, she said, "Thank you so much. I think maybe you saved my life." She leaned in and kissed me on the cheek.

"I hope your ride is just like your dream," she said.

She walked to where Gizmo stood and threw her arms around his neck, hugging him and kissing his face. "Goodbye, Gizmo. You are such a fine horse. I'll miss you."

With that, she made the effortless vault into the saddle that is born of a lifetime on horseback. She swung the bay gelding around to face me. The sun was at my back now, and I could see the glow of happiness on her face. It was brighter than the desert sun. She looked at me for a long time, sharing a quiet smile, then turned and cantered off in the direction she had come, leaving me to nurse a wounded ego and a broken heart.

Later that evening I talked it over with Gizmo.

"I'll never understand women, that's for sure"

He paused with a mouthful of dry bunch grass and looked at me, waiting for me to continue.

"And y'know something, bud?" I said, "I don't even know her last name."

# HERD MENTALITY

We were riding a back trail in northern Arizona, far from civilization. There weren't any small towns or settlements nearby. Truth be told, I didn't even see any cattle grazing in the area, nor any sign of cowboys and ranching activity. We made steady progress along the four-wheel drive service road that followed an underground gas pipeline operated by the El Paso Natural Gas Company. El Paso was hundreds of miles away, and in studying my maps, I could see that this pipeline headed nowhere near El Paso or South Texas. Instead, it gradually turned toward the northeast until it disappeared off the upper right-hand side of my topographic map. I never found out the pipeline's origin, nor its final destination. I had no idea what it had to do with El Paso, but it was enough for me that we could follow it for a distance.

The greatest advantage of following a pipeline road was that I didn't have to continually verify our whereabouts on the map. I could relax and ride along while enjoying the scenery. I still referred to the maps several times a day, but I wasn't worried about getting lost. I knew where the pipeline was going, and simply followed it.

The road itself could hardly be called a road. In most places, it was nothing more than a bulldozer path left after they'd covered the pipe, and it often traveled straight up and over a steep hill or mesa, which had me wondering how in the hell the builders had managed to get their equipment up there to lay the pipe in the first place. There was no way to navigate the road on a horse when it headed straight up the side of a mountain like that, so I had to find ways around. Still, when we could, we followed the pipeline and relaxed.

It was along one such section of the trail that we jumped a herd of elk, or rather, they jumped us. The year being a relatively dry one, the animals were beginning to congregate at lower altitudes in search of feed and water. We had seen a lot of antelope on the grassy plains through here, which I had expected. These prairies were their home, and the antelope stood like sentries, watching us as we passed. Often twenty or thirty of them would spread across the grass like statues, their heads poised high and unmoving. They blended marvelously into the background of the brown buffalo grass and sage, and had I been alone, I would have passed most of them without noticing them. But Gizmo served as my own sentry, never missing anything, and when his ears—and then his eyes—turned toward them, I always knew they were there, even before I could finally see them. And when I did manage to spot an antelope, I could suddenly see them all, as if I had turned the lens on a telescope to just the spot that would reveal a star cluster in sharp focus. This happens when you hear birds in a tree but can't see them until finally you spot one and are suddenly able to see all of them.

As we traveled through the mesas that made up the foothills of the pine forests of the Kaibab, we found ourselves in the shadow of the San Francisco Peaks to the northeast. We had not seen anyone for several days, so I had let down my guard and was not paying much attention to Gizmo as he cocked both ears forward and looked intently at the trail ahead. We continued at his slow, smooth trot.

We topped a small hill and started down the other side. We were riding along the side of a long mesa, about halfway up its face. The ground rose to our left and dropped away to our right. We were traveling through a forest that hadn't made up its mind about what it wanted to be. It was a mixture of big pine trees—ponderosa, sugar pine, white pine and fir—and smaller trees—pinion, juniper, mesquite and willow—along with various brushes like sage, creosote bush, salt cedar, and mountain mahogany. As I said, I wasn't paying attention, but Gizmo was, and I nearly came off over his head when he unexpectedly stopped short, his attention riveted ahead. I heard a strange noise, a rustling of branches, and then a big elk sprang from the brush on the high side of the road to our left just ahead of us. Within seconds, elk began pouring down onto the road. Some kept moving across and off the other side, but most stopped on the trail and stared at us. The road was soon filled with them.

Folks who ride horses know what it feels like when a horse freezes up and gets ready to spook at something. He becomes rigid and stiff, standing there focused on whatever it is that has spooked him or is about to spook him. The horse's head, which has been hanging low on a loose and relaxed neck, has been raised so that it is higher than his withers, and it seems to fold itself into his neck a bit. The neck gets shorter and grows fatter with this compression. It becomes very firm, stiff, and inflexible. He has stopped moving, and his legs become like table legs, unbending and rigid, because he has hunkered down imperceptibly, in a stance that readies him for quick retreat. In a fight-or-flight situation he will almost always choose flight, since that's what he's built for.

Your horse's body is compressed, and as you sit there you can feel this compression along with the stiffness and rigidity that runs all the way through him. If you're sitting in a saddle, you are not in direct contact with him, but this doesn't matter if you're an experienced rider. You can feel all of this through the saddle, through your own legs as they rest against his sides, and in the balls of your feet as the shift in energy is transferred through the saddle to your stirrups. The horse is sending signals that feel like electricity, and any horse person knows them well. His ears are forward, listening to the source of potential danger. All of this takes place within a split second. Unless you do something to force his hand, you have lost his attention, and he will most likely spin around, away from the danger, and run off with you.

By this time in the journey, Gizmo was rarely upset by anything, so it caught me by surprise when he froze, then shied backward a few feet upon seeing the elk. He assumed the stance I described, but only for a few seconds, while he assessed the situation. There were at least two dozen elk, and they leaped out of the bushes in ones and twos, straight across the road and down into the ground cover on the downhill side. There were bulls and cows and a few youngsters mixed in with them. Several stopped in the middle of the road to watch us, ears up and eyes alert. I'm guessing they were as surprised to see us as we were to see them. They didn't seem particularly afraid, though, and I wondered whether they might think Gizmo was some strange relative of theirs as he stood stock-still, taking in the growing numbers of long eared animals who had come calling.

For his part, Gizmo promptly realized that he wasn't in danger, and his initial fright quickly changed to curiosity. The tension in his body evaporated, and he dropped his head slightly then sniffed the air. He was still cautious, but had relaxed considerably, and as he relaxed, so did I.

Seeing those elk made me glad, partly because they had come out of nowhere and partly because I hadn't expected to see them in the lower ranges, knowing they should be high in the mountain parks by late April. I noticed several very young calves with their mothers, born a bit earlier than normal, but because of the draught, this wasn't exactly a normal year.

One small critter moved toward us, evidently as curious about Gizmo as Gizmo was about him and his family. He got to within a few yards of us, approaching slowly and tentatively. Gizmo stuck his head out and sniffed loudly while I sat as still as I could and made no noise. The young one's mother finally made a loud snort, which caused him to turn and run back to her. A large buck—I assumed he was the leader of this harem—grunted and urged the herd on. He stood watching us, all the while prodding and badgering the herd to move.

We sat there for several minutes as the herd passed in front of us and down to the lower reaches of the hill below. The bucks were beginning to grow new sets of antlers, so they weren't as impressive and intimidating as they would be in a few months, once they had their full racks to show. But they were impressive nonetheless, and I sat in the saddle, amazed at the scene we had witnessed. They seemed to sense that Gizmo and I maintained a live-and-let-live philosophy and didn't seem afraid of us. When they had finally migrated across our trail Gizmo once again found his feet and continued down the road. I asked him if they had been relatives of his, and he just snorted and watched them moving down the slope as we headed past them on the trail.

Two hours later, we had reached the bottom of the mesa and found a water tank next to a windmill. There was a small clearing with big trees for shade, so I made camp. It was late afternoon as I staked Gizmo out on some decent looking bunch grass then settled in to read my tattered paperback. I spent the next three or four hours reading, writing in my logbook, practicing gun tricks with the Colt, and going through my saddlebags to find excess items to discard. The darkness settled in quickly and absolutely since no moon shown that night. Finally, I turned in and fell asleep.

Sometime later—I wasn't sure how long—I heard the sound of a vehicle coming up the road. I immediately sat up in my sleeping bag alert. We were camped down below the road, so I hoped that whomever it was would drive past without seeing us. My hopes were not realized, however. The headlights made their way toward us, bouncing and jogging with the ruts in the road, until their shadows revealed a pickup truck approaching. Instead of driving past, the truck slowed then turned toward us. They had seen Gizmo.

The pickup stopped, and the doors opened. I could see four of them as they got out, two from inside the truck and two who climbed out of the bed. They were talking loudly as they headed toward Gizmo, and they were clearly drunk.

"It's a god damn horse!" one shouted. "What the hell's it doin' out here?"

"That's a ranch horse," another answered. "That there's a ranch horse."

"Ain't no ranch horses out here," replied the first man. "He's tied up. Why the hell's a horse tied up out here?"

I was getting tense. I was glad I had kept my pants and shirt on, though my boots were on the ground next to me. I reached inside my bedroll and pulled out the Colt. They were drunk, and they looked like trouble, but they had not seen me yet.

One of them said, "Hey, let's ride the sumbitch."

"Shit, you can't ride that horse, James," another said. "You ain't no cowboy."

"Hell, I can damned sure ride it if I want to," the one named James responded. "C'mon, help me get on the sumbitch."

Gizmo shied as the men advanced toward him. I pulled back the hammer of the Colt with an audible click, and they stopped, and suddenly grew quiet at the sound.

"Don't get any closer to that horse," I said calmly.

"What the …? Who's there?" one of them demanded.

"You fellas just turn around now and go and get back in your truck and get on out of here," I said. "I don't want any trouble. Just leave the horse alone."

"And what the hell do you think you're gonna do about it?" James challenged.

"It ain't what *I'm* gonna do about it," I answered, in a quiet voice. "It's what this Colt here is gonna do about it. You want to find out, you just keep right on. Otherwise, pack it on outta here. Like I said, I don't want any trouble."

"Fuck all, James …. he *does* have a gun! Fuck this, I'm gettin' outta here," one of them shouted.

Being the leader, James stood his ground. The other two added their own remarks about getting the hell out of there, but James didn't budge. He was the bull elk in this herd, used to being in charge. But he was stumped at having his authority challenged. He and his friends could barely see me, but my eyes were well accustomed to the dark, so I could see them clearly. I wouldn't have shot them, but they were drunk, and I could fire over their heads to scare them if push came to shove. Through it all, Gizmo eyed them warily. As it was, James finally gave in.

"C'mon, let's go," he ordered, as if it were his idea. "But you ain't heard the last of this, asshole." They stumbled back to the truck, piled in, and drove off.

As soon as their headlights disappeared over the hill, I pulled my boots on and went to Gizmo. I moved him far away from where he had been, afraid they might have a gun in their truck and would come back and shoot him. I gathered the gear, saddled him quickly, and led him away from the camp.

We had to follow the road for a ways, so I kept looking back for them for a mile or two. By then, the moon had risen and there was a bit of light. I pulled Gizmo off the road and down into a small swale around an outcropping of rock and into a clearing that was well hidden from above. I made another camp and staked Gizmo close by. I spent the rest of the night sitting up, my back against a cottonwood, my Colt in my hand inside the bedroll. I nodded off for a few minutes here and there, but kept a vigil. They didn't return that night nor the next. A couple days later, we left the pipeline road to follow a small trail higher into the mountains. I left that herd to their own rut.

# START OF DAY

I come awake after a restless night's sleep in the foothills of the mountains of northern Arizona. Out of habit, I reach to find my single action Colt that lies next to me inside my sleeping bag. My thumb instinctively checks to see that the hammer hasn't been accidently pulled back. Then I slide the pistol gently up and out into the morning air, where I check to see that the hammer still rests on an empty chamber. I reach over and slide the Colt into its holster, which lies draped over the saddle next to my head. Finally, I drag myself to a sitting position, my upper body now exposed to the cool morning breeze.

Gizmo sees me stirring and immediately issues his early morning whinny to let me know that, yes, he is still there and ready to face the day.

"Good morning, pal," I say and climb out of my bedroll.

It's a three-pound down sleeping bag, lightweight yet sufficient to keep me warm in temperatures well below freezing, or so they claim. It has done its job well, and I've suffered no discomfort from the chilly night air here in the mountains. In fact, it was warm enough last night to take my pants and socks off, and I retrieve them now from inside the sleeping bag. I don't like having to step into cold pants in the morning, so I usually store them with me inside my bedroll.

I pull myself out of the bag, stretching a bit and trying to shake off the sore back and stiff limbs of a hard night's sleep on the ground. My bedroll has drifted off the ground cloth I had laid out beneath it, so there is some dirt to be wiped off. The ground cloth is just my rain slicker doing double duty. I can lay it flat out and put the sleeping bag on top of it. It's not exactly a padded mattress, but it does serve to keep the morning moisture away, and I like to think that it discourages rattlesnakes and other critters from crawling into bed with me during the night. So far, the only evidence of this is that they haven't done so.

I extract myself from the sleeping bag and slowly get up. Gizmo whinnies again when he sees me stand and walk away from camp to find a place to pee. Upon returning, I check my boots for scorpions, snakes, spiders, or other critters. Finding none, I pull on my socks and boots. I have no mirror, so I run a comb through my dirty hair by feel. I pull my toothbrush from the saddlebags and pour a bit of water on it from the canteen. I have cut the handle off the toothbrush to lighten the load, so I have to hold it between my fingers and reach into my mouth to brush. I have no toothpaste (again, to lighten the load). I simply brush with cold water. It's better than nothing.

If we were staying over, I would make a fire and boil some water for coffee or sweet grass tea, but since we're continuing our travels today, I won't do that. I like to do most of our riding in the early hours of the day and usually dispense with coffee and breakfast in the morning to hit the trail.

To pack up camp, I shake out the sleeping bag then push it down into its small cotton stuff bag. I slide the paperback novel I was reading the night before into one of the saddlebags. When that gear is stowed, I pull my knife out of its small scabbard attached to my gun belt. It is an old Case folding knife. It has a single blade that folds open on one end and a marlinspike, or fid, that folds open on the other. It's handy because I can open cans with the blade and use the fid as a hoof-pick. I grab the brush for Gizmo.

I walk over to him and give him a pat to say good morning. I look him over to make sure he hasn't cut himself on anything sharp during the night. I pick up his feet one by one, examine each hoof, and run the knife's fid between the sole and frog to clear any rocks or pebbles lodged there. I check the condition of the shoes and make sure the nails that hold them are still tight.

I brush him down, starting with his face (which he loves) and moving down each side of him in turn. I scratch each ear and spend some time running my thumb inside them to eliminate any deer flies, bugs, or crud that may be lodged in them. I wipe away any snot or grime that has collected in his nostrils and lick my finger to wipe away the sleep from his eyes. I look for cinch galls and saddle sores or any other marks or scratches he may have. If he'd had any, I would doctor them with whatever appropriate medicines were on hand. This might include spraying them with Furox, dobbing them with purple Gentian Violet, applying Bickmore's gall salve, or using congealed bacon grease from a small jar kept in a saddlebag. This morning Gizmo is fine, so I don't need to doctor him.

Satisfied that my horse is clean and ready for the day, I turn to put my gear in order. I gather anything left lying around from the night before and clean up the camp so that I leave no trace. I pick up eating utensils, my logbook and other writing material, socks and shirts left out to dry. These are packed in my small day pack or in the saddlebags and, after taking a last look around, I am ready to saddle up.

I shake out the orthopedic saddle pad, making sure no dirt is on it. I use it as my mattress, or as a half-mattress, by putting it under my upper body during the night. It helps to soften the hard ground and to mediate the rocks and bumps I come into contact with. Then I drag my saddle and pads over to Gizmo. I throw the ortho pad onto his back, straighten it, and lay a piece of foam rubber across his withers. This will keep the saddle up off them so he isn't pinched or rubbed. I swing the saddle across his back and adjust it, the pommel over his withers and saddle bars resting in place along his back. The girth has an orthopedic sleeve to prevent cinch galls. I wipe it to make sure it's free of dirt, thorns, and other foreign objects. I run the latigo strap through the cinch ring and pull it up so that it's snug, but not overly tight, before I tie it off using the over-under-sideways method of tying a normal western latigo knot. I leave the billet end of the latigo hanging down.

The saddle is a German caisson type, made in Czechoslovakia during World War II. It was used with teams of horses to pull cannons. They didn't use a driver, as with a normal wagon or carriage, but instead the horses were ridden. The saddle has a raised seat slung between the pommel and the cantle that sits high above Gizmo's back and allows airflow. It is an English style saddle, with free swinging English style stirrup leathers. I modified the English girth system, by replacing the buckles with western style latigo straps for more adjustment options. I use a breast collar to keep it from sliding back, and a britchen to keep it from sliding forward on Gizmo. I have modified it by adding rings, footman loops, and other fittings that allow me to attach various gear, like saddlebags, bedroll, rain slicker, canteen, and picket rope, easily and securely. I have added a western saddle horn to it. It isn't strong enough to rope cattle with, but it's handy for hanging my canteen and other odds and ends from time to time.

Once the saddle is cinched, I reach around to the off side (right) and catch the breast collar, which has been looped over the saddle horn for the night. I pull it beneath Gizmo's neck and across his chest and buckle it to a ring on the near side (left) of the saddle. It is a small collar, narrow—not wide like those on western roping saddles—and hangs loosely across his chest, like the ones on English saddles. It is not fastened between his legs to the cinch, but instead rides freely. It forms a V with a ring in the middle, so that it rides above his shoulders on either side. It is meant to keep the saddle from slipping back but allows Gizmo free movement of his neck and shoulders.

With the girth and breast collar attached, I fasten the britchen. This is a strap attached to the back of the saddle on each side that goes under the horse's tail and across his hips. A britchen strap is used mostly on a packsaddle to keep it from sliding forward. Gizmo doesn't mind it under his tail and has never made any fuss about it, not even the first time I put it on him.

All this time Gizmo stands quietly, still staked by his front foot and free to walk around if he wishes. He knows the drill, so he stands patiently while I tend to the morning chores. I throw the McClellan saddle bags on behind the saddle and buckle them with two short straps that slide through brass footman loops. A long strap on the lower front of each bag attaches it to the girth and keeps the bags from flopping up and down when Gizmo trots. This is the same way that these US Cavalry bags are fastened to a McClellan saddle. I buckle the bedroll on top of them using a pair of one-inch leather straps that are fixed to the saddle. These have sliding spring buckles on them, making it easy to cinch the bedroll down quickly without having to tie anything. Regular saddle strings will come loose, causing things to fall on the trail during the day. These buckle straps pull down tight and never get loose.

I fold and roll my rain slicker and drape it over the pommel of the saddle, where there are two more straps. These are smaller than the two holding the bedroll, but they have the same sort of sliding buckles on them and are perfect for attaching the slicker to the front of the saddle. There is also a small brass ring that I can clip the canteen to, on the off side of the pommel. Once these are in place I grab the long nylon rope I use for reins and clip each end to the cheek pieces in Gizmo's halter. I remove the hobble on his front foot and roll it up with the thirty-foot picket rope, then clip this to the near side of the pommel. I sling my canteen over the saddle horn and we're ready to head out. The last thing I do is a dummy check—a final glance around the camp to see that I have everything—before I step into the saddle and turn Gizmo toward the east.

# A FIRST ATTEMPT

I stop to unsaddle Gizmo at a small wooden cattle feeder that rests at the edge of a meadow nestled in the pines of the Kaibab forest in northern Arizona. The place is familiar because I have been here before. It is located far back into the mountains on a remote trail that breaks away from the abandoned rail line we have been following. We are forced to backtrack when we come to a trestle that was destroyed years ago, probably by rail workers using dynamite.

I find a small trail that switches back and forth down the side of the mountain and down into the canyon the trestle had crossed. This lonely path is nothing more than a wildlife trail, but it takes us down through the canyon, across a small stream, and eventually leads us back up to the rail line on the other side. It is a two-day detour around a bridge that would have taken us a few minutes to cross.

The trail empties into a meadow where I spot the wooden feeder on the far side, up against the tree line, and we make our way over to it. It will do as a campsite for the night. There is plenty of grass for Gizmo to eat, a stream nearby, and easy access to kindling and firewood. Plus, the great ponderosa pines provide some shelter from the weather if we need it. I see no sign that anyone has been here for a long time. Cattle haven't grazed in these mountains in years, and this place is too remote for backpackers to wander into.

The feeder is nothing more than a manger with a roof on it. It is supported with four-by-four posts on each corner, and the posts sit on two flat boards that act as skids. So the whole rig can be pulled to other spots by a team of horses. Grass has grown up around it, and it looks as if it hasn't been moved in ages.

I stake Gizmo to one of the corner posts and set about organizing the camp. I notice something in the far side of the feeder and walk around to retrieve it. It is a book, and it is familiar to me. I know the book because I had left it there. It is *Cities in Flight* by James Blish, a collection of short science fiction novels. Its cover is bleached from the sun, and the pages are curled and puckered from exposure to the elements. As I pick it up, I look down and notice hoof prints in the dried mud beneath the feeder. I recognize those prints, too. They were made by a mule named Sammy.

**********

In 1973, the year before Gizmo and I made our ride, I set out from Santa Barbara, California with a Quarter Horse named Wayward and a big bay gelding mule named Sammy. The three of us were headed for the Atlantic Ocean in North Carolina. We followed a different trail, but inevitably, Gizmo and I crossed it a few times, and this was one of them. As I've mentioned, Wayward was Gizmo's dam, an old fashioned "bulldog" type chestnut Quarter Horse mare that belonged to my mother. She plowed ahead through anything I pointed her at, fearless and competent, sure footed and capable.

Sammy was timid and fearful, having been used and abused as a logging mule in the mountains of northern California for much of his life. He still had a few scars on his hind legs where the trace chains had slapped him over and over while he dragged logs out of the forest. I bought him from a mule breeder and trainer up in Browns Valley for three hundred dollars and trailered him down to the Santa Ynez Valley where I was living. Gizmo was not quite a two-year-old at the time and was still a gangly adolescent. I made attempts at breaking Sammy to ride but was only half successful. I could ride him, but I never trusted him under saddle, and he unloaded me more times than I care to remember. Still, he was an honest sort for the most part. He had no problems with the packsaddle and britchen strap and would carry quite a heavy load if I had wanted him to. He was touchy about his hind legs and feet, and I would sometimes have to tie his hind leg up to trim and shoe the foot.

Sammy, Wayward, and I left Santa Barbara in late March 1973 and headed out across the Mojave Desert. We crossed into Arizona at Needles and followed a gas pipeline past Kingman and into the Hualapai Indian Reservation, to the north of my trail with Gizmo. It was tough going much of the time, and it seemed I was constantly discarding gear until the panniers on Sammy's packsaddle were all but empty. He became more of a liability than an asset by then, but I was determined to keep him with me, more out of loyalty to him than out of good sense.

We had reached the middle of the Painted Desert, far out into the Navajo Reservation, when both Wayward and Sammy got sick. It was a constant battle against cinch galls and saddle sores, and Wayward finally turned up with a back sore one day and we were forced to stop. Her eyes and nose ran, and she was obviously not feeling well. Sammy began to show the same symptoms. I contacted a large animal vet from Holbrook who serviced areas on the reservation. He gave them each a shot of combiotics (penicillin) and said it was all he could do for them. I got the feeling he used this treatment on all his patients. He left me with a supply of the medicine, some syringes, and instructions for giving them shots once a day until the medicine ran out.

Wayward's back sore was near her withers, and it became infected. There was nothing to do but call the trip a failure, cancel it, and trailer the two back to California. We had covered nearly a thousand miles, and my companions had taught me more than I could have learned otherwise in a lifetime. They had paid for my lessons with their own hard work and suffering. They were fine friends and compatriots, and I was indebted to them.

Back home, and I nursed Wayward back to health over the following weeks. When he regained his health, Sammy was turned out to pasture for a year while Gizmo and I made our journey. Afterward, he spent several years with me, but I wasn't using him and felt bad about it, even though he seemed quite content to live in a big pasture with nothing to do but graze and hang out with other equines. Eventually, I gave him to a friend who had a string of donkeys and mules that he packed into the wilderness behind Santa Barbara, and Sammy spent many more years there, living a good life. He never had to pull a log out of the forest again.

When I made the decision to make the journey again with Gizmo, most people assumed I would begin where the ride with Wayward and Sammy had ended, in the Painted Desert, hundreds of miles from the California coast. Somehow, that seemed like cheating to me. The main point of the ride was to do it all at once, and not piecemeal, in sections. And though several people emphasized that no one would think the less of me for picking up where I'd left off the previous year, I stubbornly stuck to the idea of doing a "complete" ride.

The journey with Wayward and Sammy is its own story, with its own set of trials and troubles, good times and bad, and its own adventures. It's a story that I keep mostly to myself, not because I am ashamed of failing or that I did anything wrong (though I was green and ignorant, for sure). I

100

have a special place in my heart for Wayward and Sammy. Both are gone now, and I am forever indebted to them. Gizmo and I would not have succeeded if not for them, nor would this book have been written. Without them, I most certainly would have been a lesser person.

**\*\*\*\*\*\*\*\*\***

I pick up the book from the feeder. Even with its crumpled pages, it is still in pretty good shape. The feeder has protected it. I need some more reading material, so I slip it down into my saddlebags. I look again at the hoofprints in the dried mud. They are muleshoe prints, unmistakable because of their elongated oval shapes. And they are large, probably a size three, the size Sammy wore.

I look at Gizmo. "Your mother and your buddy Sammy were here last year, y'know." He stops chewing and looks at me. "Yep, right now, you're literally following in your mother's footsteps," I tell him. He goes back to picking at the clover.

As I watch my horse eat I realize I haven't exactly learned what to do from Wayward and Sammy. But I have learned a lot about what *not* to do. I have learned that a cross-country ride is not a pack trip, just as running a marathon is not the same as backpacking. Traveling cross-country on horseback is closer to an endurance ride, though it's not really the same thing. Traveling light is the key. A pack animal is not only unnecessary, but it is a liability in the long run. And it creates an exponential curve, a sharp increase on a graph of how much work you must do and how much you have to carry, with no benefits to you or your animals. The pack animal doesn't save you from work; it creates it.

That night I make a small fire, cook my dry macaroni and powdered sauce, and play the harmonica. Gizmo lies down near me and listens. He relaxes, closes his eyes, and sighs contentedly as I play. I am happy at this moment. I don't know if this ride will end up like last year's, but I know we have an advantage, and that Wayward and Sammy have given it to us. Our trails will diverge tomorrow, as I choose a different route, but our four lives will always be inextricably linked.

I play a little more then put the mouth harp back in the saddlebags. I look up into the night sky to see Castor and Pollux, the Gemini Twins, shining overhead. It is somehow fitting that I think about Wayward and Sammy as I look at the twin stars. The pair are connected with equines in literature. They are also the patrons of sailors and wanderers, and as I watch them in the southern sky, I say a little prayer out loud to the mare and mule.

Over the years since that first attempt, Wayward and Sammy come to mind whenever I see the Gemini Twins in the night sky, and I'll think, *Hello you two. I hope you're doin' well and enjoying yourselves out there in that big pasture. Happy trails to you both.*

# THE BEST JUKEBOX IN TOWN

We spent several days traveling along an abandoned railroad line, winding our way high through the Kaibab and Coconino National Forests in northern Arizona with the San Francisco Peaks towering above us to the northeast. There were a few of these deserted rail lines around the country back then, emptied of their purpose and fallen out of use for various reasons. Some were originally built for narrow gauge trains, but became obsolete in the twentieth century. Others had been bypassed by newer, easier routes in much the same way that an interstate highway displaces an old two lane road like Route 66. And some had simply outlived their usefulness.

Today they have enjoyed a bit of a resurgence in popularity in some areas due to the growth of recreational industries and the expansion of outdoor sports into places that had once been too remote for easy access. The demand for hiking and bicycle trails has revealed the old railroad beds as perfect infrastructure for these activities, largely due to their lack of steep grades, as Gizmo and I experienced firsthand. Trains can't climb steep hills, so their tracks are laid on roadbeds with a gradual incline. Instead of the straight through approach taken by highway designers, railways tend to wind through mountainous areas, taking every turn and switchback. Travelers are not subjected to rapid changes in elevation. And though it might take longer, mileage-wise, to reach a destination, it is much easier on a hiker, bicyclist, or a horse.

This particular railroad line was not on any register of trails back then. I stumbled on it by sheer luck, coming out of Seligman and headed toward Williams. The steel rails and railroad ties had been removed, and most of the trestles and bridges that spanned small streams and canyons had been dismantled. Some sections of the rail bed were missing—demolished by nature (erosion) or humans (dynamite), and I sometimes found myself having to divert when Gizmo and I reached a drop-off or other obstacle we couldn't navigate. But the path was mostly an easy one and was all the more welcome because I had anticipated hard going through the Arizona mountains. We were passing through the tallest and most rugged mountain range we had yet encountered, and I was glad that we found a bit of relief for Gizmo. The abandoned rail line placed us in remote areas where no other people had been for many years. We were completely alone, and I relished it, though I knew in the back of my mind the consequences of one of us getting seriously hurt.

I drew Gizmo to a stop on the trail. As I sat in the saddle studying my map, he lowered his head to graze then raised it with a mouthful of grass. He suddenly shook himself, as horses do sometimes. It's something every rider has experienced, sitting on your horse when he decides to shake off an itch. It's like a dog shaking water off his coat, except that dogs do it in a rolling, back and forth motion that sends the water flying. Horses employ a violent shaking movement that feels like a giant vibrating machine. It takes everything you have just to keep from falling off, even though the horse is standing in one spot. A horse often does this when he stands up after rolling in the dirt. Gizmo decided to shake himself for no apparent reason, and it almost sent me down the side of the mountain. Though I laughed and teased him about it, I knew I had been lucky. I don't know which would have been worse, the broken neck or the embarrassment of falling off my horse while he was standing still.

Flagstaff is nestled in the high country of these mountains. At seven thousand feet above sea level, it rests in the shadow of peaks rising to over twelve thousand. The area experiences severe weather during the winter months. It was late spring when we arrived at the western edge of town, but there were still great patches of snow on the ground, and the nights remained cold and brisk. I was hoping to steer clear of the city's populated area and skirt around to the northwest onto the Navajo Reservation. I unsaddled at the old Indian Pow Wow Grounds on the northwest edge of town. The grounds comprised a rodeo arena and a small camping area. They sat empty for most of the year, the facility's primary use being the place to hold the Indian Pow Wow Rodeo every summer.

The rodeo arena was the central feature of the grounds and stood in a stand of pine trees near what was then called City Park. Spectator stands faced the bucking chutes on one side and the announcer's box on the other. The crowd could sit in covered stands or, as they often did at small rodeos in those days, perch on the fence around the arena. Over the course of four days in July the place would be a hotspot of activity. As I rode up to the arena fence and climbed down off my horse, it seemed to me a fitting end to our travels along the abandoned rail line. The rodeo grounds were as empty and deserted as the railroad had been.

It was still early in the year, and there were no tourists around. There was a single groundskeeper, an older Navajo man named Billy who greeted me graciously and showed me where to find feed and water for Gizmo. I asked if it would be all right to bed down in one of the stock pens, and he told me I could stay as long as I wanted. I chose a bucking chute next to the announcer's stand. If it rained, I could move my gear up the stairs and into the covered booth. I made up my camp in the chute and put Gizmo in the pen behind it. We spent a peaceful night under a moonless sky.

I awoke to feathers—mountains of them all over me and the bucking chute. I figured a quail or some other bird had been caught and killed by something, and I sat up to look around for it. But then I noticed that my sleeping bag had been caught on a nail on the chute's gate during the night and was torn. Rather than quail, they were goose feathers in the process of emptying out of my bedroll and into the morning Arizona air. I managed to corral most of them back into the bag, which I then stitched up in a crude fashion using a small sewing kit I was glad I'd kept.

It was early morning, and I decided to take a walk downtown. Billy said he'd keep an eye on my horse and gear for me. It was a little over a mile to Santa Fe Avenue where I went into a small store and traded two novels I had for three more paperbacks. I often found places that had a shelf of books to trade. They could be found in small shops, old fashioned truck stops, or sometimes in a small town's public library. You could leave your old books and take others with you, in a sort of honor system, and I did this quite a lot during the ride. Even though I didn't like carrying the extra weight, those paperback novels were a luxury that saved my sanity at times.

*LOGBOOK:*
*Flagstaff. The first real city we've come to. Not exactly a big metropolis, but it seems like one after being alone for so long. Might stay an extra day, just to rest Gizmo. Maybe pick up a box of donuts to share with him, though he'll probably eat most of them like he usually does.*

I walked by an old-fashioned diner, hidden on a side street off of Santa Fe Avenue. The establishment didn't seem to have a name. The battered neon sign simply read *Diner.* It was a classic deco style eatery that had been there for many years. They make cafes like that on purpose these days, with artificially weathered signs and furnishings to create fake ambience and make things look old. This place was the real deal. Old diners were out of style back then. They weren't the sort of places that attracted tourists. This cafe was off the beaten path. I've always been a sucker for a mom and pop diner. You never knew what you were going to find in one. Sometimes great food, sometimes not so great. The place was run-down and somewhat dilapidated. The exhaust fan on the outside of the structure had been doing its job for years, and had produced a wave of congealed cooking grease that flowed down the wall near the back of the building. This one drew me in like a magnet.

I sat down at the counter and looked around. The place was wonderful. There were dozens of old license plates nailed to the walls—plates from all over the US. They even had some from Mexico and Canada. They dated back to the 1920s and '30s. Two large elk heads were mounted on opposite walls, like sentinels. Six barstools stood at the counter and four booths, two on each wall, sat beneath the elk heads. On a busy shift, the place could seat twenty-two people, but at that moment I was its only customer.

The waitress looked as if she were still in high school, but it was a weekday and too early for school to be out, so I figured she had either recently graduated or dropped out. She was cute and friendly and looked like she was fifteen going on twenty-five. I decided I liked this place.

I ordered a cup of coffee and some bacon and eggs for eighty-nine cents and checked out the tunes on the old Seeburg Wallbox, the jukebox selector that sat on the counter. They'd placed one at each end of the counter and others on the tables. I scrolled through the music. The entire playlist was made up of old country and western and cowboy music, and I thought I'd died and gone to heaven. The old jukebox resided on the floor in the corner, with an ancient black pay phone hung on the wall above it. It was a nickel a song, so I asked the waitress if she could make change for a half dollar.

She just smiled at me. "For the jukebox?" she asked.

"Yeah. You have some great music here."

She giggled. "You're silly," she said. "It doesn't cost anything. Just push the buttons."

Free music. Now I *knew* I had died and gone to heaven. I punched up "Movin' On" by Hank Snow, and while it played, I added a long list of other songs. The catalog was amazing and included cowboy music (Roy

Rogers, Tex Ritter, Smiley Burnett, Gene Autry, Ken Maynard, Patsy Montana) and classic style country (Hank Williams, Kitty Wells, Lefty Frizzell, Bob Wills, Spade Cooley, Roy Acuff), and what was then the "new" version of country music (Buck Owens, Merle Haggard, Loretta Lynn, George Jones & Tammy Wynette, Red Sovine, Barbara Mandrell, Slim Whitman). I could see I was going to be here awhile.

The waitress refilled my cup as the music changed to "Why Baby Why" by George Jones. She had bright red hair and freckles, and in some ways reminded me of Liz, the rancher's daughter. Of course, she was one of the only women I had spoken to since then, so that certainly influenced my judgement. She was short—petite is the word they use in the fashion world—and had a sweet, self-conscious smile that had probably broken a million hearts. I got the feeling that I might be next in line.

She told me her name was Lu, and I asked her if it was short for Louise.

"Lucinda," she said. "I used to be called Cindy when I was growing up, but I never liked it. So I changed it, and now everyone just calls me Lu."

"I like Lu better," I told her. "It sounds a bit more grown up."

She smiled again, and I let her friendly energy just wash over me. There was something calming and reassuring about her. She had the gift of making a person feel at ease.

"Do you work around here?" she asked. The sounds of "She's Gone Gone Gone" filled the room.

"Nope, just travelin' through," I said. "Might be here a day or two though," I added. "I'm traveling on horseback, headed back east. Stayin' out at the Indian rodeo grounds."

"Wow! You're riding a horse across the country?"

It felt good to have the chance to brag a bit to a beautiful woman. Not that I overplayed my hand, though. The fact was, I was more the "yup, nope" type and kept my boasting to a restrained minimum. I tended to talk about Gizmo a lot. I felt safe talking about him. I kept the conversation aimed away from me for the most part and asked Lu about herself.

"I'm from down near Cottonwood," she told me. "I came up here last winter. I'm hoping to start college next year, so I'm just workin' and tryin' to save up some money."

Merle Haggard's new song "If We Make It Through December" came on with Roy Nichols playing the melody on a gut string guitar.

While we talked, a man came in and sat down at the other end of the counter.

When Lu went to the back with his order, he asked me, "I overheard what you were saying about riding your horse across America. Is that true? Are you actually doing that?" There was a pause as the jukebox reached for another record. It fired back up with Red Sovine's "Giddyup Go."

"Yep," I replied.

"How many of you are there?" he asked.

"Just two," I answered. "Me and my horse."

"By yourself? You're doing this all alone? Damn, that's really fascinating," he said.

"No, there's two of us, like I said," I replied. "It's me and my horse."

"Would you mind if I interviewed you for the local newspaper? I do some writing for it."

"Yeah, sure," I said. "That'd be okay."

He moved to the stool next to me and pulled a small notebook from his coat pocket. "It Wasn't God Who Made Honky Tonk Angels" came on the box. He asked most of the usual questions about when, where, and why. How many miles a day; does your horse get tired; do you carry extra feed and water; what happens when you get to a fence? He asked if he could take a picture of Gizmo and me, and we made arrangements to meet later out at the rodeo grounds.

"That is so *great*!" Lu exclaimed, when the reporter had left. "You're gonna be in the paper!"

"Yeah, well … I did tell him that this place has the best jukebox and best waitress in town. So, maybe we'll make the paper together, no?"

She blushed. "Aw, I don't know …" She looked at me and grinned. "I've never been in the news before," she whispered excitedly, as if sharing a secret.

"I'll bet you have," I replied. "You just don't know it."

She blushed deeper, as Floyd Cramer played "The Last Date."

There must have been a cook somewhere back in the kitchen, but I never saw him. It was just a waitress and me in our own world, all alone there in that diner. A bottomless cup of coffee, endless conversation, and a continuous stream of the best country music anywhere. We talked until it was time to head back to my horse. I wanted to ask her out or walk her home, but I was Kaw-Liga and she was the Indian maid.

Unrequited love to the sound of a steel guitar.

# THE BLIND MARE

*LOGBOOK:*
*Hard year out here. What little grass there is has no*
*nutritional value. Dry and white looking, with no life to it.*
*Have seen a few dead horses and cattle through here. Wild*
*horses keep coming around at night, trying to lure Gizmo*
*away. Maybe they're just looking for something to eat and*
*figure he has food somewhere. It's a hard life for any critter*
*living on the land out here.*

I saw her from a half mile away, standing alone amidst the dry sage and rabbit weed. Truth be told, Gizmo spotted her first and signaled to me as he always did, with his ears. He didn't take his eyes off her as we trotted slowly in her direction. I could see that her head was down, neck drooped and sagging, as if she were asleep on her feet. She didn't move as we got closer. Gizmo began to call to her, and by the time we had closed the gap to a hundred fifty yards, I knew something was wrong.

I didn't ride straight up to her for fear she was sick and might infect my horse. Instead, I reined Gizmo off to the side and stopped to tie him to a small acacia tree. Some dry scrub grass distracted him, and he began to nibble on it while I walked over to check on the troubled horse.

I approached the mare slowly, extending my hand until it met her sagging neck. I spoke softly the whole time, "Here, girl … easy … I'm not gonna hurt you … easy girl." She flinched a bit when I first touched her, but once I began to stroke the side of her neck, she settled, as if it were too much work to be frightened. I could see she was blind. Her eyes were a cloudy, whitish blue and stared ahead, unresponsive and unseeing.

She was a sorrel mare, a wild horse without facial markings, stockings, or brand. She would never have passed as a fancy horse, conformation wise, with her parrot mouth and Roman nose, but to me she was beautiful just the same. Her tail was knotted and filthy, and her flaxen mane hung in clumps down both sides of her neck in a haphazard hairdo, separated in places as if it had been parted that way on purpose. Her breath came in short gasps, husky and labored, with a rasp on the inhale and a wheeze on the exhale. Her tongue hung from one side of her mouth, and I ran my fingers down her face until I could take the tongue lightly in my grasp. It was dry.

I walked back to Gizmo and fetched my canteen from the saddle, then returned to the mare and poured a small amount of water onto her parched tongue. She lapped at it eagerly. I began to dribble it into my cupped hand so that she could drink. She slowly gained a sort of rhythm, sucking and lapping the water as I poured it very slowly, until the canteen was empty.

It was impossible to tell the mare's age by looking at her. She seemed old, well past twenty, but that was because she was skin and bones. I managed a cursory look in her mouth. She still had some small cups on her uppers, and by the angle of the teeth, I could tell that she was well past a mature eight-year-old, but probably not much more than twelve or so. Her black hooves were those of a wild horse on the range, dry and hard, but in good shape and kept short by the rough miles she traveled. Her skin hung off in hunks, dry and lifeless. She was a skeleton with a hide draped over it, her extended backbone and ribs were the most prominent features. She wasn't a big horse—I guessed her nominal working weight should have been about eleven hundred pounds, but I doubted she weighed much more than half that.

She was completely dehydrated, and god only knew how long she had gone without water. I knew what was wrong with her because I'd seen it several times in the past weeks out there on the Navajo Reservation. It was a tough year, dry, almost no spring rainfall, and what little grass grew was parched and empty of nourishment. Many of the wild horses had taken to eating locoweed. Gizmo and I had passed a few corpses along the trail. I knew that even if I could somehow move the mare to food and shelter, her condition was not curable. She had been loco'ed for too long. It was ironic how the plant seemed to thrive as the environment became drier and more inhospitable. While everything around it was drying up and dying, the weed was lush and moist, displaying its vigor with a sort of arrogance, its shiny green leaves and beautiful blooming purple flowers a stark contrast to the dull browns and beiges of the surrounding prairie plants. The locoweed exuded a healthiness that offered an empty promise of well-being to any critter attracted to it.

I sat down next to the mare and started talking to her for what ended up being over an hour. Gizmo didn't mind the break, and he finally dozed off. I spoke to her about what a great world we live in, and I told her how I wished she could see it all. I talked about the ocean Gizmo and I had left, and I described the mountains back to the west, with snow on the peaks and great parks of lovely green grass in the meadows. I spoke of railroads and automobiles and of other human things. I told her how people love each other and how they kill each other all at the same time.

I described a waitress I had met in Flagstaff who was waiting tables at a little cafe, and told of how pretty and friendly she was, how she had flirted with me, and how the place had a great jukebox full of fine old country music. I told the mare what it's like to ride across the southwestern desert through the night on a freight train with no company except the sound of the boxcar's wheels clicking against the steel rails. I don't remember what all I talked about, but I kept talking, and I know I sort of unloaded on that little sorrel mare. I asked her about her life and what trails she'd seen, and if she had any family nearby. I told her I hoped all her babies had grown into fine horses and that they were safe and healthy. Finally, I told her how happy I was that our trails had crossed and how honored I was to meet her.

I stood up, laid one hand on her withers, and reached to scratch her behind the ear with the other. "You see ol' Gizmo over there? Well, he's still a youngster, and he's just startin' down the trail. But I reckon you've about come to the end of yours, haven't you, old girl?" As I reached down, I said, "I guess all of us come finally to the end of the trail at some point. And I suppose none of us really gets to choose when that happens."

The mare's eyes were closed now, and she had relaxed and become used to my voice. "It's just that, well … I'm guessin' those coyotes out there will come for you tonight, and I'm thinkin' you deserve an easier way out. And maybe I was put here to see to that …"

I pulled back the hammer as I raised the old single action Colt and placed the end of the barrel just behind her ear.

"Safe travels, old girl. Rest easy now. I love you." Tears welled up, and I couldn't stop them.

Gizmo jumped as the gun exploded and the mare went down. He looked at her warily for a few seconds then dismissed her and went back to nibbling at the surrounding plants, as if killing the horse was all part of a normal day's work. I holstered the pistol then knelt to make sure the mare was dead. I was sobbing now.

"Goodbye, sweet lady," I said. I walked back to my horse and untied him. As I stepped up into the saddle I looked back at her. "Goddammit," I whispered softly.

The coyotes would have her tonight, but she was past caring.

# 1974

Ιt was such a long time ago. I'm old now, road weary and weather beaten. Rode hard and put away wet, as the cowboys say. The years have left their marks. This body of mine seems like it belongs to someone else. It sags where it once was drawn taut; joints that moved swiftly and fluidly now ache from the simplest of labors; a young mind that was quick and sure, eager and open, is now old and rests from long fatigue, no longer confident and certain, but managing to stay open just the same. The somewhat boyishly handsome face that held a vigorous smile and saw life through two inquisitive eyes has long surrendered to an old one— recognizable, but with its youthful glow replaced by the seasoned countenance of age. Wrinkles and all, I still see that young man sometimes when I look in the mirror.

I was young in 1974, and I look back upon that youth with a grateful fondness for the opportunities it offered, and how I stumbled through them largely unscathed. Which is not to say that I traversed them unaffected.

No mobile phones or World Wide Web in 1974. There was pretty much no digital anything for the average person, except for microwave ovens and pocket calculators that did simple math and cost as much as a small farm. It would be another five years before I got my first computer and first logged on to what was then the internet, using a three hundred baud modem that had a cradle that held the phone receiver. Nixon resigned that year. The war in Vietnam wouldn't officially end for another year, though US troops had just pulled up stakes and headed home, leaving a disillusioned and defeated South Vietnamese populace behind. The Apollo moon landings had only recently occurred, and the Space Shuttle hadn't been invented yet. Patty Hearst had her picture taken holding an M1 carbine. Muhammad Ali knocked out George Foreman.

Some of the people born that year included Kate Moss, Robbie Williams, James Blunt, Penelope Cruz, Cee Lo Green, Alanis Morissette, Hilary Swank, Amy Adams, Jimmy Fallon, Joaquin Phoenix, Ryan Adams, and Leonardo DiCaprio. Pretty impressive list.

And among those who left us were Samuel Goldwyn, Adolph Gottlieb,

Chet Huntley, Bud Abbott, Agnes Moorehead, Duke Ellington, Charles Lindbergh, Cass Elliot, Walter Brennan, Oskar Schindler, Ed Sullivan, Walter Lippmann, and Jack Benny. Not to disparage those born in 1974, but I'm thinking that, all up, the world took a bit of a loss that year.

But I digress while attempting to draw a backstory. Suffice it to say, 1974 compares with life today about like we would have viewed 1934 back then. The sojourn that Gizmo and I experienced took place in another universe. Once out on the trail, we were cut off from everyone back home. We were pretty much cut off from everyone most of the time. Even riding alongside a highway, the cars and trucks passed us by as if we weren't there. We shared no communication except an occasional wave; we had nothing in common with them.

Letters were mailed to me via general delivery, to whatever small town we might pass through in the weeks ahead. I instructed friends and family to address letters this way:

To: John Egenes & Gizmo
Care of: General Delivery, (Name of Town, State)
"Please hold for man on horseback"

I suggested they send letters to arrive well ahead of us, and normally I figured on a month or more of lead time. I learned early on that our mail shouldn't be sent to large towns or cities where I would have to lead Gizmo through town—oftentimes far out of our way—through traffic and crowds, to get to the post office. Instead, I filled out the post office forms so that our mail would be forwarded to very small towns that I thought would have only one or two streets and a handful of residents. Without Google Maps or any sort of satellite steering gadgets, the only way to choose which towns to send mail to was to pick the ones with the smallest lettering on the map. I stayed away from the ones in bold print, or those that were circled or marked by a star.

Because of our isolation, if I sent a letter, I couldn't expect an answer, and the likelihood was that I wouldn't get one. I wouldn't even know if the person had received mine. No phone calls, no email, or texts, and no posting selfies of Gizmo and me on social networks. Those paths to self-indulgence didn't exist then.

For whatever it was worth, Gizmo was my sole company, and I was his.

The connections we now take for granted were unimaginable back then. The wireless umbilical that links us today would wait almost three decades to manifest itself. A letter was a rare and precious thing to me, and a phone call even more so. Human contact was something that occurred in real time, face-to-face. My social networks were located around campfires, cafe tables, and at impromptu stops on the side of the road.

I relied upon dead reckoning to steer our course. Since GPS devices wouldn't be available for more than twenty years, the idea of looking down on Earth from space by using software on a handheld contraption wasn't even a dream. Paper maps served this purpose. But maps don't put the areas they cover into the larger context of the entire earth. Maps focus upon your own area of interest, and your world becomes limited to that. The advantage of this is that you aren't distracted by places and objects that lie outside the boundaries of your map. You concentrate upon your own trail and not upon options and possibilities that are offered elsewhere. The paper map limits your choices because you can't zoom in and out.

To while away the time, I spent countless idle hours twirling my single action Colt, practicing gun tricks, and listening to my companion's incisors tearing blades of grass from the ground. Gizmo spent his off hours grazing, dozing, watching and listening to the world around him. We talked quite a bit—or rather, I talked, and he acknowledged through a series of grunts and sighs and by snorting loudly through his nose. I talked a lot, but it was Gizmo who had the most to say. After a time on the trail, I learned to listen to him.

In 1974, riding a horse across the continent was both a reason for, and a method of, disconnecting from society at large. It was a *physical* disconnection for Gizmo and me. I wanted to divorce myself from my culture *on purpose*. Today's digital ecosystem doesn't allow for that. Smart phones and internet connections *insure* that a traveler today is always connected—daily, hourly, and minute by minute—to friends, family, and anyone who subscribes to their social network pages and feeds. It doesn't matter if the horse and rider don't have a smart gadget and an internet connection. Passersby will certainly have them and make sure the pair are always connected by posting pictures of them and commenting on social media. More photos can be taken and sent from a handheld device in a few minutes than were taken on our entire journey.

Attempting a long ride today would still be a long and difficult process, but being truly *alone* is no longer possible. Forget about privacy and seclusion. Technology has left its footprints on our reasons for following our dreams and has even altered the dreams themselves. We no longer have a say over that part of it. One can be alone, but one can no longer be in the wilderness.

When I was a kid, a family would climb into their old Nash four-door sedan and take off on a trip through the American Southwest, traveling along Route 66. It was just a narrow two-lane highway that took them to sparsely populated (if at all), empty lands. Gasoline stations were in short supply, so the travelers made sure to fill up at every opportunity. Bottled water wasn't yet available, so they carried drinking water in a canvas bag with the name "Desert Water Bag" stenciled in bold red letters across its front, and they hung it from the front bumper of the car. This bag could, quite literally, save their lives if the Nash broke down in the middle of the desert.

The Desert Water Bag wasn't a kitschy, retro item. It wasn't hung on the bumper to look cool. It was a necessity that was meant to insure the family would live through the trip. Driving out west was still an adventure, a trek into the great unknown. It was a time before the gentrification of the American Highway, before the Stuckyfication of America's empty lands; passing beneath an arch meant that you were headed into the Utah wilderness and not into a fast food scullery. When you pulled off the two lane to gas up, you got a twenty-five cent pass to see two headed snakes and real mummies in the bargain.

For Gizmo and I, things still weren't all that much different from the nineteen fifties and earlier, and we saw a world unlike anything shown on the nightly news. We saw real people, real wildlife, and real countryside. We even saw a couple of two-headed snakes. None of it was filtered through the screen of a smartphone. We saw mountains and valleys, rivers and deserts. We traveled freely across the land and squeezed tentatively through crowded cities. We slept on the prairie with coyotes under the stars. We were guests in big, fancy mansions tended by servants and grooms, and spent nights in abandoned mines that had long outlived their bounty. We slept with the dead in graveyards and pondered our existence with truth seekers in clandestine meetings. I came to know that more animal slaughter is performed with an automobile than with a gun, not on purpose but through indifference. There were times when I longed for company (and I

116

know that Gizmo did, too), and times when we couldn't leave crowded civilization fast enough. Wild horse herds tried to steal my young horse away, and humans threatened us. But more often, the wild horses left us alone, and sometimes a complete stranger would bring me a plate of hot food and some hay and grain for Gizmo. Through all of this I came to know that Americans were different from what was depicted on the nightly news, that they were the people you pass on the street every day, people who mostly shared life with a live-and-let-live philosophy.

Traveling across America by car, you become like water flowing through a clear pipe. You see your surroundings at a distance, and the inhabitants see you, but neither actually connects with the other in any meaningful way. Handheld digital devices magnify this effect. They disconnect you from your immediate environment. When walking, riding a horse, or even bicycling, you remain within physical grasp of your surroundings. Slow travel requires a physicality that produces a far different view of the world, one not possible with the automobile and the handheld.

We no longer know what it's like to be removed from constant contact, even temporarily. We no longer experience a life without instant gratification or know the need for time to pass to solve a problem. We don't know what it's like to *not know the answer* to something.

When Gizmo and I made our journey, 60 percent of today's world population wasn't born yet. That seems a bit staggering to me. It means that most people alive right now didn't exist then, and it makes it a bit tougher to fully explain how it felt to be isolated the way Gizmo and I were. Smartphones, iGadgets, Droids, tablets, Bluetooth, wireless dongles, camera drones, GPS, wearable computers … all these digital contraptions serve to place each of us squarely in the center of our own universe. Each connections is immediate; every call is a local call. These digital connections allow no direct reference to my place in the overall scheme of things. I cannot see where I fit within the whole. The scenario distorts my importance so that I no longer need to adapt to the world around me. Instead, I command it to adapt to me, and it does. I have become the center of my universe.

In 1974, walking step by step, foot by foot, mile by mile, I always knew where I was in relation to the grand scheme of things because that grand scheme amounted to what I could see and feel around me. It something that hasn't changed for me. Today's digital connections are wonderful, but being face-to-face still beats staring at a screen. And all this is coming from me, a very early internet adopter and die-hard computer geek.

Today with a smartphone, Gizmo and I would never be lost—I could never manage to *get* us lost, as I did a few times—because GPS devices wouldn't allow it. I could point my handheld at the night sky to find out what stars I was seeing. There would be no need to memorize where the pole star Polaris is or to know which one was Sirius, the brightest star in the heavens, or to know how to find the summer triangle of Vega, Deneb, and Altair because my device would tell me. In 1974, in order to tell Gizmo the names of the constellations, I had to know them.

Photographs serve as our memories. The act of taking them causes us to relinquish our responsibility for remembering. I'm grateful for having the pictures I took during our journey. They serve the same purposes that today's digital photos do and enhance my memories of the seven months we were on the trail.

I took about three hundred photos during our ride. Since I had to wait unti the ride was finished in order to have the film developed and view the pictures, and it turned out that almost half of them were out of focus, badly exposed, or otherwise useless. I don't know how many were taken by others and given to me, but I'm guessing I ended up with a little over two hundred photos. With a digital camera or smartphone, I could easily have taken that many pictures each morning *before we saddled up.*

Shooting thousands of photos seems to offer a more detailed accounting of the story, but in fact, it has the opposite effect. By taking that many pictures you end up experiencing life through the device's screen, leaving no room to savor it. The device steers the experience. You are directed by your camera. You change your behavior—your itinerary, your *plans*—to suit the way you collect photographs and videos. Your memory of the experience is watching a small video screen. You take thousands of digital pictures, and the more pictures digitally recorded, the less you experience the real world. The total number of pictures I took in the seven months we were on the trail amounted to an average of fewer than two pictures per day. When I did pause to take photographs, I usually took several photos at a time, but I would often go days or weeks without pulling my camera out of the saddlebags. Scarcity makes things precious and serves to focus our memory. If I had taken thousands of photos of our ride, no room would have been left for contemplation, no time set aside for deliberation.

You could still get away with stuff in 1974. Not as much as you could have twenty years earlier, but still, lots of things slipped under the radar of the powers that be. You could drive a car without registering or insuring it (though you might get caught if a cop pulled you over for something). You could still sneak into a movie theater. You could still hitchhike most places. Sometimes I feel as though Gizmo and I got away with making the ride. I'm not sure if we would be allowed to do it today, with pressure from various agencies and groups. And I'm not sure they wouldn't be right in their opposition to it. There were aspects of our trip that were environmentally unfriendly and terribly cruel to Gizmo (and to me, but I don't count).

We were not then the paranoid, frightened people we are now. It wasn't a perfect world, by any means. America was already well on its way to losing its innocence in the year that Nixon resigned his presidency. And so were Gizmo and I. It was a time of great turmoil, yet it still held the promise—a fading promise left over from the heady idealism of the sixties—of a better life for all.

The parents of today, who now have children in their teens and twenties, were babies in 1974. The ten-year-old girls who wrote to me after the ride asking for pictures of Gizmo (never of me) are now in their fifties. We've moved on from 1974 and left that sweet, naïve innocence behind. The vast, empty, isolated wilderness is now accessed instantly—through a disembodied vision on the screen of a smartphone. The past becomes just another selfie.

# PASSING THE TIME

We rode for three hours this morning. I pulled Gizmo up and unsaddled for the midday break well before noon. We spent two hours resting, letting his back cool and letting my feet cool when I pulled off my boots. We hit the trail again for a couple more hours, and we were finished with our twenty-mile day in the early afternoon. We're camped in the hollow of a small hill, beneath a grove of cottonwoods. There's a windmill here, but not much else. I doubt anyone is within twenty miles of us. As usual, I have a lot of time on my hands.

Had I been hiking across America, I no doubt would have walked from morning until night, spending the entire day on foot and passing the time by traveling. But it's different having Gizmo along. We are limited in the number of miles we can ride each day and how many days in a row I will ride him. Idle time is built into the journey.

Having to pass the time wasn't something I thought much about when I planned this ride. It was merely incidental, a minor diversion from riding and seeing places, meeting people and having adventures—the *real* stuff I thought the ride would be made of. Turns out that passing time takes up most of it. It's a lot like the dark matter that makes up our universe. They're both invisible, and you don't think about them much, but they end up being pretty important.

The travel itself is its own form of discipline. By now, I have forgotten about reaching our final destination, and the ride is no longer just a mode of transportation. Instead, each day has become our reason for being, a sort of Zen setting that's self-contained. Within each day, the ultimate goal (the Atlantic Ocean) has been forgotten, and the events and surroundings of the day have grown to be our only purpose. It's no longer a matter of trying to get through the day; rather, when we awake the next morning, we simply know that we have survived the previous day and the outlook shifts to the new one. It's seamless, and I don't give it much thought.

If there are ants nearby, I watch them. I pick out a single ant and follow him, sometimes for an hour or more. I watch as he leaves the anthill and traces his progress until he finishes what he was doing and returns to his home. I often see myself as this ant. He doesn't worry about his destination nor the time it will take him to get there. He sticks to a route and simply follows it without question. Time is meaningless to him. He goes about his business, day by day, and I try to emulate him as best I can.

Before we started the ride it was easy to predict the sorts of activities I would involve myself in, but I find it's a lot more difficult to convey the sense of time that passes so slowly, and the ability to stay occupied with one of them for an entire afternoon—or an entire day if we don't happen to be traveling. I sometimes read an entire book without stopping. It generally takes five or six hours to do this. I have no distractions. There aren't any other people around. I can't get up to go to the refrigerator for something to eat, but I can get up and walk around if I want to.

My everyday activities are predictable. Washing clothes, sewing and repairing clothes and equipment, tending to my horse, cooking meals. But the truth is, they don't take up all that much time. After finishing any chores, I still have hours on my hands each day, and I have learned how to slow myself down, to purposely lengthen the time it takes to finish a task to synchronize my own body clock with that of my environment.

I set short range tasks for myself that help me get through the day. I write a poem every day for a week and then set myself the task of writing *five* poems in an afternoon. The next day I will set myself to memorizing all of them, and the following day I'll try to recite them to Gizmo while we're on the trail.

Sometimes I take my single action Colt pistol apart and put it back together. I clean it thoroughly, but I don't have the proper gun cleaning supplies. I have to do it while sitting in the dirt, and if I drop a tiny screw, I might spend an hour looking for it. Once the pistol is cleaned and reassembled, I spend an hour or two practicing gun tricks. I twirl it, throw it up over my shoulder, and then catch it while cocking and firing it all at once (it isn't loaded). I balance it on my hand by the end of the barrel then flip it up and twirl it back into the holster. I do that for two hours, take a break, and then do it all over again. I spend a lot of hours spinning that old Colt, and I've gotten pretty good at it.

I spend hours talking to Gizmo, philosophizing and asking him questions and then answering them. We discuss the books I read, or the wildlife around us, or the grass he eats. I've tried to teach him how to cook macaroni with powdered sauce, but he hasn't been much interested.

I often practice humming a tune while playing the harmonica at the same time. Once I have figured out how to do that, I practice humming a tune while playing a *different* tune on the harmonica. A variation of this is humming and whistling a tune at the same time, like Jimmie Rodgers. Sometimes I do this for a couple of hours without stopping or until it looks like Gizmo is going to kick me.

This all sounds easy, whiling the time away, and it is—for about a half hour or so. Then it starts to get hard, and the longer I go, the more difficult it becomes. I keep going then ask myself, "Have you passed two hours?" I tell myself to go for six. Go for eight. I don't have a watch, so I have to estimate by watching the sun or moon. Eventually, I get a sort of second wind, and I fall into the groove of it all. Of course, it has taken weeks— months, even. It doesn't happen in a day.

> *LOGBOOK:*
> *Took the day off today. Gizmo needs a breather, and his back could stand a rest. A small bump appeared on his back and I don't want it to turn into anything serious. So, we just wasted the day. I managed to sew up the straps on my day pack. They were almost ripped out. Put some wheel bearing grease on Gizmo's feet. It's dry through here and I don't want them to crack. Spent the day reading (a bad western called Freewater Range) and doing gun tricks. Watched a pair of redtail hawks for a long time, just circling overhead. One of them finally dived down and caught something...probably a field mouse. Gizmo's new tooth is growing in and he licks at it all the time. I rub his gums a lot, and he loves that. Who'd have thought a gum massage would feel that good? Lazy day today.*

The upshot of it all is this: I do whatever it takes to pass the time. I don't much care about spending it wisely or constructively, except for getting things done that need doing. I've learned how to slow down, to pace myself. I first slowed to a crawl then to a standstill. Ever since my teenage years, when I started hitchhiking and spending hours stuck at lonely crossroads waiting for rides, I have known that it's a lot harder to slow down than it is to speed up. It's best not to look ahead to see how much time you must fill. The real trick is simply to live in the moment (I know, a bit cliché, but it's true nonetheless) and allow yourself to focus on what's in front of you without worrying about how long it will take to do something or how much time you have before sunset. It's a lot easier to move from the country to a big city than it is to move from the city to the country, that's for sure. And Gizmo and I have definitely moved to the country.

Simple things have huge impacts. I can twirl the single action Colt, toss it in the air and catch it after it rolls two and a half times, cock the hammer back as it lands then pull the trigger and fan it with my thumb and middle finger to fire off three quick shots. The ability to carry this off doesn't mean I'm anyone special. Those who see me so this think I'm clever, but only a few will understand the hours of practice I have invested in learning this stunt. Those select few will know, because they will have put in long hours perfecting something. And they will know that it's not the trick that's important, it's the discipline and the dedication to task. The road is the experience; the destination is only the result of that experience.

It's the ability to pass time without interruption or diversion that matters. It's the experience of *aloneness*. It's the capacity for *spending time,* the ability to be alone, the power to be by yourself. You don't need to pay anyone to show you how to do this. It's not about fitting this ability into your life. It's about creating a life that allows nothing else to happen, where focus is important and diversions are eliminated. By now I know I'm allowed to take things as they come. There's no hurry. Gizmo has taught me that.

# THE PAINTED DESERT

The wind picks up in the afternoon. We can't get away from it out here. A lot of miles between things. Summer storms are starting a bit early this year, and they hit us every afternoon for an hour or so. The storm always comes out of the northwest. I can usually see it a few hours before it gets to us. It builds in the distance, clouds gathering to cover up a clear blue sky. There's no noise, no wind. We move along slowly, and I listen to the small squeak that my saddle makes as Gizmo trots along. The sound of water sloshing in the canteen moves in rhythm to the swish of my jeans against the seat jockeys and the rustle of my poncho tied across the pommel. A small chorus playing to a steady beat, using the silence of the desert as its auditorium.

The day's ride takes me over a saddle between two large buttes (I've learned that a butte is taller than it is wide, and a mesa is wider than it is tall). As Gizmo and I reach the top of the gap, I stop and turn him around, and we look back upon what has taken us several days to cross. The Painted Desert is aptly named. The buttes and mesas extend to the west until they seem to mesh with the San Francisco Peaks, the tall dark blue sentinels far in the distance. It seems ages since we rode through those mountains. The mesas are a painter's canvas—no, a painter's pallet. The pale blue sky blends with the greens and purples of the plateaus, fading into yellows and browns as I look down along the incline we have been ascending for so long.

"There you go, bud," I tell my horse as we pause to face back to the west, "That's what we've been doing for the past few weeks."

We are looking into the past, the same way you would look at a distant planet. If my eyesight were keener, I might be able to see our tracks going back for several miles. As it is, my eyes can follow them for only a short way before the marks on the trail become invisible. I rein Gizmo back to the east, toward the future.

"Look at it out there, Gizmo. That's our home for the next few weeks." I reach down to give him a pat on the neck and urge him into a walk. We have trotted most of the morning as we gradually climbed to the top of the saddle, but I will keep him to a walk as we head back downhill. It will be slower going, but it's too hard on us both if we trot when going downhill. It's likely he would injure his back.

The weather begins to assemble into a recognizable storm in the distance. White clouds have thickened and turned grey. Parts of them are turning black. They move slowly and steadily toward us. I look for a likely shelter to escape the oncoming rain. Stabs of lightning begin to flash in the distance every so often, and their frequency increases as the storm grows closer. Within an hour the leading edge of the clouds is overhead, though it doesn't bring the threat of rain just yet. It is still a way off, and I can now see the rain itself, falling from the clouds but evaporating before it reaches the ground.

We are lucky today. There is an overhang wedged into the face of a small bluff. Though it is facing the storm and open to the incoming rush of wind and rain, the small hollow should give us some relief from the coming monsoon, and hopefully protect us from the lightning. There are some large tree roots embedded in the walls of the makeshift cave, strong enough to tie Gizmo to. I have had to tie him out in the open several times during these summer storms, and I always pray he doesn't get hit by lightning. Being out on the prairie during a lightning storm without shelter brings new meaning to the word *vulnerable*.

I unsaddle and improvise a quick camp. I shove our belongings beneath the rain slicker as I watch the storm roll toward us. I can see lightning striking the ground. Gizmo and I have been through this many times already, but it isn't something you get used to. I have learned to resign myself to fate, to accept that the lightning will either strike me or spare me and that there's nothing I can do about it. I just hope that if a strike takes one of us, it's me and not Gizmo.

The lightning is close enough to seem like explosions now. The flash and the detonation are simultaneous. I can no longer count "one, two, three, four ..." to figure out how many miles away they are because they are upon us. It seems as if the storm is concentrated right on our spot only, but I know that the lightning strikes across many miles around us. Some of the flashes are so close I can feel them. I smell ozone in the air and feel the heat. My hair stands on end. Gizmo fidgets nervously while I stroke his face and neck and speak reassuringly to him. We both hope for the best.

A few nights back, we had camped at a windmill with a metal water tank next to it. There were no trees around, and the windmill tower was the only object in the area that I could stake Gizmo to. I had watched in horror as the lightning struck it. He had jumped frantically, and the picket rope jerked him off his feet. He fell, and I thought he was dead. I had been blinded by the flash, but I ran to him through the driving rain, and he jumped to his feet as I reached him. He was covered in mud, but that was the extent of the damage. He was reasonably calm about it all, but I was shaken. I had bad dreams about it that night.

Our luck holds again today, and the storm leaves us soaked but unharmed, frightened but grateful. I watch as it rolls away to the southeast, toward the Mogollon Rim. For some reason it doesn't seem as spectacular as it did when it approached us, though as the evening settles it produces a magnificent sunset. The desert turns orange then purple at the close of day.

More colors in the pallet, more paint on the canvas.

# SHEARING SHEEP

Gizmo and I spent a few days with Johnny and Rose Cook on the Navajo Indian Reservation, near Indian Wells, Arizona. They had graciously invited us to stay with them for a much needed rest. While we were there I pitched in to help with shearing, though I knew nothing about sheep. We worked in a remote sheep camp far up a box canyon. It was comprised of a small hogan and some holding pens. The canyon was closed on three sides by steep cliffs, which offered shelter and containment for the sheep, and enabled the family to better protect them from predators. I sat in the pickup truck's bed with two others as Johnny drove us up the winding route to the camp. We set out before daybreak and followed an old wagon road—nothing more than two dirt ruts—and arrived at the camp just at daybreak. We wasted no time in gathering and shearing the sheep.

The five of us worked all day in the sheep camp. My pants and shirt had bits of blood on them from where I had wiped my hands as I tried in vain to shear the critters without cutting them. There was no electricity, so electric shears were useless. We trimmed over six hundred sheep that day— or, I should say, *they* sheared the sheep, and I mostly abused them with the hand clippers. I hadn't known how thin skinned sheep were until that day, and I ended up lacerating just about every animal I attempted to shear. The Navajos around me were a good-natured bunch and joked incessantly, mostly at my expense.

"My cousin could shear almost as good as you," Cecil commented. He was quiet and thoughtful and rarely talked, so I tended to listen when he did. He went on. "He finally got his promotion."

"Oh? What did he get promoted to?" I asked.

"He works in a butcher shop now," Cecil replied with a straight face.

The other three waited for several seconds then burst out laughing. I took it in stride. They had been merciless all day.

"Oh, I don't know," I said. "I was just gettin' the hang of it. I think I'd be gettin' pretty good by now if y'all hadn't run out of sheep."

They looked at me with deadpan expressions.

Johnny responded, "Yeah, my uncle says he's a good mechanic. He has seven cars at his place, and none of them runs."

The others thought this was hilarious and began laughing once more.

"Okay, I get it, I get it," I said.

The day before, I had driven Johnny's sister to the chapter house at Greasewood for some tribal business. She didn't know how to drive and Johnny's father had asked me to take her in his old pickup truck.

"You know I'm going to have to take that horse from you," Johnny said seriously.

"And why would that be?" I asked.

"Yesterday you drove alone in the truck with Dezba." He paused to look at me thoughtfully then continued. "It is the law of my people that a man cannot be alone with a single woman unless he intends to marry her. If you don't marry, there is the need to pay a dowry. This is usually done by trading sheep or cattle, sometimes horses or mules." I could see that he was dead serious, and the smiles had disappeared from the faces of the others.

"Uh … I don't know what to say," I said. "I didn't know anything about that,"

"The horse will be enough. You do not have to give your saddle or other belongings," Johnny said, gravely.

"Oh boy," I muttered, "I don't know … I just can't give you my horse. I'm sorry. Isn't there some other way to work this out? I didn't mean any disrespect. No one told me, and I just didn't know … I'm sorry." I could feel my face burning and my pulse quickening.

Cecil spoke up. "We would not leave you on foot. We would supply you with something else to ride. Maybe not as good as your horse, but you would not have to walk."

I sat there, stunned. They all looked a bit embarrassed at having to confront me like this. They looked down at the ground, unable to meet my eyes. We sat in silence for a few minutes, each one carefully examining his feet. Finally, Johnny broke the silence.

"I think we could give you one of those big sheep to ride," he said earnestly.

I looked up at them.

"One of the big ones. Your feet might drag a little, though." Then they all burst out laughing until they cried.

"The Big Sheep Cowboy!" Johnny cried, laughing hysterically. They all got a good laugh about it at my expense. I had always thought I was good at practical jokes and pulling people's legs, but I was a rank amateur compared with these guys. They continued to laugh while I just sat and shook my head. They made "sheep cowboy" jokes all evening and all the next day.

Two days later, I had saddled Gizmo and was ready to hit the trail again. Johnny, Cecil, and several others were there to bid me farewell and wish us good luck. I had stepped into the saddle and turned my horse to leave, when Cecil commented.

"Y'know, I went back east once."

"Oh yeah? Where'd you go?" I asked.

"Gallup, New Mexico," he replied.

And they all burst out laughing.

# MY HORSE AND ME

It didn't take long for Gizmo and I to become a pair, in a sort of conjoined partnership that didn't separate into clearly defined halves. We were more a mixture of two things that couldn't be split apart. Two sides of the same coin comes to mind, but that's not exactly right. The sides can't be split apart, but they're still distinct and separate from each other. That said, I suppose it fits to some extent. Looking back over the years to the ride, I've come to view our relationship more like food dye in a swimming pool. Each one determines the other's fate, and you can't experience one without also experiencing its partner. And you damned sure can't separate them.

Dogs throw themselves into a relationship with their human partners in a one-way show of fealty and loyalty. They become faithful no matter how the person treats them. They don't expect kindness or compassion in return, but they do enjoy it when it is given. They remain faithful. They're dogs. Man's best friend. Horses aren't dogs. They don't think or act like dogs.

Hollywood makes lots of movies that have horses in them. The heroine wins over the love of a wild stallion (usually some sort of outlaw horse that is going to be killed because it's too dangerous) by feeding it sugar and carrots, petting it, talking to it, and showing how much she loves and respects it. Sometimes a horse plays a leading role in the movies, but mostly they're in the background, equine extras or props. Those of us who know something about horses can usually spot a million inconsistencies in a movie. Leaving the horse saddled, day in and day out. Riding at a gallop everywhere and never at a walk. Throwing the reins over a hitching rail and expecting the horse to stay there. Or, getting off the horse on the prairie and walking away, leaving it standing there as if it would never run off and leave the hero stranded in the middle of nowhere, on foot, and without food or water. Those sorts of things show how we would expect a *dog* to act, but they're certainly not how horses behave.

I thought about that as Gizmo and I rode across the Painted Desert with large bands of wild horses shadowing us, hoping for a chance to take him away from me. If it were a movie, I'd simply step off him, drop the reins to the ground, and expect him to stand quietly. We call this "ground tying," and many horses will do this—up to a point. Gizmo did. But I see it playing out in a different manner: I stand twenty feet from my horse, who is ground tied, while I squat to relieve myself. Gizmo decides he'd like to join that horse herd he spotted ten miles back. He begins to wander away slowly, and then more quickly. As I call to him, he begins to trot. As I shout louder still, he breaks into a gallop and heads over a hill and out of sight. I stand there with my pants down and a roll of toilet paper in my hand. Gizmo is off to join his equine brethren.

I hear his galloping hooves for a minute or so until they fade off into the distance. I am alone, a few weeks' walk from anywhere and without food or water. My horse is fully saddled. This scenario is likely to end badly for both of us. I have no cell phone or internet access, no contact with anyone, all because I trusted him to stand there, ground tied.

It didn't happen, but it could have. Turning your horse loose like that is what you see in the movies, but it's not how you live with a horse in real life, at least not on the open plains. You can trust a dog this way. He'll stay in the back of a pickup truck all day if you tell him to. But a horse would jump out as soon as he could and would probably get hit by a passing car. Horses don't maintain the loyalty to us that dogs do.

That vision on the plains was probably my worst nightmare back then, and I made sure it never happened. In writing this book, I could easily have painted a picture of the bond that Gizmo and I had (and we did have a strong one), and I could have created a world in which his loyalty to me was the same as a dog's. But the truth is, horses are more like cats. They get used to you, and they love you on their own terms—though love might not be the right word for it. It is a certain kind of loyalty, but it's not the free devotion that canines know. It comes with its own set of conditions. Anything else is anthropomorphic—placing human traits upon animals. It makes us feel good but it often does more harm than good.

Assume you take a dog, its owner, and a stranger and arrange them in a triangle, twenty feet from each other. Then have the two people call the dog. The dog will go to its owner. Then give a handful of meat scraps to the stranger and have both people call the dog again. It will still go to its owner (most times). Do the same thing with a horse, but exchange the meat for a bucket of grain. Guess which one the horse will go to? And a cat? It'll ignore them both. The thing is, when push comes to shove, the horse and the cat both look out for themselves.

I'm not claiming that Gizmo had no loyalty to me. Far from it. I was the only constant in his life. I had been a constant for him long before we started our journey. This constant companionship cemented our bond, and as I said earlier, it didn't take long for us to become a pair. We became so used to each other that it was second nature. He considered me part of his herd, and I considered him part of mine. It was a small herd of two. Still, I never would have left him untied on the open plains, not even for a second.

We each had good days and bad. We had moods, changes in temperament from day to day, from situation to situation. Mostly we were level-headed and steady, even tempered and unruffled, and we got along well together. I learned the kinds of things Gizmo enjoyed, such as massaging his gums with my fingers—because he was four years old and still teething—and scratching the insides of his ears. When I could afford it, and when we were someplace I could buy it, I got a bottle of rubbing alcohol and gave him a rubdown, which he loved.

I teased him and told him, "No smoking while I'm doing this, bud, or you'll blow us both up."

He would sigh when the cold alcohol met his skin.

For his part, Gizmo was a rock for me. After a couple of weeks in the Mojave Desert, he was not afraid of anything. We rode along railroad tracks where freight trains roared past at 90 miles an hour, and he wouldn't bat an eye. It always scared me, but after the first few of them Gizmo didn't care, and I grew to trust him.

His trot is still the best I've ever ridden. It was a slow jog, a smooth glide that covered the miles effortlessly. Horses in the wild travel naturally at the trot when they want to cover ground. It is their most efficient gait, and allows them to travel great distances with a minimum exertion of energy. During the nineteenth century, the US Cavalry generally traveled at the trot to cover ground quickly while sparing their horses.

Sitting Gizmo's trot was made even easier by using English style stirrup leathers. I rode them with both the German cavalry saddle we started with, and later, the Canadian Mounties saddle we switched to in Oklahoma City. They allowed my legs to swing freely and maintain close contact with Gizmo, something a western saddle wouldn't have done. And though I have ridden in western saddles a lot, and later became a western saddlemaker, I never did feel as comfortable in one as I did in either of those two cavalry saddles.

I usually post to the trot on most horses, whether I'm in an English or a western saddle. Posting is simply standing up and sitting down, repeatedly. You stand up for one stride (when one front foot takes a step) and you sit down for the next one (when the other front foot takes a step), all the while keeping your weight in your stirrups. It's a bit more complicated than that, but that's the general idea. It allows you to maintain a smooth rhythm with your horse's trot. On many horses, if you don't post, you'll probably bounce around like a sack of potatoes. The trot is the roughest gait to sit, and on some horses it's just about impossible. It can be bone jarring. Posting is common among English riders. Not so much among western riders, but you do see them doing it now and then. Western riders often stand in their stirrups at the trot.

I was grateful that I didn't have to post Gizmo's trot. In fact, it's another reason I chose him for the ride. I was able to sit deep in the seat of the saddle as he trotted. I call it a trot, though western riders might refer to it as a slow jog. Whatever you call it, he was smooth as silk. I kept about half my weight in the stirrups, so I didn't bounce on his back, and together we easily covered seven or eight miles an hour on flat ground. I didn't have to ask him to trot. He just did it. We almost never galloped during the entire journey, though I did have to put him into a canter for a few strides once or twice to get out of the way of oncoming traffic. If I wanted to slow to a walk, I said, "walk" in a quiet voice, and he would break to a walk. I only had to use the word "walk" in a sentence—"Hey, Gizmo, how 'bout we walk for a while?"—and he'd go along with the idea. If I said, "Whoa," he would stop dead, no matter what we were doing. So, I didn't say "whoa" to him unless I wanted to put on the brakes.

I've said before that Gizmo whinnied whenever I came out of a market or returned to him after I had been gone for any length of time. I don't know if this was herd behavior or only a habit he formed during our journey, but it lasted until the day he died. It didn't matter if he was alone or with other horses. If he saw me arrive on the scene he would whinny and come running to the fence. So, anthropomorphic or not, it's hard to believe he didn't care about me. I'm pretty sure Gizmo had some dog in him. And I *know* he was part cat.

# NAVAJOLAND

The mountains recede abruptly behind us as we enter this desert of vast skies filled with huge clouds that will bring rain and lightning during the early summer afternoons. The receding mountains have given way once again to a broad desert plain with buttes and mesas brushed with pastel colors of rust, blue, yellow, and purple, the hues constantly transforming as the light changes throughout the day. It is a breathtaking spectacle, one that I now cling to and will for the rest of the ride, and for the rest of my life.

There are no fences here, no boundaries that say *this is where my land ends and yours begins."* Gizmo and I are free to travel in any direction we wish, although nature guides us down the path of least resistance and shows us the routes that will carry us over the saddles that lie between buttes and along dry stream beds and red dirt swales, to places where we may find water. I enjoy picking out buttes in the distance and locating them on my map—or vice versa, finding one on my map and spotting it among the many that surround us. I have become an expert at visualizing the terrain ahead simply by studying the topographic maps. Unlike the Mojave, this desert's elements are well defined and unique. There is no mistaking one landmark for another as there was back in the California desert.

I can see storms coming from a long distance away in the afternoons, mostly from the northwest. The rain often takes the form of *virga,* evaporating in midair as it falls from the clouds and never reaching the ground. A storm passes over us but leaves us dry, though sometimes the cool wind that accompanies it causes me to pull my coat on. When the storm clouds turn into dark, charcoal grey thunderheads, they bring the rain and lightning with them, and we must take cover where we can. If no shelter is to be found, I unbuckle my rain slicker from the pommel of the saddle and slip it over my head as I ride. It protects me from the oncoming rain, but more importantly, it covers the entire saddle, along with the bedroll and saddlebags, and keeps the gear dry.

I can see lightning striking the ground from many miles away as the storm approaches. It is a terrifying, yet exhilarating experience, one I never quite get used to. Still, I find myself looking forward to it in a strange way during these long days without company, and I share a special camaraderie with my horse as we face these daily trials by fire together.

I have never heard of extreme sports, nor has anyone else, for it will be many years before the concept of thrill seeking will invade the public psyche, in a future when people stampede in droves to test themselves against challenges, both natural and manmade. In many ways, these ordeals will mirror what Gizmo and I are doing now, but instead of meeting their challenges in a disconnected, private environment like Gizmo's and mine, they will become normalized, their stories part of the everyday lexicon. People will share their experiences, day by day, via the digital networks that will connect everyone, everywhere, all the time. And in doing so, they will attempt to inject meaning into their existence.

I am a white man, and as I ride my horse across the reservation I know full well that in some ways Gizmo and I are trespassing, not only upon Native American land, but upon the cultural values and history of a people I know little about. The people we meet out here, though very few and far between, are overwhelmingly friendly, helpful, and supportive of the journey I have undertaken with my horse. Though they don't speak of it, I know they appreciate that I am not simply another white man seeking to experience the indigenous wisdom of native people.

I have no intention of exploiting their world for anything except my own personal experience, and to that end, I keep most of what I witness to myself and ultimately, will never reveal the extent of our true experiences in the high deserts of Indian Country. I will disclose only those surface things—superficial details that, while interesting and impressive, don't divulge what will grow inside me as a result of this pilgrimage. I know I will never be Navajo or Apache, Hopi or Zuni, Acoma or Laguna, but I appreciate the grace and good humor of these people in allowing Gizmo and me to cross their lands, and I hope we have shown honor and respect in doing so.

The constellations of the night sky have shifted, and Orion moves closer to the morning dawn until, finally, it is overhead only in the daytime and remains unseen. The Gemini Twins are setting shortly after the sun, so I catch only a short glimpse of them now. The teapot Sagittarius hangs in the southern sky, and when I look up at it, I see the glorious band of stardust that is the Milky Way, and I know that when looking at Sagittarius I am looking directly into the center of our galaxy.

The Painted Desert eventually surrenders to the mountains of the Defiance Plateau, which breaks up the desert terrain for a while and contains a defining marker for the ride—the continental divide—the line that delineates west from east in North America. Rain falling on the west side of this line eventually flows to the Pacific Ocean, on the east side to the Atlantic. It is not yet halfway across the continent in distance, but crossing this milestone affects me greatly, and I feel Gizmo and I have achieved something important. When we come to the spot on my map that indicates the continental divide I stop to unsaddle. I talk to Gizmo for a long time. I tell him how proud I am of him and how lucky I am to have such a fine companion. Gizmo eats the dry bunch grass and filaree while I talk, but his ears show he is listening.

We saddle up again and continue down the trail, leaving the Great Divide behind us as we follow the eastbound path that the water takes. The plateau gives way to more desert to the east, though its mesas are far less striking in appearance and blend more readily with the surrounding landscape. The land that is called *the Malpais*—the literal translation is *badland*—takes a terrible toll on both of us. I seriously consider quitting the ride here, but the situation renders its own paradox and becomes a sort of *Catch 22*: in order to quit we will have to reach civilization, and in order to

137

reach civilization we will need to soldier on. If we reach civilization, our immediate problems will vanish, and we will have no reason to quit. So we push on.

Once across this expanse of desert badlands, we will reach Albuquerque and later, Santa Fe. The great desert of the American Southwest will be behind us, broken up by the intrusion of the Rocky Mountains. The Sangre de Cristos (meaning: the blood of Christ) and their smaller cousins, the Sandias (watermelon) and the Manzanos (apple trees), are the southernmost extension of the Rocky Mountains, and are sometimes called the tailbone of the Rockies. When we reach the eastern edges of northern New Mexico, I will turn to look upon them, and I will see what looks to be an immense dinosaur lying on its side with these mountains making up its long tail and extending far to the south.

In a few weeks Gizmo and I will gaze out across the great prairie that lies ahead, toward the grasslands of the Texas Panhandle, as he maintains a steady trot across the buffalo grass of northeastern New Mexico.

# A RETURN TO CIVILIZATION

Gizmo and I picked a trail down along the rough sandstone ledges that wound through the foothills of the Defiance Plateau. The big pine trees had given way to the cedar and piñon found across much of the high desert. My map told me that we had reached altitudes of almost eight thousand feet as we made our way through Navajo Country, north of Pine Springs on the reservation. It didn't feel that way though. Most of the Painted Desert is over a mile high, and we were used to moving through the deceptive elevation of the high desert by then.

We had been following an underground gas pipeline across the Painted Desert, but left it back near the Greasewood trading post and had struck out across the open country to the northeast. The only fences we encountered on the reservation were corrals and small holding pastures where Navajos gathered and tended their sheep and cattle. The range was almost completely open there, and if you drove along any of the small two lane highways at night, you were in danger of hitting a horse or a cow on the road. But the unfenced land meant that Gizmo and I were free to head in any direction without a thought given to man-made obstacles, diversions, or rights of way.

What had started out as a brisk wind late the day before had worked itself up into a full-fledged windstorm, with hurricane force gales that buried us under its relentless assault. I had dismounted early in the day and had led him down through the waves of blowing sand that enveloped everything. It was all we could do to stay on our feet once the full force of the storm came to bear. Gizmo ducked his head against the wind, bending from side to side in feeble attempts to deflect some of it. I wasn't sure just where we were, and I was afraid to pull the map from the safety of the saddlebags for fear of losing it, so I resorted to dead reckoning again to keep us oriented. Once the gigantic cloud of sand swallowed us, even the dead reckoning failed. After that, I simply stumbled along and kept ahold of Gizmo's lead rope, deathly afraid that he would get loose and run off in the storm.

By dumb luck, we found a deserted hogan and managed to get inside. The entrance lacked a door, and the structure's two small windows had long since given way to the elements, but it would serve to weather the storm. I unbuckled the breast collar, the britchen strap, and the girth and let the saddle and gear fall to the ground. I turned Gizmo loose in the hogan and pulled my saddle and gear inside. As long as I blocked the doorway, there was no place for him to go. I tied a sort of makeshift gate across the doorway with the picket rope, weaving it back and forth in a crisscross pattern. The wind howled through the hogan's openings, but it was a mild breeze compared with what was going on outside.

Once settled inside, I examined Gizmo's eyes. I licked a finger and wiped the grime and crud from them. I had been worried most of the day that he could be blinded by the blowing sand, but except for a short bout of rapid blinking, he seemed to have come through it all in good shape. In fact he seemed to be in fine spirits.

I couldn't light a fire, so I'd have to skip dinner that night. I wasn't about to go out in search of water, so Gizmo and I split what was in the canteen, though he drank most of it. The wind continued to bellow in through the west facing window, but by sitting under the window, with my back to the wall, I was sheltered from the direct force of the gale. I spent the night that way with the saddle blanket wrapped around me Gizmo simply turned his butt to the wind, lowered his head, and went to sleep. Later, he managed to lie down without crushing me..

I managed a few hours of restless sleep and crawled out of my crouched position a little before sunrise. Gizmo was up and had stuck his head out the window, watching the sun come up over the hills to the east. He whinnied when I finally stirred and pulled himself back into the hogan. I gave him a pat on the head and remarked, "Damn, son. That was some storm."

The wind had blown itself out overnight, and the day dawned clear and still. I was stiff and sore and had a hard time moving as I tried to start the day. Gizmo looked tired, too. Mornings were usually his best time, when he was raring to hit the trail to see what lay ahead of us. This morning was going to be a slow one for both of us.

I untied the picket rope from the doorway and squeezed Gizmo out the door. I tied him to a nearby tree in the morning sun, brushed him down and managed to get the saddle on him. Once he was tacked up, I made a cursory check of my map. I couldn't figure out exactly where we were, but I did have a general idea. I stepped up into the saddle and turned Gizmo to face the rising sun.

We had dropped down out of the steep, mountainous country now and into a sort of rolling badlands with sage and cactus growing among the juniper and pinon. The bunch grass was plentiful through here and Gizmo reached down to tear bits off as he walked, never missing a stride. He had developed this "eat as you go" method early in the ride, and I had never attempted to stop him; in fact, I encouraged him. It would ruin his future prospects as a show horse, but it allowed him to survive on the little forage available along the trail. A small price to pay.

It turns out we were not far from Gallup. We had crossed uneventfully into New Mexico two days before without knowing it. This was our fourth state, and I chuckled to myself when I thought of how I had wanted to create some sort of ritual when crossing each state line. So far, we had traveled from California to Nevada, then into Arizona, and now to New Mexico without once bothering to acknowledge crossing the border. Back before we started the ride, I had envisioned a sign at each state border, where the pair of us would pose for a picture to commemorate the event. At this point, it seemed frivolous, and I couldn't imagine being bothered to stop for anything as trivial as a photograph to mark our progress. All the same, it felt good to know that we had passed another milestone. It felt good to be in New Mexico.

It was still early morning when we reached the outskirts of Gallup after three hours on the trail. I had no watch, but I guessed it was a little after eight o'clock when we came into town from the northwest. We met up with Route 66 on the western edge of town. The interstate 40 bypass wouldn't be built for another five or six years, so this was still Gallup's main drag, though you wouldn't have known it that morning. The road was empty, and the west end of town looked deserted. I suspected the highway was blocked, because no traffic came from either direction. The sight of Gallup's main thoroughfare looked as though Gizmo and I were entering a ghost town.

My plan was to get through town as quickly as possible, then find a secluded spot to camp somewhere to the east. We crossed the railroad tracks out near a small airfield and covered the short distance to the highway, where I paused to take in the surroundings. It felt odd to be off the Navajo Reservation and back into so-called civilization.

It was a Sunday morning, and the place looked desolate. The windstorm had done considerable damage, leaving windows shattered, signs hanging haphazardly, power poles splintered and broken, and mounds of dirt and sand everywhere. Route 66 itself was covered with sand, and I had to look twice to make sure it was paved. Litter was scattered everywhere in all manner of chaos, with pieces of roofing, tree limbs, and parts of broken signs, barrels, chairs, clothing, and other paraphernalia that had been deposited randomly throughout the area. I saw no one until a single battered old pickup truck drove slowly past, its driver concentrating on dodging the obstacles in the road.

The south side of the highway looked a bit safer and less cluttered, so I urged Gizmo onto the blacktop. A white station wagon approached from the west, passing in front of us as we crossed the road. As it drove by, I saw something fly up over the car's roof and land on the pavement in front of us. I thought it was debris that had been flipped up by the car, but it began to explode. It was a string of firecrackers, and they went off like a series of rapid gunshots and scared Gizmo nearly out of his skin. He spooked and spun around with me, and I grabbed a rein and tried to keep him from running off. He lost his footing and stumbled, nearly falling in the middle of the road. I quickly slid off him, keeping ahold of the rein. I spoke to him, reassuring and calming him while the firecrackers continued to explode.

The car was a quarter mile down the road by then, but was making a U-turn and heading back toward us. I led Gizmo to the other side of the road and looked for a place to hide. The last thing I wanted was a confrontation with someone. I saw no place to go, so I simply led him along the sidewalk. As the car reached us, it slowed. The man in the passenger seat heaved an empty bottle over the roof of the car. It sailed toward us in slow motion, and I was helpless to do anything about it. I gripped the rein tighter and waited. The bottle hit the road and shattered, showering us with splinters and shards of glass. The driver of the car gunned the engine and raced off to the west. I looked down to see a piece of glass stuck in Gizmo's left front fetlock, near his hoof. I reached to pull it out, and it started to bleed. I pulled some toilet paper out of my saddlebags to wipe the blood that was running down his pastern, over the coronet band, and onto the hoof.

During all this time, I hadn't seen another person on the street. No other cars had driven by. Gallup seemed abandoned. I turned again to see the car in the distance, making another U-turn and heading back our direction. I felt vulnerable and helpless.

Gizmo's foot was still bleeding and I could only think to lead him down the sidewalk, away from them. The car slowed as it reached us. It came up from behind and pulled up next to us, within a few feet. There were two men, obviously very drunk. The passenger shouted at me with slurred speech, "Hey you sonuva—"

I had already pulled the old Colt from its holster and had drawn the hammer back. I pointed the barrel at the passenger's face, not more than a foot away. He froze momentarily then turned frantically to the driver who hadn't noticed the gun yet. When the driver leaned forward to peer around the passenger, he saw the gun barrel and immediately stomped on the accelerator. The car's rear tires spun and burned rubber out of the gutter and up onto the road. Surprisingly, Gizmo didn't seem to mind and took it all in stride. I waited until they were thirty or forty feet away and squeezed the trigger. The Colt jumped in my hand, and the rear window of the station wagon exploded as the car and its occupants sped away.

The truth of it was, I had not shot in a fit of anger or a moment of passion. Firing the Colt was premeditated. While the car had been turning around for the last time, I was able to take stock of where I was. I could see nothing toward the northeast but the railroad tracks, with open land beyond them. There were no buildings in that direction—no train cars, no people— so I figured that if I had to, I could shoot without endangering anyone (except the car's occupants). And to this day I don't know if I hit either of them. To be truthful, I don't particularly care.

Shooting a gun like that was not something I thought I would ever do, nor have I ever considered it since. It's not something I am proud of, and I haven't talked about it much. I've never subscribed to the John Wayne tough guy mentality of settling disputes. I certainly wouldn't have used the Colt if Gizmo hadn't been with me. I haven't owned a gun in many, many years and have no use for them now. But I'm glad I had that old single action back then. And though it seems like a contradiction, it's not an endorsement for keeping firearms for self-defense. I had carried the Colt to scare away critters. I didn't bring it for self-defense, and to my reckoning, people who keep them for that purpose are fools.

I watched as the car drove east through the main part of town and disappeared around a corner. I never saw it or its occupants again. I holstered the Colt and began to lead Gizmo along the litter-strewn sidewalk toward the center of town, when a voice came from the front porch of the building we were passing.

"Man, that was *some* shootin'!"

I could barely make out the shadow of a man crouched on the stoop of the abandoned structure. He was homeless, with a scruffy beard, battered and worn out dirty clothes, and a brown paper bag in his hand that concealed a bottle.

"Sorry I had to do that," I said.

"Naw, them boys had it comin'," he answered. "You oughta get on that horse and go after 'em."

I just nodded and walked on, leaving him there to contemplate what he had witnessed. We slowly made our way along the road to the center of Gallup, with saloons and bars seemingly on every corner. The town began to gradually come alive. People appeared in the shops and businesses along the way, bending their energies toward cleaning up the mess and repairing the damage the storm had inflicted. Some stopped to chat, but most left us to ourselves, which was a welcome relief. The incident had soured me on people for the time and I just wanted to find a secluded place where my horse and I could be left alone.

I did not get back on Gizmo that day. I tied a rag around his foot to stop the bleeding and I just led him along the main road through town. It was a long day, tiring and discouraging. The sun was low in the western sky when we finally made camp in a field to the east of town. We had made a little over sixteen miles that day, and I had walked most of it. I thanked God that Gizmo wasn't lame and that his pastern seemed none the worse for wear. It had bled freely for a while, soaking the rag red, but the cut was only a surface wound and wouldn't require suturing. I doctored it with some Gentian Violet that I kept in my saddlebags. It is a vile smelling purple liquid that has been in the tack rooms of horse barns since the late 1800's, used as a universal cure-all for cuts and scrapes, thrush (foot fungus), and other livestock maladies. The lid had a built-in wool dauber attached, which stayed immersed in the purple liquid when the bottle was closed. I was always terrible at painting and not surprisingly, I ended up with as much purple stain on myself as I managed to apply to Gizmo's foot. The stain became its own form of tattoo, a semi-permanent blemish that would stay on my hands for weeks.

With my Case knife I managed to cut some wild alfalfa growing alongside the road and brought it back for Gizmo. It was a dry camp but he had had plenty to drink shortly before we got there, and I wasn't worried about him. Darkness settled in as I spread my bedroll and lay down on it. It had been a long, difficult day and my mind began to race as I thought back on the events that morning.

Shooting at someone is not something you do. It just isn't. Shooting is something you see in the movies, something you fantasize about when you're seven years old playing cowboys and Indians. It's violence that you read about in the paper, a story that you see on the nightly news. It's not something you do. It certainly wasn't me. It wasn't who I was. Or at least, it wasn't who I thought I was.

"I think I'm losin' my mind, pal. That gunfight stuff isn't what we signed up for. "

He blew the dust from his nostrils and continued to munch on the dry alfalfa cuttings. After a while, he stopped eating and came over to lie down beside me. I was angry with myself, and I was scared. Scared of what I'd become. I had set out to find myself, to get to know who I really was, out here somewhere along this long trail. But I sure as hell hadn't set out to find this.

My dreams were violent that night, and colored in deep purple.

# A HARD ROAD

T he trail from Gallup to Albuquerque steered us along a path to the north of, and parallel to Interstate 40, sometimes following what was then Old Route 66, but mostly taking the more remote routes offered by powerline roads, gas pipelines, and railroad tracks. The weeks spent across the deserts of California and Arizona had taken a toll on Gizmo, as he lost weight and suffered the various bumps and bruises from the trail. The grass had been poor back in Navajoland, but was even worse, now that we had dropped down into more populated areas. We had good days and bad days, but through here it seemed most of them were bad. For every mile I rode I walked a mile, hoping to lift Gizmo's burden and ease his suffering. Most days we barely managed to make our twenty-mile goal, and I wasn't going to push him in order to keep up with that target. We still had close to 150 miles to ride before we reached Albuquerque, and another 60 up to Santa Fe. The more tired and trail weary Gizmo became, the slower we traveled and the more time it would take to get there. It became a downward spiral—the more time we spent on the trail, the slower the pace, which meant more time on the trail. Of the 150 miles to Albuquerque, I figured on walking 75 of them. We would lose four or five days along the way. Traveling on foot meant carrying most of the burden myself, but it would save my horse from further suffering.

*LOGBOOK:*

*We stopped at the Howard Johnson's outside of Grants. I staked Gizmo out to the big flagpole in front. There was a big circle of green grass growing around it, like a lawn. Really out of place because it was so green. Especially after what we have crossed. I went inside and sat down at a booth in the little cafe there. I must have looked like a rough saddle tramp with my beat up cowboy hat and weather beaten day pack on my back and the single action Colt strapped to my side. I think I scared the waitress a bit. She asked what I wanted and I told her what I'd been dreaming about for days—weeks, even. Did they have any peaches and ice cream? She said no, they didn't serve that. I asked if they had a bowl of peaches and she said she could get me one. I asked if I could also have a bowl of ice cream. She asked, vanilla chocolate or strawberry? I told her vanilla, and a cup of coffee please. She came with the coffee and the two bowls and I poured the peaches on top of the ice cream. It was the best thing I've ever tasted. When I finished I went outside and Gizmo had pretty much destroyed the lawn around the flagpole. I didn't care. Hard to believe a company would waste water on a useless lawn in the middle of a desert. Gizmo and I rode off feeling a lot better, and I can still taste that bowl of peaches and ice cream.*

From the Navajo and Hopi Reservations we passed through the lands of the Zuni, Acoma, and Laguna people. We crossed the great lava floes of the Malpais, where every step was painful for my horse. It was a constant search for water and for any sort of feed for Gizmo.

*LOGBOOK:*
*This is pure hell. The wasteland will never be past us. I was ready to quit today. No water here. The feed is worthless. Gizmo easts mostly tumbleweeds and sagebrush. I killed a six foot rattler today. We followed a dirt road through the Laguna Indian Reservation in order to find water at some of the windmills or cattle tanks. Many were dried up, and we walked several miles out of our way. I'd spot one in the distance, only to find it dry. It was a vicious circle; the more we travel, the more we need the food and water, and the longer we do without, the slower we go.*

*LOGBOOK:*
*Today the same as yesterday, only worse. We are both dragging so bad my nerves are shot. People drive by down on the highway in their air conditioned campers, eating cookies and drinking soda pop. I hate every one of them. Lost one of my spurs. Walked back more than a mile looking for it. As I was leading Gizmo, I felt a tug on the reins and turned to look at him. He had gone down. I just fell down beside him and took his head in my arms and cried.*

We rested like that for an hour or more, until he seemed to want to get to his feet and go on. It was a turning point in the ride, and I think in both of our lives, because our luck started to change for the better after that. Later that day, as I led him along a lonely two lane road, a truck drove past and hit a bump in the road. A bale of hay bounced off right in front of us. We camped right there where the bale landed, on the side of the road.

We still had several days to go.

# GIZMO GROWING UP

I used to think Gizmo was part cat and part dog when he was a youngster. As a weanling colt and into his yearling adolescence, he'd follow me around like a lap dog, curious as a cat about everything around him.

I was living in a rambling old two-story frame farmhouse on California's central coast. In the rolling hills behind the house, there was a pasture fenced with barbed wire, home to a pair of ancient wooden water tanks that had seen their usefulness evaporate along with the water that had been in them. They sat atop impressive twin towers made of hand hewn timbers. The tanks were empty except for the small amount of rainwater that seeped in through the holes and cracks in their tops and sides. Now and then teenagers would sneak up into them at night to smoke weed, their transistor radios tuned to FM stations that played the Jackson Five or Creedence Clearwater or any pop and rock music they could get stoned to. They usually kept the level turned down where they thought I couldn't hear, but on any moonlit night I could see Gizmo standing beneath the water tower listening to the music. It was a dead giveaway, but I left them to their parties because they weren't doing any harm, and besides, the colt seemed to enjoy the music and the company.

He had the run of ten or fifteen acres which he shared this with a sad old gelding named Star and a weather-beaten Abyssinian donkey named Pancho. They both tolerated the young colt, although neither particularly liked him or his constant affections and inquisitions into what they might be doing at any particular moment. He was generally shunned as any young nuisance would be, and so whenever I appeared at the pasture fence, he came running. He kept up a constant game of nuzzle-and-run in which he would thrust his nose under one of my arms then pull back and run away as fast as he could for several strides. He would turn back to see if I was watching and then return to repeat the process again.

He enjoyed most of all the times when I would bring my old accordion to play. I'm pretty sure he thought I was playing for him alone, and maybe I was. Star and Pancho dismissed my performances as not being worth the price of admission. Whenever I played the accordion—or sometimes the guitar or harmonica—Gizmo would wander up and stand next to me. His eyes would soften, his lower lip would relax and hang open slightly, he'd lick his lips, and sometimes he would utter a quiet sigh. During these occasions, he was the calmest I ever saw him as a youngster. I like to think I instilled a love of music in him, but he was a horse, and I don't know how they view those sorts of things. Still, it was a sort of bonding ritual for me, and maybe for him as well. And many years later, when he was old and turning grey in places, he still grew soft and quiet at the sound of the accordion or the harmonica.

I spent very little time training him when he was a colt. He was halter broke and could be tied, though I rarely tied him up. There was no reason to. I could handle his feet and legs and trim his hooves without incident. That was the extent of our working relationship at that point. Nothing much was required of him except to grow and to stay healthy.

Apart from having to be sewn up by the local veterinarian from running through the barbed wire and the trauma of being gelded when he was a two-year-old, he did a pretty good job of doing nothing. He loved attention, whether from people or other animals. Horses, dogs, cats … didn't matter. He was a mirror for me, the yang to my yin. He was an extrovert who wanted to be the center of attention at any party. And growing up, life was one big party for Gizmo.

By the time he was eighteen months old, I had begun to throw a light packsaddle on him—eventually with panniers—to get him used to being saddled. At the same time, I taught him how to be tied by his front foot, an invaluable thing for any horse to know. I had no idea he would eventually take me across the continent, so I wasn't preparing him for anything specific. I just fancied that I might want to take him on a pack trip or two someday, and picketing a horse by the front foot allows him to graze without the picket rope wrapping around his hind legs and leaving rope burns.

Gizmo didn't much balk at anything I threw at him. He took his first saddling with good humor, and merely bent his head around to look at what I had fastened to his back. He didn't mind the longe line or the driving lines I attached through the stirrups of the saddle to ground drive him. As I said, I figured he was part dog in that regard. I didn't try to get on him until after he was three years old because it's not good for a young horse to carry that kind of weight. I was living in Los Angeles at the time, and Gizmo was stabled at a local barn. I had managed to get him used to the idea of being saddled, and by the time I finally climbed on him it was more or less anticlimactic. No bucking, no fear or fits of anger. Just a casual acceptance. Though he wasn't a "finished" horse at that point, I did manage to coax him to pack me along as a passenger.

One of the tricks I employed in training him was to use his curiosity to my own ends. He loved to see what was on the other side of the hill, and I rewarded this by leading him, then ground driving him on short adventures down the trail, away from the home pasture and the other horses. Many horses become what is called herd bound, which means they don't like to leave the barn or the horses they live with. Things can get a bit frantic when you take them off by themselves. They tend to travel a lot faster returning to the barn than they did when riding away from it. But Gizmo seemed to be just the opposite and loved to go wandering whether other horses were around or not. He didn't mind that the others stayed back at the barn and wasn't in a rush to get home once we turned around. He socialized with others in the corral, but when I took him out, a little switch seemed to flip in his brain, and he became a different horse, with the mind of a wanderer.

By the time I started to ride him, I merely pointed him down the trail, and he was happy to take me anywhere I wanted to go. Of course, like any young colt experiencing their first rider, he had a bit of trouble figuring out where his feet were. He stumbled a few times, unsure of just how to go about carrying this accordion-playing, harmonica-blowing animal that he'd grown up with, but as the weeks went by, he quickly turned into a sure-footed, confident, and self-assured horse. I don't think he ever saw our relationship as a master-animal, or boss-worker, and I know I never did. We were always equals, and I knew that Gizmo didn't exactly *obey* me. It was more like he allowed me to steer most of the time. And through it all, he never lost his insatiable curiosity.

# HIPPIE GIRLS

Gizmo and I are feeling good. It's early June, and we've hit the trail after a layover in Santa Fe. We're both well rested, though I'm not quite as perky as he is. My ribs and leg are hurting pretty badly from a fall with another horse.

While staying with my friend Eliza I had volunteered to try a young pinto mare for her that she was thinking of buying from a neighbor. The man had ridden the mare over and was obviously pretty hard on the horse. His spurs had big, sharp rowels on them, and I knew that he used them liberally because they had left their marks along the mare's flanks, in small trails of blood. The mare was frightened and edgy, and when I stepped up on her, she reared up and flipped over backward with me before I could catch my offside stirrup.

In a series of events in slow motion, I felt the mare rise up and her neck and head slapping into my face as we both fell backward. She landed on top of me then rolled off to one side and stood up. I dragged myself to my feet and dusted myself off, but at the time, I didn't let on about how badly I had been hurt. And even though it has been a few days now, I feel as though I probably broke a rib or two, and my right side is all black and blue. It hurts a lot when I breathe deep or cough, but I'm not coughing up blood anymore, so I think I'll live. When we got hurt as kids my grandmother would tell us we were fine, and she used to say, "It's a long way from your heart." The fact is, this isn't all that far away from my heart, so I guess I'm lucky.

*LOGBOOK:*
*After almost 2 weeks in Santa Fe we're finally back on the trail. Gizmo is a new horse. He's gained at least 100 pounds or more. Not exactly fat, but a lot better than when we got here. Vet wormed him and gave him a vitamin shot. He has new shoes. I've repaired all my gear. Aside from my ribs that are killing me, we're ready to go. It was good to hit the trail again this morning.*

Gizmo is feeling great. He gained weight during our stay in Santa Fe, but he's still thin. After worming and vitamin shots I'm feeling better about him. The horseshoer shod him with borium welded onto his shoes. They'll last a lot longer that way.

He was feeling no pain and even had a little hump in his back as we left, day before yesterday. Good thing he didn't unload me in front of the TV cameras. We stopped at a little cafe about ten miles out of town to get some water. The woman who works there recognized us and came out with a piece of apple pie for Gizmo. She had read in the paper that he likes it. She ended up going back in and getting the rest of the pie for him, and we talked for a while. I noticed how shiny and curly her hair looked in the morning sun and was struck by the deep turquoise color of her eyes. She told me her name is Shelly and invited us to stay at her place out near Pecos. I don't like to make Gizmo detour too far, so I told her I'd think about it, if it's not too far out of our way.

That was two days ago and now we're near where she said her place was. I'm not sure about her directions, and after thinking that we've missed it and giving up, I spot the house, a small adobe back in the woods a little way up an old four-wheel drive forestry road. It's late in the afternoon when we ride up, and I step down off of Gizmo at the front porch. Two women come out to greet me. Shelly from the cafe is there, and she introduces me to her roommate, Jen. The two are what I could only call hippie girls because they are like the live-off-the-land types I have known who lived in communes. Shelly is tall—*statuesque* would be the right word—with golden hair that hangs down just past her shoulders in lazy curls and waves. She is almost a head taller than Jen, who is petite and slim, with dark features and a brilliant white smile that you can see a mile off. Both are barefoot and wearing short summer dresses, and their deep tans make it obvious they spend a lot of time outdoors.

They show me around back to a small shed that serves as a guest house. Next to it there's a wire corral with a lean-to attached that houses a couple of goats. I unsaddle and turn Gizmo out with the goats, who are very happy to see him. He gives me a look that could kill and resigns himself to his fate as the goats begin nudging and pestering him.

I drag my gear inside. There is a small dining table and a couch in the corner where I toss my bedroll. I leave my saddle and day pack on the floor. There is no electricity here, but I find some coal oil lamps I can use, and a small log burner hugs the wall opposite the couch in case it gets cold at night. The place has running water and a shower, but no toilet. There is an outhouse set farther back that I can use. After organizing my gear, I take a look around the back of the building and find there is a small stack of alfalfa hay that they feed to the goats. I toss a big flake of it over the fence to Gizmo, and he chases the goats off and begins to eat. I take a quick shower before I head over to the main house and knock on the back door.

Jen lets me in, and I find myself in the kitchen, where she offers me a bottle of *Pacifico*. I gladly accept the beer. I tell her that I am happy to pay for Gizmo's hay, but she will have none of it, so I thank her and tell her how much Gizmo and I appreciate it. She is cooking enchiladas on the stove and has a pile of sopaipillas on the counter, ready to fry. I stand in the corner and watch. She has long black hair that hangs down her back in a single braid that ends just below her waist. She is wearing a skimpy summer dress that emphasizes the fact that she probably has nothing on underneath it. She pauses and looks at me for a moment with her coal black eyes, intense and silent, and I can feel myself blush. She is a strikingly beautiful woman. It occurs to me that I am now alone in a house with *two* strikingly beautiful women, and I'm suddenly nervous. I begin to wonder if coming here was such a good idea.

Shelly comes in from the other room, and the way she puts her hand on the small of Jen's back makes me realize that they are more than just roommates. I experience the slightest bit of disappointment at first, but then I am surprised at how relieved I feel. It's as if a small pressure valve has opened inside me, and suddenly, I am relaxed and smiling and joking. I begin to feel at home with them.

Jen asks how long we were in Santa Fe and mentions that she saw us in the paper there. Some of the normal questions about the ride come up.

Then I ask Jen what sort of work she does. She says that she's an artist and works mostly with textiles. She gives a sort of self-effacing shrug. Shelly jumps in and talks about how talented Jen is and then grabs my hand to lead me into the other room to show me Jen's work.

I find myself looking at several marvelous sheets of fabric hanging from the living room walls. They look like intricate tapestries, and Jen explains that these are what is called batik and that she uses old newspapers to roll up the cloth and put wax on it somehow to come up with the intricate designs. I have no idea what she's talking about, but I'm very impressed with her work. I don't think I'm as impressed with her as Shelly is, though, because I can see the glow of pride in her eyes as she watches while Jen is explaining her work. If I had any amorous thoughts about either of these two ladies, they have evaporated now, and I find that I'm very happy and comfortable here, sharing this space with these two lovely people.

We have a wonderful meal of traditional enchiladas—cooked flat in layers of blue corn tortillas, with green chile, cheese, sour cream, and guacamole. We have another round of *Pacificos* and sit at the kitchen table where we talk for a couple of hours. The two have made this their home and have done all the work on the place themselves. They have a small garden out back and grow a lot of their own food. Shelly says that they manage to get into Santa Fe fairly often on the weekends for fun. They are genuinely friendly and hospitable, and neither is star struck or in awe of what Gizmo and I are doing. Even though they both think it's interesting, they take a sort of matter of fact attitude toward it all. I find this very refreshing, and I love them for it.

At first, Jen appears to be a bit of an airhead, but she's astute and extremely smart. She talks about positive energy and vibrations and all those sorts of things, and how love puts us on the right spiritual path, automatically. Shelly is more of an Earth mother type, grounded and sensible, but she agrees with Jen about the love stuff, and I like that. Gizmo and I have been existing in survival mode and living rough for so long that I guess I've forgotten about how to care for anyone but my horse and myself. It's nice to feel this way, and nice to spend an evening sharing emotional things, rather than talking about practical matters.

As it gets dark, I excuse myself to go out and check on my horse, and Jen comes with me. We find him lying down in the corral with the two goats piled up against him. He whinnies when he sees me but doesn't get up. I check to make sure he hasn't colicked, and he looks fine. He's just resting. He seems to have made friends with his two stablemates, and I feel better, knowing he's content. We start back to the house, and Jen links her arm in mine and rests her head against my shoulder as we walk.

We all sit down on the couch together with me in the middle, and the two ladies snuggle up to me. I start to get nervous again, and I'm wondering where all of this is heading, but I stay put and allow the women to sort of attach themselves to both sides of me. If they were cats they'd be purring. As it is, they're making contented sounds like lambs. I think to myself that, right now, Gizmo and I each have a couple of adoring companions. There's something very sweet about it all, and I find myself relaxing again and just enjoying their company.

We sit together like that for a long time, no one speaking, until I feel myself starting to fall asleep. I finally break the silence by apologizing and saying that Gizmo and I have an early start in the morning. I gently extricate myself and stand up, and they stand up too. I thank them again for their wonderful hospitality and friendship.

Jen says, "You're welcome to stay in the house tonight." She pauses, then continues. "You can sleep with us. We would love it if you would."

"Yes, we would love for you to stay with us tonight," Shelly says.

I'm a bit taken aback and don't know what to say. I pause to think about their offer and then, even as I mentally kick myself, I respond by telling them how lucky I am to have met them, and that I'm really, *really* flattered and tempted, but that maybe it wouldn't be such a good idea. "I'm sorry," I say.

They both smile and say, it's okay, that they understand. I'm glad they understand, because by this time I sure don't.

I turn to give Jen a hug goodnight, and as we start to embrace, she leans in, and the hug suddenly becomes a kiss, hard on the mouth, and it lasts a long time. She holds me in a tight embrace that seems almost desperate. When we are finished, I turn to Shelly and she repeats the process, holding me very tight and kissing me passionately.

"The offer still stands," she whispers when we separate.

"It's awfully tempting, but I have to decline, sorry." At the same time I'm telling them this, I'm telling myself that I am a complete and utter moron.

I head out to the shed and stop to say hello to Gizmo once again. He is standing up now, his two new pals lying at his feet. He steps gently over them and comes to me, sticks his head over the fence, and puts his nose under my arm to see if I have any treats.

"Sorry pal," I tell him, "not this time. Looks like we're both outta luck tonight."

I go inside the shed, light one of the kerosene lamps, sit down on the couch, and think back on the evening. My ribs are hurting from the hugs, though I didn't notice the pain at the time. The women were the best kind of anesthetic. No sane man would pass up what I just have. I pause to consider the person I have become, and I wonder if the lonely trail we have been following has somehow damaged both of us in ways I don't understand. I think I might have already succumbed to the pressures of being alone, and maybe I have turned feral and just don't realize it or care. I fear the same applies to Gizmo. But the more I think about those two beautiful creatures back in the house, the more I love them for who they are. Simple, unassuming, and free with themselves. Giving, sharing, loving.

*********

I can still remember when we used to use the term "free love" back then. The years have taught me that the term is the very definition of those two ladies, and that they embodied it. It's not the sexual part, though it was certainly a factor. In the larger sense it's all about how they gave freely from their hearts to strangers like Gizmo and me, letting us into their lives. They opened their home and their spirits to us, and as delicious and seductive as they were, they were my sisters, and I loved them for that. I was their brother, and I still am.

# ANOTHER SUMMER STORM

As we left Las Vegas, New Mexico, we turned straight eastward and climbed up onto a high plain. For the first time I began to feel our passage through the southwestern desert. The Rocky Mountains were receding behind us, though we would see them for many days and still catch glimpses of them in the distance in the weeks ahead. We had arrived at the top of what would have been a giant mesa had nature carved it out with a bit more definition millions of years ago.

*LOGBOOK:*
*A man stopped his Winnebago camper along the road. He had a horse trailer on the back with 2 horses in it. Gizmo and the horses whinnied at each other. He said his name was A. Kelly Pruitt, and that he was a cowboy artist. He seemed in no hurry, so I tied Gizmo to the side of the trailer and Kelly gave him some grain. We sat and talked for about an hour. He had lots of wonderful paintings that he had done, and a bunch of great old cowboy horse gear in his camper. He asked me if he could take some pictures of me on Gizmo, to use as studies, and I said sure. Was a nice break, visiting with him.*

We traveled along a little-used two lane road that headed straight toward Texas and took us across an enormous flat prairie that was covered in grama and buffalo grass, with some bluestem and others competing with the cholla and rabbit weed against the wind and draught. It felt as if we had set sail on a great brown ocean beneath pastel blue skies that spread to the horizon in all directions and disappeared behind the great mountains behind us. I could see a windmill for many miles before we got to it, and they dotted the landscape here and there. No trees were to be seen, except those that were planted on purpose for shade next to the few ranch houses in the distance.

The land reminded me somewhat of the Painted Desert, though it lacked the striking buttes and mesas that had surrounded us there. Instead, the Sangre de Cristo mountains lay behind us to the west—the tailbone of the Rockies—and the land began to give way to a flat plain in front of us, with a chain of rugged hills doing its best to block our trail to the headwaters of the Canadian River. But it still felt *big* and *open*. Once we had climbed up onto the great plateau, we lost sight of Las Vegas and of anything else that tied us to civilization. Save for a ranch house and barn here and there, it was empty, open country.

> LOGBOOK:
> *I watched a coyote stalk and kill a rabbit today. We were cutting across some foothills and were camped at the edge of a large draw, up near the tree line. I was reading a paperback and looked up to see a big, healthy looking coyote trotting across the meadow below. His coat was shiny and he was fat and looked like he was having a good year. He stopped, then began to move slowly. His eyes were focused on something ahead. I couldn't see what it was. After a minute or so he broke into a run and I saw a cottontail leap from a bush just in front of him. After a few twists and turns he landed on the rabbit and killed it. Then he trotted back the way he had come, the dead rabbit flopping in his mouth. For some reason, the whole scene had a certain elegance to it and I felt as though I had witnessed something special.*

On our third day out on this flatland, we camped at a windmill with a metal water tank and a small wooden creep feeder nearby. The mill was an old Dempster ten-footer that sat on a thirty-two foot, four-legged tower. Most water pumpers in these parts were made by the Aermotor Company, so this Dempster, while not exactly uncommon, created a unique silhouette against the New Mexico sky as it spun with the wind. The mill's wheel and tail both creaked and groaned in the wind as its sucker rod slapped against the guides with every stroke, a small bit of water leaking from the stuffing box as it pumped water into the tank at two or three gallons a minute. It was a reassuring sound to me, one that will always be connected with survival. A windmill means water, and water means life.

The grass in this part of the country had been overgrazed until there wasn't much left but dirt, so Gizmo didn't have a lot to eat. There was some tall green rye grass growing around the shady side of the water trough, so I staked him to the windmill where he could reach the grass and the water. I made a crude camp, then took a bath in the trough. It was big enough to swim in, so I floated on my back, naked, looking up at the wispy clouds forming in the afternoon sky. The water was icy cold but refreshing after several hot days of trail dust and sweat. I washed my clothes and hung them on the windmill tower to dry, which they did in a few minutes in the dry New Mexico sun. I sat and read for a while then noticed a storm front moving toward us from the northwest. It was miles off, but it was very black and threatening. I could see lightning hitting the ground as it grew closer, and I quickly rounded up all my gear and moved it to the creep feeder.

Creep feeders are used for feeding calves, and sometimes for horse foals that are still nursing. They are too small for the mother to fit into, but big enough to allow a foal or a calf through the opening. They allow the rancher or horse breeder to feed supplements to the young ones without their mothers taking it instead.

Creep feeders are constructed in various ways, sometimes just some fence panels strung together with a small opening and some, like this one, built of wood with a tin roof and railing around it, high enough for a calf to walk under, but too low for a mother cow to pass beneath. I crawled into the wooden feeder and dragged my saddle and all my gear under its small roof as it started to rain. I ducked back out and headed to fetch Gizmo as the rain began to pour down in earnest. It arrived suddenly, with a vengeance, much sooner than I had expected. The lightning exploded when it hit the windmill tower where Gizmo was picketed. I was knocked off my feet as the light rain turned to a downpour within seconds. I watched as he jumped around, staked to the metal tower, and I jumped to my feet and ran to him. As I reached him and took ahold of his halter I rubbed his nose and talked to him to calm him down. It was the second time lightning had hit a windmill that Gizmo was tied to, and I felt like we had run out of luck. The lightning hit again, very close, and he reared up and jerked me off my feet.

I managed to hang onto the halter. The downpour suddenly turned to hail the size of golf balls. They were giving us both a pounding, but my hat took the brunt of the punishment. Gizmo was being beaten pretty badly by it all, and I knew I had to get him under shelter of some sort. I unclipped the rope from his front hobble and clipped it to his halter. Then I untied it from the windmill and led him back to the creep feeder. I couldn't get him inside, but I could coax his head and neck in, so he was partially protected from the hail. It lasted a few more minutes then reverted back to a steady, driving rain for another half hour.

Most of the afternoon summer showers in that part of the country come and go within an hour or two. This was a full-fledged storm that looked to be settling in for the night. The creep feeder did a poor job of keeping the gear dry. Everything was soaked. Gizmo and I were both muddy and drenched, and there was no place to sit or stand to get away from it. I decided to saddle up, and we set off for a building I had seen in the distance.

As we walked, I asked him, "What're the odds of *two* windmills you're tied to getting hit by lightning?"

He dropped his head and walked along, pretending he hadn't heard me. I led him a couple of miles to where a large hay barn stood by itself near a dirt road. The barn doors were open, so we slipped inside and out of the storm.

As I was unsaddling and spreading my gear out to dry, I heard a pickup truck pull up outside. I looked out to see the truck's doors opening, and two men stepped out and came into the barn. The older of the two (I figured for the father) asked me what I was doing, and I told him we had gotten ourselves trapped in the lightning storm. He was a bit stroppy and aggressive at first, but when he saw that we were traveling and meant no harm, his bearing changed and he became friendly. He told me it was fine if we spent the night and to help ourselves to some of the grass hay that was stacked in the barn. I told him I wouldn't break open a new bale, but would find one already broken. We talked for a while, the younger man asking questions about where we'd come from, the older one offering suggestions for how to navigate the country ahead. They said their goodbyes and left us to weather the storm in the barn. It rained well into the night.

The air was crisp and clear when we hit the trail early the next morning. We had taken a bit of a detour by heading to the barn so we had to backtrack to find our way along the fence line to the east. We had covered a quick six miles at Gizmo's smooth trot when we came upon a large truck and a couple of pickup trucks parked alongside the road. There were several men at work along both sides of the fence and it wasn't until we were almost upon them that I realized what they were doing.

Several cattle were dead, piled on top of one another inside the barbed wire fence. Gizmo snorted in fear as we pulled up to the scene and stopped.

The rancher and his son were there, along with several others. They were butchering the cattle. They wrapped the pieces in white butcher paper from a roll in one of the pickup trucks. They set the meat inside the large truck, which was refrigerated and used to haul meat and produce. The rancher told me that thirty-two head of cattle had bunched up against the fence. When the lightning hit the fence, it had killed all but three of them. He told me I had made the right choice, taking cover in his barn. I asked if they needed any help and he said no, that they had it all under control. He spoke in a matter of fact manner, as if this was just part of the job of raising cattle. And I suppose it was. I turned Gizmo back up the road, and we left them there, trying to make lemonade out of lemons.

*LOGBOOK: June 23*
*Camped at an abandoned schoolhouse outside of Trujillo. Last night I saw a mother sparrow making a nest. This morning she was dead, caught in some sort of nylon webbing she had brought home. She had flopped around until she died. I cut her loose and buried her. For some reason it made me sad and I cried.*

# DEAD PEOPLE MAKE GOOD NEIGHBORS

The ride didn't mark the first time I had slept in a graveyard, though it did for Gizmo. I have mentioned that I did a lot of hitchhiking and riding freight trains during my youth. That activity continued almost up until the time of the ride. And during those times, graveyards were my friends. The first of the many cemeteries I spent the night in was outside of Salinas, California, while I was thumbing my way back to Los Angeles from San Francisco in 1967. I was stranded at a place called Spreckles. In those days, Salinas was still a wild cow town, and Spreckles wasn't even on the map. As was often the case when hitchhiking in a remote place, you could easily be stuck in one spot for hours—oftentimes for an entire day or more—while you waited for a benevolent soul to stop and pick you up.

I found myself alone on Highway 101 with the sun having set over the Monterey Penninsula to the west. In most cases, I would try to find a drainage culvert to squeeze into or a bridge to crawl under, so I could sleep the night there, near the road. They were easy to find along major highways, but the small two lane road that was Highway 101 back then didn't provide anything for me on that particular night. So as darkness settled, I picked up my grip and my guitar and made my way along a dirt road, away from the two lane. I knew that if I didn't find a place to hide, I would likely wind up in the local jailhouse as I had on previous occasions. The two most popular offenses used by police back then to put away hardened criminals like me were vagrancy and loitering, both of which I was, technically speaking, guilty of.

After I had covered a short distance, it occurred to me that I was walking through a cemetery because I stumbled over a bulge in the ground that turned out to be a grave. I could barely see the headstone, which lay flat on the ground at one end. Not one to let that stop me, I wandered between the graves until I saw a massive oak tree nestled within some large bushes, and figured it could hide me for the night. I wasn't sure how exposed I might be the next morning when the sun came up, but as it turned out, I spent a restful and uneventful night there and was able to flag down a semi truck on the two lane early the next morning. I filed the idea of "graveyards as sleeping quarters" away for future reference.

The first time Gizmo spent the night in a graveyard was when we were in northeastern New Mexico, out in the badlands east of Las Vegas and almost to the Texas panhandle. We were crossing open range, along the headwaters of the Canadian River, following a line on my topographic map that indicated an old wagon road, but which was nothing more than faint wagon wheel ruts that appeared at intervals, left over from the days of the great trail drives. The so-called road wound around the north side of a small mesa, often coming to an abrupt ending when it would disappear into a canyon or a washout. It was slow and tedious going, and we had to backtrack frequently, sometimes for several miles. Toward the end of the day, we came to an old settlement, or what was left of it.

I was surprised that it wasn't on the topo map, though it did show a well nearby. There were four buildings still standing. The settlement consisted of two houses, a large barn, and another small outbuilding that looked to have served as a corn shed or workshop. Corrals were set up next to the barn, with one still mostly intact, so I dismounted and turned Gizmo out into it while I scouted around.

"Hello, is anybody here?" I called. I shouted several times but received no reply, nor did I expect one. There were no tracks—animal, human, or vehicle—anywhere to be seen. There had been no one there for a very long time.

I unlatched the barn door and dragged it open far enough to squeeze through. It took a few minutes for my eyes to adjust to the faint light that came through the slits between the weathered siding. The light shone in strips along the dirt floor and onto the walls. There were a few items hanging on the barn walls—an old harness, a couple of sets of collars and hames for horses or mules, a length of log chain, sets of singletrees and doubletrees, and an old tarp—along with various items that were scattered about: some buckets, a pickaxe, a horse-drawn plow blade, and various implements and tools.

Three horse-drawn vehicles were parked inside. Directly in front of me was a typical farm dray used for carrying heavy loads. Next to it sat a buckboard, or what might pass for a buckboard. It was actually a light carriage that had been modified by removing the original body and replacing it with a flat bed and a single spring seat and footrest.

The one last really caught my eye. It was a beautiful enclosed carriage that was hanging from the rafters and tied there with four lengths of old manila rope. I found out after the ride that this carriage was a Clarence. It was black (as most carriages from the late nineteenth century were), and its graceful driver's seat sat perched atop the front axle and two undercut front wheels. The seat gave way to an enclosed cab that held four people (six if they were small). The windows were still intact, with curved glass panes that created the refined front end. The wheels looked to be in very good condition, if a bit dried out from the northern New Mexico weather. A set of black shafts and singletrees that matched the vehicle were hanging on the barn wall behind it. It was an elegant vehicle and seemed out of place in this remote spot.

I exited the barn, making sure to latch the door securely, and made my way to the first of the two houses. The old building had taken a beating from the elements, but it was still serving its purpose. I shouted as I approached the house and again received no answer. I stepped onto the front porch and turned the door handle. I was amazed, and a bit unnerved, by what I found inside.

The house had two rooms—basically, a living room and a bedroom. There was a kitchen area that had a sink built into the counter, although there was no indoor plumbing. Shelves filled with old cans of food, dishes, stacks of old newspapers, and other odds and ends stood against the wall. The masthead on the newspapers said, "The Santa Rosa News," and the papers all dated from 1934 and 1935.

The two small beds in the other room were made up, though they had long been home to packrats and other critters. The old quilts that covered them were full of holes and had been stuffed with all manner of paraphernalia that the rats had collected. There were some bits of clothing—a work shirt, a blouse, and a pair of pants—hanging on a hat rack in the corner of the room. A very weathered pair of lace-up work boots rested on the floor beneath them.

I checked the other house and found much the same—a fully furnished home, complete with dishes, clothes, and furniture, with no one living there. They had even left an old treadle sewing machine, with thread still in the needle and extra thread and other sewing notions in its drawer. Cans of food—mostly beans and peas, from what I could read of the bleached labels—were stacked in the cupboards as well.

At first, I had thought this place was a line camp, used by cowboys when gathering cattle. But I had seen no cattle sign for several days, and besides, there were signs of women here—clothes, nice dishes, and sewing items—so I figured it was a settlement and not just a line camp. There was no evidence that anyone had been to this place for a very long time.

The whole place spooked me. The people had up and left without packing anything, without saying goodbye to their own home. I had a very bad feeling about it all, a sense that something terrible was going to happen if we stayed here, and I decided that Gizmo and I wouldn't stay the night. I had never had a premonition like that before. I had never been frightened that way. I wasn't a believer in ghosts, and I still don't believe in them. But there was something about that abandoned settlement that made my hair stand on end, and as I threw my leg over Gizmo, I was glad to be shut of it.

This is supposed to be a story about graveyards, and it turns out that this settlement had its own graveyard, which was located a couple of miles to the east. As we followed the wagon ruts away from the buildings, Gizmo and I came upon it, nestled in the cup of a small confluence where two dry arroyos met. Several large cottonwoods grew, which meant there was water there regularly, so I looked around until I found the spring that fed them. The water formed a small pool, and I found animal tracks all around. It would serve us for the evening, so I made camp away from the water to allow the wildlife to drink.

Three marked graves and what looked like two others that were unmarked lay nearby. The markers, made of wood, were no longer legible. What was left of a small picket fence still formed the line that once enclosed the graves. The fence was strong enough at one of its corners to picket Gizmo, and I decided to sleep there. We spent a quiet and peaceful night under the stars. I felt comfortable there, sleeping with the dead, and I decided that if any troubled ghosts lingered about, they were probably back at the settlement.

Gizmo and I slept in more and more graveyards as we traveled east. There were a couple of reasons for this. One was that we were moving into more populated areas to the east, which meant fewer open areas for Gizmo to graze at night. The other was that, as we traveled east, we encountered more and more news media who interviewed us and spread our story. And as the story spread, it became more difficult for us to find places to be alone. I became more and more protective of my horse as the daily search for water in the desert gave way to a daily search for solitude in civilized areas. So, what better place to hide?

Cemeteries vary in size, shape, location, and condition. Some are huge, with hundreds—maybe thousands—of people spending eternity in them. Others are like the lonely graveyard back on the New Mexico prairie—just a handful of graves surrounded by a picket fence. Some cater to rich people, some to paupers, some to Catholics, Baptists, Jews, Methodists, or what have you. Some have manicured lawns with fancy water fountains and crews of workers tending them, while others are neglected and left to decay in lonesome patches of history, untended and forgotten.

But all graveyards have one thing in common: their residents are the best neighbors you can have when you're traveling across the country with a horse. They don't complain if you rest your head against a gravestone. They don't mind if a horse wanders across their eternal resting place and eats the grass and recycles it on top of them. They don't make noise, and they don't mind if you do.

Also, no one comes to visit them at night—ever. In all the nights Gizmo and I spent in graveyards, I always felt at ease, at home, and welcome. I would often turn him loose so he could wander around. He would roll and lie down between the headstones, nibbling on flowers and leaving his hoofprints across the burial places of countless lost souls. I rested with my back against a tombstone, reading aloud or playing my harmonica for the dead. And the truth is, I very much respected those who were interred there. But graveyards service the living, not the dead. And since Gizmo and I were still very much alive, I was glad that we had a sort of carte blanche. Sometimes we find our deliverance in the least likely places.

# THIS AIN'T NO BED AND BREAKFAST

Some folks need a plan when they travel. They shy from spontaneity, especially when it comes to finding a room for the night. They want reservations so they know when and where they'll bunk down each night during their journey. They don't like surprises. They want to know—in advance—exactly what to expect when they are traveling to unfamiliar places. I used to scorn people like that. I'd scoff at their timidity and cowardice. But over the years I've come to appreciate the comfort of predictability, the reassurance of being forewarned, and the absence of stress that comes from knowing where you're going to lay your head for the night. I'm still pretty much a fly-by-the-seat-of-your-pants kind of guy, so piling up on a stranger's couch that I found on the internet works just fine for me. But sometimes it's nice to be able to check into a hotel that you booked months beforehand, one that you know will have a lobby and room service and internet access and all the requisite things that you expect when you're planning ahead.

Although I planned the *general* route that Gizmo and I followed, I didn't plan a specific trail. I didn't pick a detailed path that we would stick to each day because I knew that it would be a recipe for failure. We had to be flexible and adaptable if we were going to weather the difficulties that seven months on the trail would throw at us. Instead, I picked an undefined route that gave me plenty of latitude for change. I chose a few places I wanted to stop for longer periods—a couple of weeks in Santa Fe, a week in Oklahoma City, and a bit of time in Nashville—because they were places where I knew people and where Gizmo and I could rest. But there were many options available for getting from one to the other. I made the journey up as we went along, picked the next day's trail, and hoped for the best.

Since I didn't know exactly what route we would be traveling most days, it followed that I had no idea where we would spend the night. I simply had to pick a spot when I found one and call it home. Those who need to plan their travels would not do well on a ride like this. Each day was a new adventure, each night a crapshoot. Spontaneity always looks good on paper, but in the real world, it can be a bit troublesome. Fortune smiled on Gizmo and me for the most part, as it always has. But it didn't smile every day or every night. It could be tightfisted and callous, sometimes leaving us without food or water or shelter—and sometimes without all three. It could be bighearted and generous, providing us with places that were so beautiful they would make you cry and with people so wonderful they made you proud to be a human being. But either way—good or bad—I learned things, I experienced things that no one else ever would, and I was fulfilled in ways I would never have thought possible.

Spontaneity is the sister to Serendipity. They are twins. They dance together in a playful ballet to the music that fills our souls. When the music is good, it's very good. And when it's bad, it can be spectacularly bad. But either way, when you have them together, you are assured of something special in your life, and the reason it's special is because you have no idea what's going to happen. Every day for Gizmo and me was spent with Spontaneity and Serendipity, the sisters riding along with us every step of the way. I danced with them both back then, and I still do today. I'm forced to plan a bit more now than in my youth, but I still rely upon having a heavy dose of those two women in my life.

Back in the 1960s and long before Gizmo and I hit the trail, both *Goodwill* and the *Salvation Army* used to have these big metal bins out on the street where you could drop off your old clothes to donate to the needy. They were enclosed bins with a metal flap on the front through which you shoved your old clothing. The opening was just big enough for me to squeeze through and pull my guitar and bedroll in after me. It was pitch dark inside, but filled with clothing and blankets, so there was always a soft, dry bed for the night, and sometimes you even left with a new wardrobe.

If I was stuck in the city, I could go to a used car lot and sometimes find the car keys hidden on the cars—usually on top of a tire or inside the bumper. Once the lot was closed for the night, I would climb in and sleep in the car, but I had to wake up before they came to work in the morning. This trick also worked well on freight trains that were carrying new automobiles. I could climb into a car, turn the engine on, and run the heater (or air conditioner if it was hot outside) until the car ran out of gas. When that happened, I climbed into the one next to it. Of course, there was hell to pay if I got caught, but I never did.

Without the sisters Serendipity and Spontaneity, those seven months with Gizmo would have been a living hell for both of us. The upshot is I was well prepared for thinking outside the box, so to speak. I wasn't afraid of where we might end up at the end of each day, and I wasn't too concerned with where our next bed would be.

We slept in so many diverse places and situations that it's hard to remember them all. There were abandoned gold mines in the desert, where my main concern was rattlesnakes. We used abandoned sections of highways—including the Mother Road, *Route 66*—that stretched for miles and were completely empty. While traveling on these old roads, we stayed in deserted motels and ancient gas stations and felt the ghosts who lived in them. We camped exposed, completely out in the open, without shelter of any kind on so many nights I lost count. Coyotes, wild horses, and bears were our neighbors, along with other critters, like rabbits, foxes, and night owls. The animals seemed to know that we were just passing through, so we all got along.

We camped alone, mostly, with the stars for company. I love the stars, and I would lie awake and talk to Gizmo about them, pointing to constellations and planets. I showed him the difference between a shooting star and a satellite, and the differences between the planets of our solar system and the stars in the heavens. All my life I have had a choice, and weather permitting, I have chosen to sleep under the night sky without a tent, which proved to be an inconvenience only a few times during our trip.

*LOGBOOK:*
*Camped along the road, down in a swale and out of sight. Managed to pull another of Gizmo's incisors today. I was practicing gun tricks when I saw him sticking his tongue out in a weird way. I checked and felt the loose tooth, so I worked it until it finally came out. Bled a little but didn't seem to bother him. I'll keep it along with the other one, for good luck.*

Since Gizmo was a Quarter Horse, he and I were invited to visit the headquarters of the American Quarter Horse Association in Amarillo, Texas. We arrived at the outskirts on a Saturday afternoon and headed into the central business district, where I found a large park with a small lake in the center populated by lots of trees and picnic tables. I picked a likely spot and set up camp, and we enjoyed a leisurely Sunday, mostly to ourselves. I practiced gun tricks, played the harmonica, wrote in my logbook, and managed to read a little. When nightfall came, we had the entire park to ourselves, and no one came to bother us.

In the middle of the night, it started to rain. It became a torrential downpour that immediately soaked everything we had. There were bathrooms across the park, on the other side of the lake, so I saddled Gizmo and threw the gear on top and set off in the darkness, leading him around to the building. It was a small, concrete block structure with toilets for men and women toilets. We were drenched by the time we got to the building, but the lights were on, and I hoped it was unlocked. I tried the door and was relieved when it yielded to my push. I tied Gizmo to a nearby tree and stripped the saddle and gear from him then dragged it all inside.

The men's room was quite large with several toilet stalls and urinals and half a dozen sinks. Although the floor was slippery, I went back outside and untied Gizmo and led him into the bathroom. He had started to shiver out there because he was soaked to the bone. It was a bit warmer inside, but not by much. I shut the door, turned him loose inside the bathroom, and hoped he wouldn't slip on the tiled floor. I threw the saddle against the door, so he wouldn't escape if someone opened it. I draped the saddle pad and my bedroll, along with clothes and other wet items over the walls of the toilet stalls to dry.

There was an electric hand dryer on the wall next to the sinks, so I pushed the big chrome button and let it blow hot air into the room. I sat down on the floor beneath it and reached up every few seconds to hit the button each time the dryer shut off. After repeating this countless times, it struck me that I could tape the button down. So, I pulled some tape from my saddlebags and was able to keep the button depressed and the dryer ran constantly. Within a few minutes, steam was filling the room, and it started to heat up. Eventually, it became like a sauna in there, and I had to shut the dryer off for a while before taping the button down again.

Once again I found myself thinking about how peculiar this all was, and yet how *normal* it seemed. I knew there was something wrong with me, but I couldn't really put a finger on what it was. I couldn't quite grasp where or when my own soul had taken a turn, or who the person was who now inhabited my body. I was sitting in a restroom with a horse, our belongings strewn about the place as if we owned it. We were in the middle of a city, probably breaking the law—probably breaking any number of laws—and I found that I really thought nothing of it. It was no big deal. I never considered that it as a good story to tell later. It was only a place to spend the night. It was survival for the moment and nothing more. I didn't see myself as a rebel, a maverick who set out to thwart the rules of society. I gave it no thought whatsoever. But as I had always done, I questioned my motives and I tried to make sense of my purpose in all of it. What was I doing, spending a rainy night in a bathroom with a horse? No sane person would have ever considered it. I didn't have the answer, but I suspected I was going off the rails a little bit. Still, I knew I was still the honest, good hearted person I'd always been. And I knew that I was doing it for my horse, and that was the main thing.

Gizmo dried off after a time and quit shivering, and when the rain stopped, I led him back outside and staked him to a tree where he would be more comfortable and could eat and lie down. I propped the door open so I could see him, then shifted my gear around to dry. By morning, it was mostly dry and warm. I took a sponge bath in the sink and put on my cleanest dirty clothes for our appearance at the Quarter Horse Association. The day dawned clear and bright, and after I said a small prayer of thanks for the bathroom and the hand dryer, I stepped up onto Gizmo, and we set off in search of a local cafe where I could grab a cup of coffee.

# WEIGHT ISSUES

I am normally a pretty laid-back, easygoing guy. I've always practiced a live-and-let-live philosophy in my life. I try not to sweat the small stuff, so I don't worry too much about minor things. But as they say, the devil's in the details. And some of those details can kill you, or in our case, put an end to our journey.

Gizmo and I began the trip with more weight than we had when we finished, and that included our own bodies. For him, the gear included saddle and blankets, saddlebags, hackamore bridle, halter and lead rope, picket rope and hobbles, and a few odds and ends for maintenance, such as extra horseshoe nails, a hoof pick and brush, and gall salve.

My own paraphernalia consisted of a minimal amount of clothing, a rain slicker, a canteen, a bedroll, a book or two at any given time, my logbooks and writing utensils, a small amount of food and cooking utensils, a few topographic maps, a Case folding pocket knife, a Colt single action revolver and gun belt with a few bullets, a denim jacket, a cowboy hat, and various other odds and ends. I didn't carry a tent because of the extra weight. I could create a makeshift tent with my rain slicker if need be. And besides, I preferred sleeping under the stars.

I never forgot that everything I carried myself—whether in my small backpack or on my person—was also Gizmo's to carry when I was riding him. Early in the ride—within the first two or three weeks—I began to discard things and soon became preoccupied with lightening the load for him. I figured since he had no say over the burden he carried, the least I could do was make it as small a load as possible. My fixation on this process quickly deepened into an obsession, one in which I found myself scrutinizing the smallest of articles and abandoning them if I felt we could do without them. And this obsession lasted the entire ride.

The weight issues started with the heavy things, the first being the box of ammunition for the Colt that I carried. I had brought along a carton of 50 rounds that I kept hidden in one of the saddlebags. Gizmo and I were in the Mojave Desert somewhere northeast of Barstow when it dawned on me that I was asking him to carry a bunch of bullets that neither he nor I needed. So, I took the Colt and the box of ammunition out of camp about fifty yards, set up several sticks as targets, and commenced to shooting them. Gizmo didn't like the gunfire at first, but after a couple of rounds, he ignored it. I used up the entire box, except for the four or five cartridges that I kept. I also held on to three of the .410 shotgun shells I had cut down to fit the Colt. They were meant for snakes, and I kept one loaded in a chamber at all times.

176

Having unloaded several pounds of unnecessary baggage, I began to sift through my gear and personal belongings to ferret out any other likely candidates for expulsion. There were two paperback books that I'd already read, so I used them to start my campfires for the next few nights. I was given to unconsciously collecting various small items, such as rubber bands, paper clips, small rolls of tape, tweezers, a couple buttons that someone had given me, and so on. Occasionally I would pile them together and, as I had no scale, I would guess at the weight. It always seemed significant when I collected a hoard of unwanted things. I felt proud of myself when I discarded it, and I always showed it to Gizmo first and mentioned that I was doing it for him (as if he cared).

I cut most of the handle off my toothbrush, so that only an inch or so remained, and I was forced to reach into my mouth with it to brush my teeth. The billet on Gizmo's halter was buckled, with the excess hanging down from the buckle six or eight inches. So, I cut this off too, along with most of the extra straps that were buckled to the saddle. I shortened every piece of leather and nylon to its minimum acceptable length. I got rid of scraps of paper I had scribbled notes on by compiling all the notes onto a page in my logbook. I decided the hackamore bridle I had made for Gizmo, with the braided rawhide bosal and the horsehair mecate reins, was unnecessary. So, I simply rode him with his halter and used the lead rope as reins, and I sent the bridle home.

Along with the disposal of extraneous articles, I found myself walking and leading Gizmo more and more as we covered the trail. It allowed his back to cool and helped to prevent scalding and saddle sores. As a side benefit, it gave me a rest from riding and Gizmo a rest from having to carry me and everything that I carried. It felt good to get off and walk, and I did this religiously for ten to fifteen minutes every hour or so. Oftentimes, I walked for several miles when it felt good, or when I thought Gizmo needed an extra break.

I don't really know how much weight Gizmo had to shoulder, as I never had an opportunity to measure the burden. I know that by the time we had covered a thousand miles and were into our third month on the trail, I had dropped thirty-five pounds from my own starting weight of 165. The idea of requiring a horse to carry needless extra weight has remained a pet peeve of mine ever since. At a training clinic once, I asked a world-renowned reining horse trainer why he thought "the heavier the saddle, the better."

His answer was that he believed it stayed put on the horse's back better than a lighter one would. I thought that putting a heavy saddle on a reining horse was a lot like making a sprinter run the hurdles wearing combat boots, but I kept my mouth shut.

I don't know if Gizmo appreciated my obsessive behavior or not, but then, he was just a horse, and horses are going to make up their own minds about things regardless of what you do. I reckon it made his life a tiny bit easier, even if he had his mind on other things.

# PREDATORS

I was giving Gizmo a drink from the radiator filler hose at a run-down Shamrock station outside of Briscoe, Texas. Grain elevators rose like launchpads in the distance, towering above the flat Texas Panhandle and clearly marking the route of the defunct Panhandle and Santa Fe Railroad. The rail line had long been a staple of the area with its concrete silos and sidetracked gondola cars.

The summer day's clammy heat was diminished slightly by a welcome breeze. Gizmo had learned to take the curved black nozzle of the radiator hose between his teeth while I pushed the spring trigger to open the water flow. He could drink without spilling a drop, something that often amazed bystanders. I'm not sure just when they disappeared, but you don't see those radiator filler hoses anymore.

"Hell, I got a horse that can do that," the man said annoyingly.

I looked over at him but didn't reply.

He wore a Texas Tech ball cap and a snap down western shirt with no sleeves. It looked like a wife-beater version of a cowboy shirt, so I thought of him as "Wife-Beater." His Wrangler boot cuts covered the tops of brown work boots, and the right rear pocket below the leather insignia was burnished with a faded circle made by the round Red Man snuff can that lived there.

He drove a red Ford F-250 pickup, late sixties model. The truck was a three-quarter ton four-wheel drive with full floating axles, split rims, and an eight-foot bed that had seen its fair share of hard work and abuse. There were three gun racks bolted inside on the back of the cab that covered the back window and held various rifles; each served notice that this wasn't a truck or owner to be trifled with. A blue heeler sat in the truck bed with his chin resting on the side, quiet and still, observant and intense, waiting for someone to cross the invisible vertical plane that separated the outside world from his own domain inside the truck's bed and made them fair game.

"Ain't nobody gonna mess with that truck," the man said. "Hell, I don't even lock the sonuvabitch."

"He'll pull a beer out of a cooler and open it, too. Just like that," he

179

said, snapping his fingers. "That horse don't look like much of a rope horse," he commented, looking at Gizmo.

"He's not a rope horse," I answered. I didn't like Wife-Beater and tried to concentrate on watering Gizmo so we could be on our way.

"What the hell good's a horse if you can't rope off him?" he replied.

He was trying to be funny but was rubbing me the wrong way. I didn't answer.

"You travelin' or something? What's with the rig?"

"Yep, travelin'," I answered. "Just headin' cross-country."

"What the hell kinda gun you got there?" he demanded, indicating my Colt.

"Just an old single action Colt. Nothin' special."

"Got me a forty-four magnum under the seat there. It'll put a hole in an engine block. Stop a car dead. See them rifles?"

I looked over at his pickup truck.

"A thirty-thirty, a three oh eight, and a little twenty-two long. I use 'em for *KIE*-oats." He pronounced the word without the Spanish *E* on the end.

"You shoot coyotes with those things?" I asked.

"Yep, as many as I can find. Ain't nothin' better'n a dead *KIE*-oat. Got no use for 'em."

I had seen thousands of rabbits every night out here on the flat prairie. They seemed to fill the plains with their numbers, eating the grain from the ends of the grass and devouring much of the feed that was meant for cattle in this part of the country. I only had to shine my flashlight into the darkness to see the pairs of eyes stretching into the distance, lit up as if electric. I wondered at the wisdom of killing their predators.

"Seems like there's a lot of rabbits around here," I mentioned.

"Yeah, hell they're just a pest. I shoot them, too, but they don't really hurt nothin'," he replied.

"You don't think they eat up the feed for the cattle?"

"Naw," he said, "they couldn't put a dent in all that pasture. It's them damned *KIE-oats* we have to worry about. Them bastards'll take down a young calf. And I seen 'em hamstring a two-year-old heifer. Sons-uh-bitches ain't no good fer nuthin'. That's why I keep them guns in my truck. I kill every one I find."

"How many head you lose this year?" I asked.

"The outfit I work for didn't lose any, but that's because I've run most of the bastards off."

I was used to this mindset, though I'd never gotten used to the outlook of killing and conquering anything that constitutes a threat. I've never been a bleeding heart, so I've never seen coyotes and other animals as poor victims so much as I see them as fellow travelers in our universe. I'll admit, my first instinct was to wish the coyotes had guns, so that Wife-Beater could know what it was like to be hunted and driven from his home, have his family killed for no apparent reason, and face elimination by a foe who he hadn't chosen and had no quarrel with. Sure, my initial reaction was to hate him. But I didn't really see him as the bad guy, any more than I saw myself as a good guy.

I had done some reading back then, and I've read a lot more since. I knew that coyotes accounted for killing less than half a percent of all cattle in that part of the country, and that once a calf was over six or eight months old, there was pretty much *no* chance of a coyote getting him. So, a rancher would lose a calf for about every two hundred head he owned. Much as I don't want to see calves killed, I figure that's a pretty small price to pay for taking over another creature's home. And it occurred to me that if things were reversed—if I wanted to take over the rancher's home, if he were the "coyote" and I was the settler—I doubt he'd be as acquiescent as the coyotes had been for him. I'd have to fight him for it, and the price would be damned high.

"You kill a lot of coyotes?" I asked.

"Already got twenty-six of 'em this year. Got forty-two last year," he replied. "Best year I had was fifty-seven. I get 'em at night with a light. Gub-ment pays me to kill 'em."

There wasn't anything I could say to Wife-Beater to convince him to change his mind about killing coyotes. It didn't matter that they were (and are) my favorite critters, that I think they're the smartest species alive, and that waking up surrounded by them, listening to their plaintive cries—in the Mojave, the Painted Desert, the mountains of Northern New Mexico, and even here in the grasslands of the Texas Panhandle—is the best way anyone could start their day.

Coyotes kill—it's what any predator does—but they don't set out to systematically eliminate a competing species from the face of the Earth. They take what they need and nothing more. They become the aggressor only when they have to. This is universally true of all creatures. A predator is a creature that kills and eats other creatures. Simple as that. But when applied to humans, its meaning defines a person who ruthlessly exploits others. Those who experience the world through Wife-Beater's eyes somehow transpose the two meanings and come to believe that the animal is the ruthless exploiter.

The water began to flow out the side of Gizmo's mouth, signaling that he was finished drinking. I pulled on the water hose, causing the coiling mechanism to click and automatically wind it. I turned toward a grain elevator in the distance, hoping for some loose oat or barley grain for him to eat.

Wife-Beater climbed into the cab of his truck and called out, "Hey, I'm goin' out shootin' tonight. You're welcome to come along if you want."

I shook my head, waved, and pulled Gizmo alongside me as I walked. I watched the predator drive away. Up until then, I hadn't thought of us as *prey*.

# IT AIN'T AS EASY AS IT LOOKS

My life isn't a lot different from anyone else's in most ways. I'm an eternal optimist, but I've never been what you might call naïve. That is, I don't blindly believe in luck or karma or any of those sorts of things. Well, maybe I do to some extent, but I don't *count* on them. I don't *rely* on them. I prefer to retain a bit of skepticism about how things might go. If I've learned anything through the years it's this:

> *It'll always be harder, take longer, and cost more than you thought it would.*

I could give endless examples that help to prove this statement, but I don't really need to. You can look at your own life and know it's true. I studied up a lot, pored over books, magazines, maps and other things to learn as much as I could before setting off on that foolhardy adventure. I learned about horses, saddlery, horseshoes, but also trails, compasses, map reading, guns, and ammunition. I even read up on things like astronomy and natural foods and such. I didn't pretend to know it all. I knew I didn't know it all, but I thought I had a pretty good grasp of things. It turns out I knew hardly anything.

I remember saying, in one of the countless ongoing conversations I had with myself, that Gizmo and I were on what could be called the *Calvinist Ride.* I called it this because, according to the Calvinist doctrine, life's objective was not to have fun or enjoy yourself. Life is supposed to subject you to the travails of nature, as a metaphor for all the hardships and cruel times that life is supposed to present you. You're meant to continually bang your head against a wall, and then it feels so good when you finally stop.

In a lot of ways, misery is a comfortable thing. That's why so many people seem to prefer it. It's safe, predictable, and dependable. It's easy to find. If it's not right in front of you, it's easy to create it. You know where you stand when you're in misery, even if you don't exactly know why you're there. You can count on it to produce the expected results. Happiness is a lot harder. It takes effort. And it usually takes time. You have to be patient to be happy. Gratification isn't the same thing as happiness. It's momentary and fleeting, and when it disappears (which it always does) you're left feeling a bit empty and—yep, you guessed it—miserable. Yet we tend to reach for instant gratification instead of working for long-term happiness. It really is the little things that count. Life's tender mercies.

*LOGBOOK:*
*Made camp in a little park. Grass ain't the best, but it's okay. I walked out to the road and cut a big bunch of wild alfalfa and brought it back for Gizmo. Gave him an alcohol rubdown, which he loved.*

I chose a long and tedious ride like this on purpose. One of the things I *did* know beforehand was that it would be tedious. I knew I would need patience and some luck, and quite a bit of faith to make it to the finish line. Without the patience, though, the luck and the faith were worthless. A long ride does not make for instant gratification. There are surprises (lots of 'em) and a few spontaneous rewards along the way, but they're not the ones that stick with you. Sure, you remember them, but they don't mean as much as those rewards that you earned from crossing an entire desert or mountain range, or nursing your horse against illness and injury over long periods and seeing him come out of it in good health. The things that make you stronger, that feed your soul, are those that take a long time and require so much patience that you think you're going to burst. In some ways, they're the Calvinist things. They're hard, on purpose.

Gizmo and I stopped at a construction site in western Oklahoma for water. I spoke with the foreman while Gizmo drank out of a hose. During our conversation, a young man drove up to the site pulling a backhoe on a trailer behind his truck. He came over to let the foreman know he was there.

"Where the hell you been?" the foreman demanded.

"Sorry, boss. I got tied up on a job, and it took a little longer than I expected." the young man replied.

"You were supposed to be digging those footings an hour ago! I can't have men standing around waiting for you while you're off on some other job, dammit." The foreman was furious, and continued. "What's so damned important that it couldn't wait?"

"I had to dig my mother's grave," the young man answered apologetically. "Sorry. We're burying her later this afternoon, so I'm afraid

I'm gonna have to leave early today, if that's okay." He said all of this in a stoic, matter-of-fact way.

Now, just that very morning I had been grousing to Gizmo about how hard we had it. It was getting hot, and we were traveling a bit slower than usual, and I was feeling depressed and sorry for myself. I had been asking *Why me?* and basically venting my frustration. (Gizmo, of course, was having none of it, nor did he care what I thought.) But on hearing that young man's account, two things occurred to me: The young man had just suffered a terrible loss and was taking it in a stoic manner by being strong and resilient, and he saw his boss's ire as a dilemma that was as great as his mother's burial.

Witnessing that vignette changed something in me. I held on to it for the rest of the ride, and I've never forgotten it. Or at least, I have *mostly* not forgotten it. I still grouse about inconsequential things. I still complain and moan about my lot in life sometimes. Who doesn't? I reckon it's a safety valve that helps to keep us sane. And it might even help to make us happy, as long as we don't let misery take over and become the norm in our life. Like I said, misery is a comfortable thing.

The ride was hard as hell. There's no other way to put it. There were easy days, and there were fun days, but I'd never describe the ride as easy or fun. I wouldn't describe it as joyous, though I experienced some of the most joyous moments of my life on that journey with my horse. This is how I *would* describe it: *fulfilling*. Fulfillment only comes the hard way, the Calvinist way. You don't get it for free. It's not something that's bestowed upon you by virtue of who you are or where you are, even though they may play a part in it. It's also about what you do and how you do it. Patience and perseverance are a part of it, too. Fulfillment is *hard*. If it were easy, it wouldn't be fulfilling.

But here's a secret. When faced with something daunting—like getting a vaccination shot when you're seven or eight, or taking tests in school, or an obstacle course in boot camp—I've always taken the view that, since a lot of others have done it before me, I should be able do it. I just keep in mind that if they can do it, I can do it … like a mantra. It doesn't make the doing of it any easier, but it allows you to attempt it in the first place without chickening out or giving up before you try. But the ride, well … that was something else again. The fact that Jeff Spivey had done it was a shot in the arm for me because at least I knew it could be accomplished. But it wasn't as if thousands had gone before me. Other than Spivey in 1968, and Tschiffely way back in the 1920s, I didn't know of a single person who had done what I was doing, so I had to make it all up as I went along. I knew there was no magic bullet, no single thing that would see Gizmo and me through it all. Patience and perseverance were what was needed. Fortunately, I possessed both a solid determination and a profound ignorance of what I faced, and these allowed me to step up on Gizmo and take our first steps eastward.

I didn't think of myself as brave or especially capable (I still don't), but I figured if anyone could do it, I could. It wasn't so much a vote of confidence; it was a way of saying there's no reason *not* to. It's odd, the things that go through your head when you set out to do the impossible, or what people say is impossible. In my case, it wasn't a matter of trying to prove them wrong. Just as it was with the other kids back in my school days, I didn't much care about proving myself to anyone else. It was never a matter of "I'll show *them*," or "Just wait till they see what *I've* done." It never occurred to me to worry about what others thought.

> *LOGBOOK:*
> *Stopped at a place called Reptile Village to water Gizmo. There were more people outside looking at Gizmo and me than there were inside looking at the snakes. I did my laundry in a nearby laundromat. Had to wash everything, then change clothes in the bathroom and wash what I had on.*

I'm sure there were many who believed that taking a young horse across the country was an act of cruelty, that I was stupid to try it, or that it was foolhardy and selfish. And they would be correct. It was all of those things. I wasn't defensive because it never occurred to me that people might be opposed to our ride. Since I didn't think about it, it was never an issue.

As things went, I was armed with a dream and a large pile of dogged determination, and that's what ultimately launched Gizmo and me on our way. It's interesting, the sorts of circumstances and events that can set you on a new path toward a destination you never thought you'd seek. They can be little things that change your life in small ways, or they can be big things that forever alter who you are.

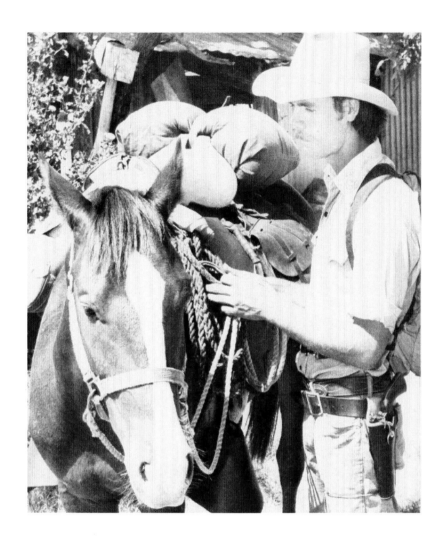

# THE WEST

We are veterans of the trail now, and after covering more than eighteen hundred miles we're beginning to feel the fatigue that accompanies our slow progress across the continent. Gizmo and I have left the Rocky Mountains of northern New Mexico behind as we enter the vast prairie of the Texas Panhandle. The rough country that surrounds the headwaters of the Canadian River in northeastern New Mexico becomes our gateway to the flatlands of Texas. The mesas have gradually yielded to the pressures of erosion and the geomorphic results of rain, snow, and wind, as their edges become progressively softer and smoother. We are crossing the great grassy plains where buffalo once traveled in herds so large that it took several days for them to pass by. My horse and I leave the mesas, standing in the distance like sentinels, and begin to drop steadily in elevation.

The sky is huge here, and once we reach the flat panhandle country in Texas, it feels as if I am back in the Navy at sea. The horizon is a three hundred sixty-degree flat border between the grass and the sky, and the only interruptions are the tall grain silos in the distance and the occasional windmill pumping water at a gallon and a half a minute in the Texas wind. Trees are scarce here, and where a copse can be seen, there will be people. The land is stingy with its water out here, and the trees and people live side by side because they both need it. Birds have a long way to go to find homes out here, and some build their nests atop telephone poles and road signs along the highway.

The night sky comes alive with the Milky Way and its distinct teapot constellation, Sagittarius. I love the great summer triangle of stars—Altair, Deneb, and Vega—that spread out across the sky. I smile when I see the familiar Cygnus, the swan, which I also know as the Northern Cross. Scorpius, the great scorpion, dances in the sky and its brightest star, Antares, looks like a shining broach upon its chest. As always, the Little Dipper (Ursa Minor) can be seen rotating around the star at the end of its handle. The star is Polaris, the North Star, and all the heavenly bodies rotate around it. Two stars that form the side of the Big Dipper (Ursa Major) point toward it, and its handle points to Arcturus, the great red giant in the constellation Bootes.

Once on the flats, we make good time. Gizmo covers seven to eight miles per hour at his smooth trot, and the twenty-miles-per-day limit I have set will usually be met before noon, even with a break to unsaddle at the halfway point. I am left with many hours to fill, and I spend them reading, playing my harmonica, writing in the logbook, practicing gun tricks with my single action Colt revolver, and having long, one-sided conversations with my horse.

*LOGBOOK:*
*Camped at a little roadside park. I found an unopened bag of lemon crème cookies on the picnic table. Gizmo and I ate it for dinner. He got the lion's share, though.*

We are traveling parallel to and north of Interstate 40 on farm-to-market roads and across large pastures where there are no roads. Cattle guards are becoming more and more common, and I spend quite a bit of time cutting and repairing fences as we make our way past the countless barbed wire barriers. It becomes frustrating at times, but I think back to the terrible stress Gizmo has endured in the deserts of Arizona and New Mexico and the inconvenience doesn't affect me. My patience has been tested every day of the ride, so I keep the larger picture in mind when faced with these annoyances.

The land has been overgrazed. There is a remarkable difference between the grass that grows along the roadside and what's left in the pastures just across the fence line. It is a stark contrast and one that can be easily seen, even by those who travel quickly past in their cars and pickup trucks. I don't see how cattle can even exist on the other side of the fence, but there they are, by the hundreds, browsing for sustenance. What was once a vast grassland, a great prairie where millions of buffalo traveled and fed, has become a dirt patch that resembles the parking lot of a honkytonk bar on the edge of town. The grass is a pale brown against the red color of the dirt and has been bitten off to ground level. The cattle make small dust clouds as they wander single file toward their watering hole late in the day. At night, the rabbits come out by the thousands to eat what they can find, robbing the cattle of what's left of the nourishment the land provides. The rabbits thrive, in part because the ranchers have set themselves to trapping and shooting the native coyotes in an attempt to exterminate them.

I manage to gather grain for my horse at the silos along the way. Some is wheat, and I am not sure if it is good for horses, so I let him eat only a small amount at first. The other grains—oats and barley, mostly—are fine. I do not free feed the grain because I'm afraid of foundering him, so I keep track of how much Gizmo eats. But I am generous with it because he needs the extra nourishment. I am glad my companion has finally gained some of his weight back and seems to be retaining it.

The summer storms still come through for an hour or so on most days, but they are not as intense as they were in the Painted Desert, and the lightning doesn't strike the way it did back there. I am aware that we are in the middle of tornado country during tornado season. Should one develop, there is not a lot we can do about it. Resigned to our fate, I hope for the best as the two of us make our way eastward.

As the first real heat of summer sets in on us, I keep a close eye on how the saddle is fitting. It would be easy for my horse to become scalded and blistered, so I stick religiously to my regimen of unsaddling and resting in the middle of the day. This allows Gizmo's back to cool and dry out and prevents injury. So far, there are no dry spots near the withers or other places that might indicate the saddle isn't riding correctly. I feel relieved, but I know I have to keep this vigil up daily through the end of the ride because a back sore can appear within minutes and put a stop to our adventure.

Most people think that food is the biggest concern for Gizmo and me, and it is certainly a major one. But saddle sores, cinch galls, shin splints, and other mundane ailments cause me the most worry because any of them could end the trip in a single day.

There is population here. I don't think of it as *civilization* so much as the fact that we see people every day now. I know that my horse and I will not be alone again for the rest of the ride. We will spend many nights by ourselves, hidden away from public view, but we will never be truly alone again. And I realize that in some ways, we will never be alone for the rest of our lives.

> *LOGBOOK:*
> *We're camped out behind an all night restaurant. Able to hide in the trees here. Went in for coffee this evening and sat at the counter until late, flirting with the cute waitress. There was a crazy old man who had a laugh box. He would tell a stupid joke, then press the button and the box would go hahahaha... Joke example: [question] Why does a cow give buttermilk? [answer] What else can she give, but her milk? [press button, hahahahahaha....] It wore thin after a while, but I put up with it because the waitress was worth it. We had a beautiful conversation and it sort of made my heart ache, thinking about what a lonesome road I've chosen.*

The flat Texas plain is eventually broken up by the hills of Oklahoma, and the grass returns to a greenish color. It contains more moisture and is taller and healthier looking through here. Gizmo picks up more weight. Water becomes plentiful, though I get sick more than once because I drink from rivers and streams that are filled with chemicals and other pollutants dumped into them by manufacturing companies upstream. The water is cool and clear, and tastes good, but it sometimes hides these things. I hope my horse doesn't get sick from the water, and he never does.

We enjoy a layover of several days in Oklahoma City, where the Oklahoma Quarter Horse Association presents us with a new Canadian trooper saddle, to replace the worn out WWII German caisson saddle I have been riding. Gizmo is once again the center of attention as newspaper reporters and television crews train their cameras on him. He is checked by a veterinarian, who says that he is in good shape, although a bit anemic. My horse is given vitamin shots and a Coggins test, for Equine Infectious Anemia, which he passes. The vet floats (files) Gizmo's teeth because they have some sharp edges, which makes it more difficult for him to eat. He'll have an easier time of it now.

> LOGBOOK:
> After what felt like too long a stay here in Oklahoma City, I saddled Gizmo and we took off for Tulsa. People were kind to us, though it's good to be back on our own now. All the TV stations followed along in cars, filming us as we rode. Good to be on the trail again. Gizmo is a hell of a horse.

We follow secondary roads to the northeast, toward Tulsa. The new Canadian Mounties saddle is stiff and begins to rub us both raw in places. I am forced to stop in Tulsa for a few days so a saddlemaker can make alterations to it. We are invited to stay with a wealthy couple while the saddle is repaired.

> LOGBOOK:
> Staying with a Jim and Laurie who are only a few years older than me and are already oil millionaires. Very nice folks, but Laurie keeps flirting with me behind her husband's back. She's a lovely lady but I keep my distance as best I can. All of their friends are young oil millionaires, too. It's a strange world here. So different from Gizmo's and mine. Nice people, but it's sure not my scene. Watched president Nixon resign on TV tonight. An odd feeling, being so disconnected from world events. It's a change in the country that I know will have long lasting effects. Everyone seems to be talking about it, but I still feel disconnected from it all. So busy worrying about our basic survival out here that I'm not much concerned with world affairs anymore.

I think about where the west ends and the east begins. Most people tell me that the dividing line is the Mississippi River, but my sense is that we are already in the east by the time we reach Arkansas. The people still have the western, laid-back style of what I consider to be "out west," but the fenced pastures, the population density, and claustrophobic hills and small parcels of land everywhere don't match my ideas of what the west is. But I figure it

192

is only my definition and not anyone else's, so I leave it at that. By the time the pair of us find ourselves in the Ozark Mountains, we are in the east as far as I am concerned.

# A DAY OFF, THE HARD WAY

We're in eastern Oklahoma. Three days ago we camped beside a beautiful little river in a secluded spot. At the time, it seemed like a gift from God. I found out the next morning that the stream's crystal clear water was filled with chemicals that were dumped by a big company upstream. According to a local I talked to, "Everybody knows to stay outta that water."

I was sick in the morning but forced myself to travel. Gizmo and I managed to make another twenty miles and ended up at this unremarkable spot, where we have been staying for the last couple of days.

We're camped next to another creek, about a half mile down the hill from a roadside tavern-cafe-market. Yesterday I got sicker and couldn't travel. Thank god Gizmo seems fine. I fall into delirium with a fever and the whole works—vomiting, diarrhea, and general aches and pains. All I can think of is how I am going to water Gizmo. He can't reach the river where he is staked, and I can't get up to take him there. I have visions of him getting loose and running away, ending up on the highway where he'd be hit by a car.

I run out of toilet paper during the night, and I know I can never make it up the hill to the store. I lie on top of my sleeping bag, wishing someone would just shoot me. I feel my lower intestine kicking in again, and don't want to soil the bedroll because I know I'd never get it clean. So, I roll over onto the grass, where my body seems to explode. It is trying to rid itself of toxins by expelling everything inside—from both ends. I find myself lying on my back in the grass, my t-shirt covered in vomit and my pants filled with god knows what. My head is pounding with a blinding headache, and my face and hands are on fire with fever. I consider the possibility that I am dying and don't feel any real fear from that prospect. I am more afraid of staying alive at this point, and the only real fear I have is that Gizmo is without water and that no one will find us in this secluded camp.

After I lie here in my own waste for a time (I have no idea how long, but my pants have dried somewhat), I decide I need to clean myself, no matter how bad I feel. I don't have another pair of jeans, so I will have to wash the ones I am wearing. I stagger to my feet and stumble barefoot to the stream, where I lie in the water with my clothes on. The cold water feels good running across my feverish body. I get up, pull my shirt off, and toss it onto a nearby bush. I pull off my pants and underwear and drop them into a shallow eddy, where I scrub them with river sand. I scrub my t-shirt as well, then lie back in the water and scour myself with sand. It is all I can do to walk naked back to my bedroll, and by the time I reach it, I am shivering badly. I lay my wet clothes on the ground cloth and slip into my sleeping bag. I sleep through the rest of the day and night.

# SUSTENANCE

I was lucky enough to have been raised in a poor family. Lucky because as a result, I was never picky about what I ate, since there weren't a lot of choices growing up. I'm still not picky and will eat most anything. Having the choice of pancakes or macaroni and cheese out of a box gave me a dulled sense of culinary awareness and stifled my young palate so that it never expected much when I got older. So now, anything more than those is a bonus to me.

My mother had four children living with her, along with her mother and later, my older sister's kids. So, there was generally a house full of people. There was a saying in the house, "The first one up's the best one dressed," but it applied more to eating. My mother was less than a great cook, though she did pride herself in her ability to make a mean pineapple upside-down cake once or twice a year. She could fry an egg and make a few simple dishes, but she wasn't what you'd call an accomplished cook. The fact is, her cooking got a lot better with the invention of Hamburger Helper (and later, Tuna Helper, Pork Helper, Chicken Helper, and all the rest), but I had left home by the time that came along, and so I didn't really benefit from it.

You could make pancakes for a month with a seventy-nine cent box of Bisquick. Real maple syrup was expensive and was out of the question, but we made do with Karo Syrup, a dark pasty extract made from corn oil. If you mixed it with a lot of sugar and heated it on the stove, it made a passable maple syrup substitute, or so I thought. But I didn't know any better and didn't have much experience with anything real. In the fifties and sixties there wasn't the awareness of good nutrition there is today, and many people got by on whatever they thought tasted good. If it didn't kill you outright, you weren't too concerned about its long-term effects. Parents back then thought the brightly colored breakfast cereal they fed to their children was created by experts, and that all the sugar and food dye was better for the kids than what the parents had eaten when they were growing up, because the new colored stuff was made by scientists and was chock full of vitamins.

Cheap hamburger meat and government-issue bulk cheese often featured on the menu at home. We never received welfare, but you could shop at certain bulk stores and buy the government cheese and sometimes peanut butter (another staple at our house). The cheese would come in enormous blocks—they must have weighed several pounds apiece—that had most likely sat in a military warehouse for months, or even years, before they were finally sold to the public. They came in cardboard boxes that had "US Dept. of Agriculture" stamped on the side. The peanut butter was sold in bulk, so you had to take your own jar to scoop it into. It was usually kept in a big barrel on the floor of the store, and you used a giant wooden spoon to dish it into your container. Little kids would help themselves and lick the big spoon when their parents weren't watching. There's no telling what sorts of foreign objects and nasty germs found their way into that barrel of peanut butter, but we took it home, and as far as I know, none of us ever got sick from it.

We weren't overly grateful for the food we had as children (at least, I know I wasn't), but we never complained about the situation either. We survived on a combination of toughness, ignorance, old-fashioned home remedies, and for the most part, a positive outlook on life. So as I mentioned, I found that I was lucky when I began the ride because I wasn't much concerned with my health, my diet, or with how I was going to survive on whatever I managed to forage for meals along the way. I was certainly concerned for Gizmo, and it was a constant battle to see to his nutritional needs. But for myself, I generally ate once a day in the evening, and I was content with that. I was on what I referred to as a "low budget diet," which had always served me well when hitchhiking and riding freight trains. I suppose you could say that Gizmo was on the same diet.

There were three main influences upon my diet during the ride. One was cost. I started with a hundred dollars in my pocket and earned another two hundred during the ride. The entire ride cost three hundred dollars, plus forty for the German saddle, and a few dollars for maps and other things. Most of that money was used for Gizmo's needs. Another was weight. I couldn't afford to carry much on Gizmo and certainly couldn't carry canned goods or items with water or excess bulk. The third factor was availability. We were often in places where I couldn't find much at any cost. So whatever I carried would have to last as long as I could make it last.

Since I was on a low budget diet, macaroni became my staple. I could buy a plastic bag of it for less than twenty-five cents, and it would last for a week or more. Two or three packs of macaroni would be sufficient for a couple of weeks. Along with that, just to add taste, I bought little packets of powdered tomato sauce—the seasoned kind you mix with canned tomato sauce to make pasta sauce. I couldn't carry the canned sauce, so I simply boiled the macaroni, then added a bit of the powder and mixed it in while it was cooking. The powder blended with the water and created a sort of diluted sauce that gave the pasta some taste. Not being a picky eater, I never got tired of it, and it always tasted fine to me.

*LOGBOOK:*
*Stopped at an abandoned shack. No water, so kept going. Found an old trailer where I watered Gizmo and filled the canteen. Made another 3 miles along the powerline road to this place. We're camped under the powerlines. I staked him to a tower leg. There's only a small area of dry bunch grass that isn't worth a damn, but it's better than nothing. Didn't make a fire. Cooked macaroni on the Sterno stove. Nothing to put in it. Lousy, but filling. Gizmo even ate a little of it.*

I had a small metal pan—not much bigger than a coffee cup—that I cooked my meals in. It would produce the equivalent of a small bowl of pasta. The macaroni was devoid of protein and flavor, and I lost thirty-five pounds with all the physical exertion, but I managed to survive on it. The pasta was lightweight, would never spoil, and a dollar would buy me a month's supply of it. I cooked a single serving over a fire each evening and ate it without ceremony. As we moved eastward, I was forced to curtail my campfires, so I used a small Sterno stove. It had a folding grill that sat on top of a tiny, candle-like can of Sterno fluid, which burned slow and hot. It took a long time to boil water, but it did the job.

I sometimes shared my bowl of macaroni with Gizmo if he seemed interested or had no grass to graze. Most of the time, he was content to let me eat my own pasta. But if I happened to have a Snickers bar for desert, well … that was another matter.

# MUZZLELOADERS AND VELVEETA

I needed to pick up a couple of packages of macaroni pasta, so I took a short detour and reined Gizmo off the two lane and onto a side road that took us down into the main section of Huntsville, Arkansas. We were on the edge of the Ozark Mountains, though they seemed more like hills to me after what we had already crossed. Huntsville was the home of the legendary singer Ronnie Hawkins, which made me curious, and I figured that was as good a reason as any to make a detour. The town was largely boarded up, and I rode past many empty and abandoned stone buildings and closed businesses. The sign at the edge of town said "Huntsville, AR Pop: 1,126", but it looked as though half of them had already pulled up stakes and left.

There was a general store there, a classic place with a couple of old wooden benches out front under the porch awning and a store inventory that only half filled the shelves inside. I did manage to find a single package of macaroni, and I substituted the second one with a bag of fusilli, the twisty pasta that looks like short blonde licorice sticks. I picked up six or seven packets of powdered pasta sauce and a small box of matches and grabbed a Snickers bar for Gizmo. I asked the clerk at the counter if they had any apples or carrots, or other fruit or vegetables that they might be throwing out. He told me they didn't, so I paid and carried my bounty out to Gizmo, who was tied to the front porch railing.

He cried his usual whinny when I stepped through the front door. A few people were gathered around him, curious to see what was going on. One was a tall, lanky bearded man who introduced himself as Charlie. As I was stuffing the groceries down into the saddlebags, some of the others came over and started asking questions about the ride. They had seen us on the news and in some local papers that had carried an AP story the week before. I visited with them as I tore open the Snickers bar and fed it to Gizmo.

A friend of Charlie's walked over from across the street and introduced himself as Kurt. He said that Charlie and he had a place back in the woods, and they invited Gizmo and me to stay. After giving it a little thought, I told them, "Sure, why not?"

They wrote directions on an old paper sack, and I stuffed it into my pocket. I was tired of traveling on the two lane highway and a dirt road that took us off into remote areas sounded good to me. They hopped into an old Ford half-ton pickup truck and drove off, and I stepped up on Gizmo and pointed him in the same direction.

The road that led to their place was winding and narrow, not much more than a dirt track. I began to have doubts about this second detour. I had a hard time tracing the road on my topographic map, but I managed to discover that I could, in fact, travel a great distance through the hills here without having to follow the two lane. We would eventually end up in the same place, so I figured it was probably better for us both, even if it meant a few extra miles.

We arrived late in the afternoon. The place was built next to the Kings River, a painfully beautiful waterway, pristine and clear. It was running at a high level, and their place sat in a densely wooded area with a large clearing that extended away from the river and across the road. Charlie greeted me and said, "We don't exactly live in the middle of nowhere, but anyone goin' past this cabin ain't goin' anyplace."

There were three cabins altogether, though the main residence was by far the largest. Charlie had built the place himself, cutting the trees by hand, stripping and notching them, and painstakingly laying them in place. He had built it to last. The logs were substantial, and the place was solid. The long front porch was screened against mosquitos and other insects. The large pitched roof was covered with wood shingles that had been made by hand.

Kurt directed me to a structure next to the main house, which had a bunk and a small washroom. There was a corral next to it that hadn't been used in a long time and was overgrown with tall grass. Gizmo would make short work of it. I unsaddled, tended to his needs, then stashed my gear in the bunkhouse. Afterward, I went to join them in the main house.

Charlie was an interesting fellow. He had come down from Missouri to settle in the Arkansas mountains so he could live his dream of making muzzleloader rifles. He built a workshop where he made beautiful rifles and pistols using local hardwoods. He forged the barrels and working parts by hand. He made flintlocks and percussion rifles and pistols of various bores and vintages and was an expert on all things having to do with flintlock or cap and ball rifles and guns.

Kurt was a knife maker who made an astonishing variety of knives, from large hunting and skinning knives to small folding pocket knives. He created powder horns from various steer horns and antlers. He used the same sorts of local hardwoods that Charlie did and trimmed some of his work with silver and ornamental bone. His shop was in his house, next door. Between them, they had an impressive collection of work, and I spent a long time looking through it all over the course of a couple of days.

Charlie was a poet and homespun philosopher of sorts and was a tremendously prolific writer. There were books and notepads stacked around the cabin that were filled with his longhand writing, covering various subjects and issues. Every inch of the walls was covered with all manner of memorabilia, including tools, old clothes, photographs and paintings, animal heads, rifles, and knives. Amongst these items I noticed hundreds of scraps of paper with poetry and other philosophical notions that had been penned and pinned by Charlie. There was a large stone fireplace where a muzzleloader hung in a place of honor above the mantle and acted as a fitting statement about what it all meant. I was amazed by all of this and spent a good deal of time walking around the large main room, studying the mementos, and reading the little scraps of four-sentence wisdom. I could have stayed for a month and not have read it all.

> LOGBOOK:
> Made it to Charlie's place today. We're pretty far back into the Ozarks here. The Kings River runs right next to the shed I'm sleeping in. The river looks like God made it yesterday. Went for a swim and led Gizmo into the river. Gave him a bath and a rubdown. He loved it. It's beautiful spot here. Big storm front came in and it looks like it'll rain all night. Late to bed. I'm here in this shed and Gizmo's out in the rain. I feel a little guilty but he doesn't seem to mind it.

Despite the abundance of interesting items, the biggest surprise came when Kurt pointed me toward the kitchen cupboard to find a glass so I could get a drink of water. I opened the wrong cupboard and was met by a wall of yellow and red. The shelves were stacked two deep with boxes of Velveeta brand cheese. There were several dozen bright yellow boxes, all tightly piled with the familiar label printed in brilliant red lettering. They had caricatures of children's heads on them—a boy on one end and a girl on the other—with the words, "Full of Health from Milk!" printed beneath the logo.

I asked Kurt why they had so much of this cheese, and he replied, "We eat rabbit, and it makes good cheese sauce for the meat."

"You dang sure must eat a lot of rabbit," I joked.

"Well, we use it on other things, too," he said with a grin. "Like wild turkey. And sometimes we butcher a lamb or a goat."

"What about fishing?" I asked.

"No, we don't use it on fish. We just fry 'em with pepper and things."

"No, I didn't mean cooking the fish," I said. "I meant fishing with the cheese."

"Whatta ya talkin' about?"

"You know … using the cheese as bait," I replied.

"Bait?"

"Yeah, you know… you roll up a little ball of Velveeta cheese and put it on your hook. I'm pretty sure the fishing industry has kept the company in business for years," I said with a grin.

"I've never heard of such a thing," he said. "You mean to tell me you can use that cheese for bait? You can catch fish with it?"

"Well, you're livin' here next to a river, and I see all this Velveeta cheese in your cupboard, and I think, dang, they must fish *a lot*."

"Nope, never tried it."

"Well, what do you use for bait? Do you fly-fish?"

"We just take a net out and drag it in the river to get some minnows. Then we use them for bait. But heck, I think I'd like to try your deal of using the cheese. C'mon," he said as he grabbed a box of cheese and headed out the front door.

He walked over to a small storage cabinet on the porch and opened the door. He reached in and pulled out a rod and reel and a small tackle box. I looked at the hook that was on the line. It was a single barbless hook, similar to those used for fly-fishing, but without the fly. He picked up the tackle box, handed me the rod, and we walked down to the river bank.

"You got any treble hooks?" I asked. "They'll hold the cheese a bit better."

He fumbled around in the tackle box and found one then tied it to a piece of leader line and put it on the fishing rod in place of the old hook.

"Here's how you do this," I said and opened the box of cheese. I took a small amount between my thumb and fingers and began to roll it into a little ball.

"You have to keep it cool, so it doesn't fall off the hook," I instructed and dipped the cheese ball in the river. I pushed it onto the treble hook and squeezed it until I thought it would stay in place. Then I handed the rod back to Kurt.

"Just cast out into the river in whatever spot you like to fish," I said.

"This spot is as good as any," he muttered and cast into the middle of the river.

It was a classic fisherman's story. It took only a few seconds for a smallmouth bass to hit that cheese. Kurt was startled, but jerked the rod to set the hook then reeled it in and landed the fish.

"Good god awmighty!" he exclaimed.

"I'm guessin' they've never seen cheese before," I said with a smile.

I showed him how to bait the hook again, and he cast once more. This time it took almost a full minute to hook a fish. He caught one more before he said, "This is enough for dinner, I expect."
We put the fishing gear away and headed back to the house.

"You'll fish that river out if you're not careful," I cautioned.

"Oh hell, we never catch more than we need for the next meal," he replied. "These three will do us for dinner and for breakfast tomorrow." He looked at me and shook his head. "Damn, Charlie and I have been sittin' on a gold mine all this time and never even knew it. Of course, neither one of us is much of a fisherman."

That evening, Charlie cooked a fine meal out of a couple of those fish, and we had the other one the next morning for breakfast along with some eggs. And no, there was no cheese to be seen. But later that day, some friends dropped by. One of them, a man named Ed, raised rabbits. Everyone around those parts seemed to barter and trade with each other all the time, so Ed brought along several rabbits he had prepared and wrapped in trade for various things that either Charlie or Kurt could make for him. They did their dealings out of earshot, so I never knew what those rabbits were worth.

Several other folks stopped by, and it evolved into a bit of an impromptu gathering. They decided it would be a good time to barbeque some rabbit and shoot muzzleloaders. And so, that's what we did.

We all took turns shooting across the road at some permanent targets that Charlie had set up on the other side of the meadow. I wasn't the shot that most of them were, but I managed to make a respectable showing and didn't embarrass myself too badly.

The rabbit was heavenly—smoked and blackened from the barbeque fire and drowned in melted Velveeta.

# LANTERNS AND PITCHFORKS

The town of Cotter, Arkansas is surrounded on three sides by the White River. The water course makes a large horseshoe bend that creates the town's boundaries to the north, west, and south. Gizmo and I crossed the river from the west on the *Cotter Bridge*, a lovely structure that was built in 1930 to replace a small ferry. It was originally a toll bridge. Because they were forced to pay to use it, the townspeople ignored it at first. They chose to continue using the free ferry until the government threatened them, and they had to start paying the tolls. The bridge incorporated five large arches in what was termed a rainbow design. It was an elegant structure that was unique in its day and ushered in a certain amount of economic growth in Cotter, even as the Great Depression reached its full sway.

The old arch bridge eventually replaced the free ferry altogether, and the toll was dropped. The span deposited Gizmo and I into the old part of town. This consisted of a small market, a gas station, and a few stone and wood frame buildings. Among these buildings was the Town Hall, which also served as the Police Station, the Justice of the Peace's office, the City Attorney's office, and the Mayor's office. All were in fact one and the same office with the various positions filled by the same man. Cotter had less than nine hundred inhabitants back in 1974, and according to current census data, it doesn't have many more than that today.

Gizmo and I made our way to the far end of the street to the small market on the corner. I tied my companion to a railing outside and went into the store to see what I could scavenge for him. By then, I had figured out that grocery stores often throw away their produce as it gets too old to sell, and I had taken to looking in their trash bins to see if anything could be salvaged for my horse.

I had to be careful when rummaging for food because a horse's digestive system isn't the most robust thing in the world, and any little thing can cause the animal to colic, which is very painful and often fatal. There are certain fruits and vegetables that are not good for a horse, including celery, cabbage, potatoes, tomatoes, bananas, onions, and even grass clippings from mowing the lawn. But I often found perfectly edible items such as apples and carrots, and the storekeepers were usually generous and accommodating once they learned who the produce was for.

I went inside and asked the proprietor if he had any old fruit or vegetables I could have to feed to my horse.

He had a puzzled look on his face for a moment, then asked, "A *what?*"

"My horse," I replied. "He's outside there. Just wantin' to get him a bit of grub if I can."

He walked to the front of the store, looked out through the front door, turned back to me, and exclaimed, "You got a *horse* out there!"

"Yep. We've come a long ways, and I like to get apples and carrots and stuff for him when I can."

"You're that fella on TV," he said. "Dang son, you come a purty fur piece, ain't you?"

"Yep, we have."

"Well, lemme see what I kin find hereabouts."

I followed him to the produce section at the back of the market where he picked some apples from the stack and loaded them into a bag.

"Oh, I was thinkin' maybe you had some old ones that you were gonna throw out," I said. "Can't really afford to be buyin' 'em."

"Wouldn't think of sellin' 'em to you," he replied. "These are on the house."

"Aw, jeez … thanks a lot," I replied. "Gizmo will really appreciate 'em."

"Gizmo, that his name?"

"Yep."

"Well," he said as he started for the door with the apples, "let's get him fed up proper."

Gizmo whinnied as we stepped through the door. Several people had gathered around, and a couple of young girls were petting him. I untied him and began to feed the apples to him, one by one. He grabbed at them eagerly and chewed rapidly, swallowing them core and all.

"He likes 'em," I said.

The crowd grew steadily larger as we stood there, visiting with folks. They asked the usual questions: What kind of horse was Gizmo? How old was he? How many miles had we traveled? What does he eat? Those sorts of things. Somewhere in the middle of this, I had mentioned that Gizmo would eat just about anything I could eat, so the store owner's wife went back inside and appeared shortly with an apple pie.

"I saw on TV that he likes cakes and pies," she said. "Will he eat this?"

"Well, if he don't, I sure will." I said with a grin, knowing that Gizmo would make short work of that pie. And he did, much to everyone's amusement.

After we had been there awhile, the local sheriff's deputy walked up and joined the group.

"Please step away from the sidewalk and come this way," he ordered. I handed the lead rope to one of the girls and walked over to where he was.

"Do you have a license for that gun?" he asked, indicating the Colt in my holster.

"It's not loaded," I replied. "It doesn't even have its cylinder in it," I said, reaching for it.

"Keep your hands away from the gun!" he shouted. "Don't move," he ordered as he pulled his own weapon.

He reached over, unfastened the hammer thong, and removed the pistol from my holster.

"Where's the other part of it?" he demanded.

"The cylinder is packed in my saddlebags," I said. "I just carry the gun in my holster because it's easier that way."

The deputy ordered me to produce the cylinder for the Colt, so I walked over to Gizmo and shuffled through the saddlebags until I found it. I handed it to him. I could see he didn't know how to assemble it, so I asked, "Do you want me to put it together?" He indicated that he did, so I took the gun from him and popped the cylinder into it, spinning it to make sure it was installed correctly.

"There," I said, handing the gun back to him.

"Will you follow me, sir?" he asked, and gestured toward the Town Hall up the street. I turned and asked the young lady if she would mind hanging onto Gizmo for a little while.

The store owner started to get a bit hot under the collar and shouted at the deputy, "What the hell you doin', Carl? This man's done nothing wrong. Leave him be."

Deputy Carl ignored him and kept walking. "Just follow me," he ordered.

Since he had my revolver, I did. I had no choice.

"Leave him alone, Carl," another cried. "Fer chrissakes, you can't do this!"

More people were yelling at the deputy by this time. Halfway up the block, he led us into the Town Hall, a modest white stone structure. Some of the crowd had followed us, shouting at him and taunting. We stepped through the front doors of the building, and he shut the door behind us. He ushered us into a room, where an old man sat at a large desk.

"Here he is, Mayor," the deputy said and handed him my Colt.

"Well, whatta we got here?" the man said, examining the Colt and looking up to eye me occasionally. "You got a license for this?" he demanded.

"Didn't think I needed one in Arkansas," I replied. I knew I didn't need a license to carry a weapon that wasn't concealed, but I remained passive. I didn't want to provoke him.

"You didn't think, period," he answered. "What about that horse? You can't have a horse on the city streets like that. What's the matter with you?"

I was a bit dumbfounded and didn't know how to respond. I had never been greeted this way by a government official and wasn't sure how I should proceed.

"Whatta ya think, Carl? Carryin' an illegal firearm? Maybe creatin' a public nuisance?"

"Yeah, Mayor. I think that sounds about right," the deputy replied.

The old man went on for a while, badgering me and trying to goad me into losing my temper. He clearly had a mean streak in him and was enjoying this. I sat as still as I could, gripping the arms of my chair until my knuckles turned white.

"I'm pretty sure I haven't broken any laws," I said, frustrated.

"How much schoolin' you got?" the old man asked.

"High school, a little college," I answered, puzzled at the question.

"So, you're a big high falutin' college graduate, come here to *edicate* all us country folk, eh?"

"No, wait … I didn't say I was a college graduate, I only meant—"

"No, you just stop right THERE," he shouted. "I'm a retired Army colonel. That's U-S- *ARMY*. You understand that?" He cocked the hammer back to the first click and twirled the cylinder of the Colt as he spoke.

"Ain't no fancy college kid protester gonna come in here and try to make us look like fools, you hear?" He didn't allow me to reply, and continued. "I reckon we're gonna have to take you over to Mountain Home and lock you up for a little while. Maybe *that'll* knock some sense into you. If that don't, I reckon those jail guards will."

I started to tell him that I wasn't a war protester and was indeed a veteran, but thought better of it. I could tell that he wanted my Colt. It was a vintage piece, a second generation Army Colt made in 1902. My brother had given it to me. The words, "Army Colt" stamped on the barrel must have caught his eye, and I could see that he was set on keeping it.

"How 'bout it, Carl? I'd say sixty days on the pea farm oughta do him some good." Carl nodded.

I was starting to worry. I didn't want to lose the Colt, but I figured it was already gone. My only thought was for Gizmo, and I had no idea what would happen to him if they threw me in jail.

"Gonna hafta impound that horse too, I reckon," he said. "Evidence, and all that."

"Now wait, you can't just take my—"

"I don't think you're in much of a position to tell me what I can and can't do, son."

I began to think about fighting my way out, about charging the deputy first and then taking on the old man, but I knew that he would have a gun hidden somewhere in his desk, and he was certainly the type to use it. I decided to resign myself to fate. I kept trying to reason with him, though I knew it wasn't any use.

"Look, maybe there's some way I can just leave Cotter and not cause any trouble," I pleaded.

"I'm afraid you've already caused a lot more trouble than you can imagine," he replied. "You got your cuffs, Carl?"

Just as the deputy was about to place me in handcuffs, there was a knock at the office door and it opened. A woman poked her head in and asked, "May I come in, Mayor?"

The mayor looked irritated as she opened the door and came in, shutting it behind her. She looked to be in her late thirties. She entered in a mild manner and in a soft-spoken voice she asked, "Mayor, is there something wrong?"

"I'm afraid this man has broken a few laws. We're gonna hafta confiscate his horse and his gun."

"Now, mayor," she said in a tranquil voice, "I'm sure there's a way we can settle all of this without an incident, isn't there?" She remained calm and continued. "He and his horse have come a long way, all the way from California. Can't we just let them go on their way? I'm sure you could see yourself through to letting him go with a warning, just this one time, can't you?"

"I need to make an example of him," the mayor replied.

"Mayor, I think you need to know," she said. "He has a letter from the governor. He has letters from senators and congressmen from all over the country. He and his horse have been in newspapers and on TV. Maybe you could think about this a little," she said.

"The governor knows about you?" he uttered, not as a question but as a comment to no one in particular.

"He sent me a letter of support," I said, "It's in my saddlebags."

I could see his face fall. The woman introduced herself to me, explaining that she was a member of the town council. I felt a glimmer of hope.

"Can't we just give him back his gun and let him be on his way?" she asked, in a tone that was more of a suggestion than a question.

"It's against the law for him to cross the state line with it," the mayor answered. He was beginning to grasp at straws, but he wanted that Colt badly.

"Well, how about this …" she said, "We can let him go, and I'll drive over to Missouri and meet him there and give it back to him. Or, we can mail it somewhere for him."

The old man was losing his enthusiasm for detaining me. He had deflated a bit, and I think he was beginning to realize that he wasn't going to get away with taking the pistol.

"How about it, mayor?" she said, holding her hand out.

He answered by handing her the Colt.

"You get outta my town right now and don't come back," he ordered.

I looked him in the eye as I stood up and took the gun from the woman. I didn't say anything as we turned to go.

The woman and I stepped out of the office and shut the door behind us, leaving the mayor and his deputy to themselves.

"Thank you," I whispered, as we stepped outside through the Town Hall doors.

This little meeting with the mayor had taken place over the course of about forty minutes, and as we walked out onto the steps of the Town Hall, we were greeted by what could only be described as an angry mob. There must have been forty or fifty people gathered in the street out front. Many carried rifles and pistols, and most of the others had some sort of implement that they could use as a weapon. They were coming to storm the building with shovels and rakes and hammers, to break me out. I was stunned.

"Is my horse okay?" was all I could think to say.

"Yep, he's up the street, eatin' apples," a man replied.

Another stepped up to the front window of the building and shouted, "You ain't gonna get away with this, mayor!" That set the crowd off, and they started shouting and making a huge racket, and threatened to break into the building and take on the mayor and deputy.

"Please, PLEASE!" the councilwoman shouted. "Let's all be calm here. This man's okay, and we're out now, so let's just let it go." She looked around at the crowd, who responded by quieting down somewhat.

We started back down the street to where Gizmo was, most of the crowd walking along with us, but some staying behind to offer more comments to the mayor and his deputy. I talked to the woman as we walked. She told me she was on the town council and that several people had phoned her when the deputy had taken me in. She explained that the mayor was also the Justice of the Peace, the Chief of Police, and the City Attorney, and had been for years.

One of the men next to me said, "He's an old fool. Nobody else ever runs against him, so he always gets elected, even if nobody votes. He's just a mean-spirited old bastard."

Others began speculating about grabbing Carl, dragging him behind a building, and beating him up. After they'd done that, they said, they'd do the same thing to the mayor. The councilwoman cautioned them to keep a level head and that things would be okay. No violence, just leave it be.

"There ain't no law against carryin' a gun in open sight," declared another man. "They cain't stop us from carryin' our guns like that. If that was the case, we wouldn't be allowed to go huntin'."

"Yeah, that's right!" shouted others in the crowd.

They were beginning to work themselves up again, and the councilwoman stopped suddenly in the street, causing everyone else to pause as well.

"Just STOP it!" she demanded. "This has gone far enough! You need to *take it easy,* okay?" She looked around, catching each one's eye to emphasize her point.

"Yeah, you're right," one of them said, "but that don't mean we cain't show them two a little disrespect, does it?"

The others laughed, and an informal consensus seemed to be reached that they would test the mayor and deputy by carrying their weapons around town.

"We won't keep 'em loaded," one of them said.

The councilwoman sighed and shrugged her shoulders.

When we reached the market, I saw that Gizmo was in good hands, surrounded by a crowd of young girls who were petting him and feeding him apples and carrots. I'm pretty sure the market's supply was down to nothing. I was a bit worried that he'd get a stomach ache from eating all those apples, but I let him keep munching on them.

A local man invited us to stay with him and his family for as long as we wanted, and I accepted. It was late in the afternoon, and though we hadn't covered our twenty miles that day, I thought it best to take the bird in the hand and not try to find two in the bush. We spent the evening with him and his wife, and their two children. Many people stopped by to wish us well and to apologize for the actions of their mayor and deputy. Several mentioned that they would make up for it by beating them up, over my protests that no harm had been done. I don't know if their threats were carried out, and I hoped they weren't. I was never one for wanting to get even with folks. I do know that the next day many of the townsfolk took up arms and walked the street in front of the Town Hall, daring the mayor and deputy to try to take their guns away. They taunted and goaded and generally gave the two a hard time for most of the day. I wanted no more confrontation and stayed out of it.

The incident in Cotter has crossed my mind many times over the years. I've given a lot of thought to how I reacted and how the townspeople behaved. I have often imagined how Gizmo must have seen it. He would have remembered it as a fine day, a short ride on the trail, a nice rest in the shade outside a building where people petted him and fed him apples and carrots and pie. In his eyes, it was probably one of the better days of the ride. I saw it as a close call, a reminder that one's liberty and freedom can be snatched away on a whim, for no reason at all.

And no matter who has control of the situation at the time, sometimes it's safest to be on the side of those with the lanterns and pitchforks.

# HORSES AND MUSIC

For most of my life, I have maintained two distinct sets of friends: music people and horse people. I still live in both worlds. Up until around the turn of the twenty-first century and the advent of social networks like Facebook and Twitter, the two groups were pretty much separate. There may have been the odd horse person who played the guitar, or the musician who had a horse, but none of my friends or acquaintances has been seriously based in both worlds. I have written music for upper-level dressage freestyle riders, and that seemed to combine the two interests for me, but it didn't bring the two groups of people together. My horse friends and music friends have been mutually exclusive people who didn't know each other, and usually weren't even aware that the other was a part of my life.

I have spent my life in both camps, the two worlds like binary suns that orbit each other but never converge. I wouldn't try to discuss half passes at the canter with a bass player, nor would I attempt to offer discourse about the tone of a Telecaster through a Fender Deluxe amp to a reining horse trainer. I'm sure there are people who know about both, but I've never met any.

*LOGBOOK:*

*Took today off. Managed to sew up the torn sleeve on my jacket, and repair the billet that holds my canteen to the saddle. Nothing to read, so I mostly did gun tricks. I pulled my harmonica out for the first time in a while and just played a bunch of random tunes. Gizmo stopped grazing and came over and laid down next to me and listened. Most people would hate it, but at least my horse loves my harmonica.*

Gizmo and I were living in my horse world during the ride. Except for my squeaking on the harmonica around the campfire in the evenings, music appeared briefly only a couple times during our stays in Santa Fe and in Nashville with musician friends. It felt good to bring up that side of me for a change during those layovers, even if only for a few days. And the thing is, I didn't exactly talk horse talk with people during the ride because I met very few real equestrians. But the talk did, naturally, center on my horse, and upon horses in general. Plus, I was living the horse life every day and couldn't have gotten away from it even if I had wanted to.

It had been hard for some of my musician friends to imagine leaving music behind and taking off on a ride for several months. When you're immersed in your passion it's hard to imagine *not* doing it. Taking a temporary respite stirs fears that you might miss out on something. And to be honest, it *was* difficult to drop out of the music scene and leave it behind. It was only going to be for a few months, a year at most. But the prospect seemed like forever when we first set out on the trail.

I know I'm not the only one who has more than one primary interest. I'll bet there are nuclear physicists who skydive or drive race cars, and master carpenters who sing opera. The world is full of people who have a passion for more than one thing—enough passion to make them good at those things. We tend to discourage this idea. Actors are not supposed to be professional reining horse trainers. It's considered amazing if the leader of a country is also a world class pianist. An astronaut shouldn't be able to write poetry or paint. Your dog's veterinarian is not supposed to be able to make fine furniture. We're surprised when we find out that a person has an interest or avocation outside of how we know them. It messes up the picture we have of them. It takes their frame away.

We end up in silos, disconnected from each other. We're separated by *what we do,* instead of *who we are.* I shared our ride with everyone I met along the way, and they identified with Gizmo and me because it wasn't seen as an *equestrian* activity. It was a *human* one, one that happened to include a horse.

I'm curious—curious enough to plant my feet in several fields—music and horses are the most prominent two for me, but there are a few others, like saddlemaking and astronomy, computers and flyfishing. The truth is, you can be good at a lot of things, and they don't have to be related to each other at all. Their common thread is your own curiosity. It's your primary driver. Curiosity. Pursuing new interests is what keeps you *grounded* as a person. Following those interests until you get good at them is what makes you a *strong* person. Having the inquisitiveness and imagination to engage, and the perseverance to continue, makes you a *special* person.

Curiosity might have killed the cat, but he had eight more lives. Here's hoping that I still have a few of them left.

# INSPIRATION

The town of Steele, Missouri had seen more prosperous times. The timber industry that built it had years before succumbed to the pressures of harvest, and the newly cleared land that resulted had encouraged farmers to settle there in the heart of the Missouri Boot Heel. Highway 164 passed through town and became the main drag, slowing the cars and trucks with stop signs and traffic lights, and luring drivers to pause with promises of gasoline, home cooked meals, and hardware for the home or automobile. These hardly mattered, however, because the larger cities of Dyersburg to the east and Caruthersville to the north enticed even Steele's own residents away from its two-block central business district. The town seemed to be engaged in a slow death as its population gradually shrunk, but its residents clung to a fragile thread owing to a perseverance of farming and through a small amount of activity at the local cotton gin. Almost a third of the area's population lived below the poverty line in 1974. Neither the size of the population nor the average income has changed very much since then.

Gizmo and I found ourselves passing through what several referred to as the "old section" of town (as far as I could tell, there was no "new section"), which was comprised of several unremarkable buildings, none of which was memorable enough to pique my interest. They were constructed in true Missouri "show me" fashion, for utility and not for flash. If any structures in town had been created with an artistic bent, they weren't visible to me. Form followed function here, and the main street was meant to provide exchanges of goods and services and not much else except for the occasional conversation between residents. The town broadcast its name to the world by way of large, plain block letters painted on the side of a galvanized tank perched high atop a tower. It contained the citizens' water supply. I had seen countless water towers—each embellished with its town's name—and could by now guess how many people lived there by the size and height of the tank. Steele's was neither large nor exceptionally high above the ground. It suggested a town of under two thousand.

We had had another rough night of battling mosquitos, and we were worn-out and in need of a break. I tied him to a post on the side of a flat

216

faced building that housed a small cafe—the town's only cafe, it turned out—and went in for a cup of coffee. I sat at the counter where I could keep an eye on him while I read the local paper. The only other customer there was a young man who sat a few seats away. I nodded a greeting as I picked up the paper and browsed through the headlines. The proprietor set a cup of coffee in front of me, and the young man stood up and went to the window where he could get a better look at my horse.

"That you in the paper the other day?" he asked.

"Well, if it was about some guy riding across America, then yeah, I guess it was," I replied.

"That must be a heckuva horse you got there."

"Yep, he's a keeper."

"So, what made you do something like this?" he asked, still watching Gizmo through the glass.

"Oh, just something I wanted to do, I guess."

"You know what I've always wanted to do?" he said, more as a statement than a question. "I always wanted to go to Alaska." He returned to his stool at the counter.

"Wouldn't mind goin' there myself," I said. "I hear it's a beautiful place."

He was quiet for a moment then continued. "I been stuck here my whole life. I always wanted to go out where it's wild … you know, live in the wild country."

Sensing that he wasn't looking for a reply, I kept silent while he continued.

"I don't think I wanna spend the rest of my days workin' on a farm or at the gin," he remarked. "I'm thinkin' I might just figure out how to get up there to Alaska … yep, just up and go."

"Well …" I said, "I think followin' a dream is never a bad thing to try. Seems like that's one of the main reasons we're here, at least to me it does."

"How'd you go about doin' this horseback thing you're doin'?" he asked. "You have a lot of money? You have to save up for it?"

"Neither one, really," I answered. "I only had a hundred bucks when I left California. It don't cost much to be out here. It's not like I have to pay rent or bills or anything. I've worked a bit here and there, so I'm managing to feed myself and my horse, and that's about it. I sure ain't rich," I said with a grin then continued. "If you set your mind to something you'll figure out a way to do it. It ain't easy, but you gotta start putting energy toward something. It'll give things back to you. Sometimes they're not what you thought they'd be, but still ... it's guaranteed you're gonna get something in return."

We talked for a while. He told me he worked as a laborer in the fields and at one of the cotton gins, though work was a bit hard to come by these days. He moved irrigation pipe, drove trucks and tractors, and did what most laborers do, which is just about anything that needs doing. His name was Martin, and I asked if folks called him Martin or Marty. Martin, he told me. He said he liked the name Marty, but that Martin just sort of stuck to him when he was younger, and now everybody just called him that.

He pulled a piece of paper out of his wallet, unfolded it, and then turned it to show me. It was a ragged photograph of a snowy mountain peak. "Mount Whitney, Alaska" it said at the bottom. It had been torn from a magazine. The photo had worn spots where the folds were, and I guessed it had been in his wallet for a long time. He carefully folded it up and put it back in his billfold in a way that suggested he cared for it the way a father would care for a wallet photo of his kids.

"That's some nice lookin' country," I said.

"Yeah, I figure I could get some work on the pipeline ... or maybe fishin' or trappin' or something," he replied.

"Well, look at it this way," I said. "If a guy like me can do what I'm doin', I don't see why someone like you couldn't get himself up to Alaska. Whatcha got to lose?"

"Man, I tell you what ..." He paused. His brow furrowed slightly, and he looked down at his empty coffee cup. "I'm glad I ran into you here. I believe I might just do it ... I'm gonna figure out a way. Damn ... *thank you*, man," he said suddenly, extending his hand.

I reached out to complete the handshake as he rose from his seat. He started for the door, muttering to himself.

I called out to him as he opened the cafe's front door, "Hey, think about it this way. If you head up to Alaska, nobody there is gonna know you. You can start having 'em call you Marty."

"Yeah, that's somethin' to think about," he said, and stepped outside.

Gizmo started to whinny when Martin stepped through the door. My companion had thought it was me, but stopped short when he saw that it wasn't. Martin gave him a pat on the neck as he walked past and headed up the street out of my view.

Sometime after the ride I got a postcard with a three-year-old postmark on it. It had been forwarded several times, the postmarks covering some of the writing on it. It was beaten up from its travels through the postal service, but still legible. On the front was a picture—a cartoon drawing—of a mountain and lake with bears, elk, and other animals placed within it. It said, "Alaska—America's Last Frontier" on the front. On the back was a short note, painstakingly written in terse, upright letters that suggested an author who was not comfortable with writing:

> *I made it thanks to you.*
> *Signed,*
> *Marty*

# THE HEARTLAND

Gizmo and I travel through the Ozark Mountains in northern Arkansas now. The heat we experienced in Oklahoma has followed us and is more intense. Some days the thermometer pushes up to near a hundred with over eighty percent humidity. It's the humidity that is taking a terrible toll on us. We sweat constantly, and I wonder just how many calories each drop of perspiration contains, how much body weight escapes with every glassful of sweat. It is not like the heat on the Texas plains, where the sun beat down, and we could feel its luminance directly on our faces and backs. The sun is partially masked here. Even on cloudless days, the sunlight is diffused by the moisture in the air, and it feels as though we're in an oven. The heat seems to come from everywhere and penetrate everything. It is stifling, suffocating. We plod ahead, each day a bit slower than the previous, until every stride requires extreme effort.

The Ozarks are beautiful, and we manage to take a couple of days off, staying at a cabin next to a river. I relax in the river for long periods, enjoying the cold water. It seems to cleanse me of more than just the trail dust, and I feel revived. I lead Gizmo into the stream and give him a bath. He enjoys it, too and seems content to stand in the middle of the river while I scoop water onto his back and massage him. We are momentarily revitalized.

The mountains still harbor remote and inaccessible places that require miles of travel on unimproved dirt roads to reach. This is changing, though, and the local government is creating new farmland and housing sites by using herbicides and defoliants that were developed for the war in Vietnam. The war is ending now, and the manufacturers see a new market for their products. They use helicopters to spray sections with the defoliant, and nearly a decade's worth of aging and decomposition occurs within just a few months. Large open parcels of land are beginning to dot the sides of the Ozark hills and mountains, and they will bring a new population to the area within a decade.

This new open land comes at a price, however. The numbers of mosquitos and other insects multiply greatly. Damage from rain runoff and erosion increases, and there are problems with the new farmland that requires even more pesticides and other chemical enhancements. After being referred to as the last bastion of the old west, the Ozarks are changing rapidly and will become unrecognizable to the old timers within another twenty years. The old hillbilly culture will give way to a new urban, and modern one, as the new "amenities migrants"—well-heeled modern urbanites—bring highways, shopping malls, movie theaters, and designer coffee shops with them.

The Ozarks surrender themselves gradually, and by the time we reach the eastern part of northern Arkansas, we find ourselves on another flat plain, this time surrounded by farmland. We wage a constant battle with mosquitos, deer flies, and other biting insects. Soybeans are the main crop here, grown by sharecroppers and poor families who work for large farms. Families live in sharecroppers' shacks that were built several decades before, and I wonder how the people survive in this place. There is not much more than a minimal subsistence living to be made here, no matter what your job is. The land is dotted with these small shacks. The glass in their windows is mostly broken or missing entirely, and many have no doors on their thresholds or screens on their porches. They offer no protection against the swarms of mosquitos that engulf them at night, and most have families with several children living in them. Every person I see in them is black. The people stare in disbelief at Gizmo and I as we pass, as if witnessing first contact with an alien species.

LOGBOOK:
*Stayed up all last night, and the night before that, and so on. Too hot to cover up and too many mosquitos not to. Rode on the little ferry across Norfolk Lake. Gizmo seemed to enjoy it. Had to go 28 miles today to find a campsite. The Ozarks are dropping back behind us, and the land is getting flat and swampy. More insects than ever. We haven't slept in three or four days. Gizmo is one mass of lumps from mosquito and deer fly bites.*

LOGBOOK:
*Another killer today. Gizmo was covered with lumps from mosquitos again this morning. He is so tired. Went through Denton and Steele without being stopped by cops about my*

*gun. It rained some, and I unsaddled him and let him stand in*
*it. Sort of soothed the bites, and he seemed grateful.*

The land remains flat as we cross the border into the state of Missouri and begin to ride across its boot heel. It becomes a flood plain as we reach the eastern half of the state. It is low ground, and much of it is lower than the waters of the Mississippi River. Only the manmade levees along the banks of the river will keep the area from flooding if the great river goes on a rampage. The sticky heat remains, and we travel slowly, as if we are prisoners of war on a forced march. We seem to travel without purpose now, continuing eastward only because I know no other way and can think of nothing else. The insects swarm around us after dark, stealing any chance of a night's sleep, until each day flows mindlessly into the next, one after another.

The crossing of the Mississippi River is more than just a watershed—it is a defining moment in the journey. With it comes new hope, a rebirth, and a signal that we are truly in the eastern United States. Crossing into Tennessee, Gizmo and I leave the heat and the mosquitos behind as suddenly as if we have stepped into an air-conditioned building. The flatlands of the Missouri boot heel have been cut by the river, and we now climb into pine-studded hills on our way to Nashville. The air is decidedly cooler here, and for the first time in weeks I pull on my jacket as I ride. It feels good to be bracing myself against the cold.

Tennessee seems beautiful but tame to me. The wilderness that was once here has been conquered and replaced, fenced and domesticated by immigrants and settlers long ago. *Manicured* is the word I think of to describe it. Predictable and safe, not like the wild deserts of the Southwest. It is lovely, though, and I enjoy traveling through this part of the country.

We find only the occasional railroad spur that we can follow to pass through towns and escape the traffic, and these don't appear very often. Gas station maps actually become more useful than my topographic maps here because they show all the roads, new and old. I ultimately use both, glancing from one to the other to make sense of the populated areas we are forced to negotiate.

Now there are no more power line roads or underground gas pipelines to follow, only the small two lane backroads that will take us the rest of the way to the Atlantic Ocean. Most of these roads have no shoulder, or if they do, it is grassy but full of broken glass from bottles thrown by passing drivers. I do not want to risk injury to Gizmo, so we follow what I think of as an eddy—the intersection of the grass and the pavement—and take our chances. The cars and trucks pass by within inches of us, and I become more and more worried about the possibility of getting hit as the days go by. Every inch of the land has been fenced, so riding through pastures is not an option. We must stick to the roads through here.

*LOGBOOK:*
*Pitched camp at a school here. There was a PTA meeting going on tonight and everyone kept bringing me food. Got enough for tomorrow, too. Gizmo ate a whole ham & cheese sandwich, some cookies and crackers, and 2 peanut butter cups.*

Autumn begins to settle in as we make our way across Tennessee. We stop for a layover in Nashville and come away rested and refreshed. Gizmo almost unloads me on our first day back on the trail because he is feeling so good. The air has a snap to it now, and I can see my own breath in the morning. On many mornings frost covers the grass where we have slept, and it makes me want to stay in my warm bedroll longer, hunkered down against it. But the months have strengthened my determination and have given me a strong resolve. Habit dictates that I roll out early, and so I do.

The night sky is not spectacular here. The stars are masked by manmade light from the cities and towns we pass through, but I still look up to them every night that I can. The winter constellations are beginning to show themselves on the horizon. I can see the Great Square of Pegasus, and though it doesn't look much like a winged horse, I point it out to my companion. Cassiopeia is joined by her daughter, Andromeda, and on moonless nights I can sometimes make out the Andromeda Galaxy nearby with my naked eye. The handle of the Little Dipper points toward the pole star, Polaris, as the entire sky rotates around that single point of light.

I miss the wide-open spaces in the west. Each time we top a hill or mountain, I stop to look around and I feel disappointed. I expect to see a long way ahead, but I am greeted only by more nearby hills. In the desert, I could see where we had been a hundred miles in the distance. Here, there are no views like that. There is no vantage point where one can look back to see where they have been for the last two weeks or where they will be traveling through in the coming two. I see only short views across hollows or small valleys, snapshots of the next set of hills a few miles away. The views are pretty, but they are not inspiring to me. Still, I am happy about being here because it is new.

The people here are friendly and outgoing, and I know that the increased media coverage has helped. People recognize Gizmo and me and often stop to chat along the road. I begin to feel frustrated when these visits become obstacles to making our twenty miles a day. We camp in cemeteries at night, knowing that people won't think to look for us there, or that they won't come even if they know where we are. This gives us some space, some room to breathe and to be by ourselves, even if only for the night.

It is early October now, and the weather is cool but manageable. There is no ice on the ground during the day yet, and I am thankful for this. The trail through Tennessee is largely wooded, with open patches of farmland throughout. I see the first tobacco drying shed I have ever seen. Gizmo and I will make our camp in several of them before the ride is finished. So far, the Tennessee weather has been good to us. We've encountered only a few small rainfalls, and I have not had to pull my rain slicker more than a couple times. Without a tent, my slicker doubles as a lean-to if it rains. We have been lucky so far.

# HOW WATER WORKS

Hub Crossett was a head taller than me but probably didn't weigh a whole lot more than I did. He was wiry and sinewy and hard as the stones his grandfather had used to build his house more than 75 years before. We stood in his yard, talking as he watered a flowerbed with the hose. He reached to shut the water off and laid the hose down. Then he took a few steps away and unzipped his pants to urinate at the base of one of the large beech trees that surrounded the house.

"Does runnin' water make you have to pee?" he asked.

"Not sure," I replied, "Never given it much thought."

"It dang shore makes me hafta go," he said. "I cain't git near water where it don't all of a sudden make me wanna pee." He finished and zipped his trousers.

"Well, now that you mention it …" I remarked and stepped over to the tree to mimic what he had just done. "Maybe it does."

Hub was in his seventies and seemed ageless. Judging by the old photographs of him that hung on the walls in his house, he looked the same as he had twenty-five years earlier, though his grey-white hair was a giveaway. He had ridden endurance horses for many years and was proud of the fact that he rode all the way from his home in Huntingdon, Tennessee to Washington DC just a few years before.

"Ain't no life without water, whether it's comin' or goin'," he remarked. "You drink it, and you piss it out the other end. You gotta do both, or you die. Simple as that," he said.

"Yeah, I guess you're right," I said. "Gizmo and I have spent our fair share of time looking for water along the way."

"It's life's elixir," he opined. "It's the most valuable thing on the Earth."

"I never thought about having to pee when you're around water," I said.

"Oh, it's not just bein' around water … it's *runnin'* water. Got to be runnin', like a hose or a stream or somethin'."

"I'll have to keep that in mind," I said, making a mental note to check my urological urges the next time I was next to a river.

We stepped onto the front porch and sat in the old chairs there as we looked out at the barn where Gizmo was grazing happily on dried corn cobs. He stuck his head out the stall door, a cob hanging from his mouth, and chewed it for a little while. Once he had stripped the kernels from it, he dropped it on the ground outside, then retreated into the stall in search of another. Hub was quite taken with him.

"That's a helluva horse, right there," he said. "A helluva horse."

"Yep, he sure is. He's packed me a good long way," I answered.

"C'mere, I got somethin' I want to show you," Hub said. He stood up and motioned for me to follow.

We walked out to the barn area, where Gizmo greeted me with his usual whinny. Hub led me to a small shed next to the barn and flipped the snap that held the door closed. The sagging door scraped the floor as he shoved it open. We stepped inside.

It was a tack room filled with all manner of cavalry saddles and harness that he had accumulated over the years. He possessed quite a collection of McClellan saddles, both the plain trooper rigs and the fancier officers' models that had side jockeys and hooded stirrups. Sets of harness, most with the iconic "US" insignia on the various hardware rosettes, were hung along the wall.

"This is unbelievable," I said, "What an amazing collection you have here."

"I figgered you'd like it," he said. "Been sorta collectin' this stuff for years. On my endurance rides, I use the McClellan that you saw back at the house. That one sorta got me into collectin' 'em. Hell, I don't use 'em for anything, except showin' to people like yerself."

We spent some time in the tack room, going through the saddles and harness, bits and spurs, and other cavalry paraphernalia. I had spent quite a bit of time before the ride studying old cavalry manuals and other books related to the US Cavalry, trying to learn about traveling cross country on horseback. I had naturally absorbed some information about the gear and riggings they used, and Hub was surprised at how much I knew about such an esoteric and arcane subject.

"Not too many folks even know what this stuff is," he remarked.

"No, I guess they wouldn't. Not really something many people are interested in."

"Time was, you'd find a lot of this cavalry stuff around these parts. Mostly left over from the Civil War and afterwards," he said.

226

"A lot of the gear here is probably from the World War I era," I replied. "But those two there,"—I indicated, pointing to two saddles—"See those saddle horns? Those are Hope saddles, and they're from the Civil War. Confederate soldiers most likely rode those things. They're pretty rare, too."

We talked about saddlery and harness, and I mentioned the buggies and harness I had found in the abandoned settlement back in New Mexico.

"Maybe you oughta go back and get all that stuff after your ride", he offered, "Sounds like it might be worth somethin'."

"Nah, I don't think I'd want to do that", I replied. "Don't really want anyone knowin' where it is, either. It's kinda nice just knowin' that it's out there".

"I know what you mean", he said, "There's some things you just want to keep to yourself, I reckon."

Hub talked about driving to school in a small buggy when he was a kid and how his grandfather had built the house he lived in, around the turn of the century, by hauling the stones for it in a horse drawn dray. As we left the tack room and made our way back to the front porch chairs, the talk turned to horses and places we had gotten stuck when riding them. Hub asked me about crossing rivers.

"I don't swim Gizmo in deep water. I'd rather go for days, trying to find a way around than to put him in water I'm not familiar with," I said.

"That's a good philosophy," he said. "It's 'specially hard when the horse is carrying a load like Gizmo is."

"Yeah, and even if I thought it was safe to swim, I don't want to ruin all the stuff in my pack and saddlebags," I noted.

"How'd you get across the ol' Big Muddy?" he asked.

"Good question," I replied. "Turns out I had to study the situation—about how I was gonna cross the Mississippi—and I thought about it for a few weeks before we ever got to it. But here's the upshot of it all."

Hub sat back and listened as I gave an account of our journey across Arkansas and Missouri and our crossing of the great river:

\*\*\*\*\*\*\*\*\*

We're back in the Ozarks, staying with a couple of fellows who live way back in the woods in a log cabin. I talked to them about the best way to get a horse across the Mississippi River (which they pronounced 'mis-SIP-ee' with three syllables instead of four). It turns out that there are surprisingly few crossings of the river in this part of the country. There are a couple in Memphis, but they're major highways, and I couldn't see dragging Gizmo across a two-mile bridge in crowded traffic. Bridges don't usually have much room for horses, and if you get in a jam there's no place to go but off.

Then there's the Caruthersville Bridge on the highway into Dyersburg. Closer, but same deal. Probably too much traffic for a horse. There is another bridge at Cairo, upriver a ways in Missouri, but it's a good stretch out of the way and would add a week or more to the ride.

"How about a ferry?" one of them asked, "There are a couple of 'em."

He told me about the main ferry between Dorena, Missouri and Hickman, Kentucky. It was a few days out of the way, but closer than the Cairo Bridge, and I could probably do that. But before I settled on the Dorena-Hickman route, the other fellow mentioned something about the old Cottonwood Ferry, and his pal said, 'yeah, that's a good idea. I forgot about that.'

Turns out there's a small ferry at a place called Cottonwood Point, or Cottonwood Landing, that's on pretty much the same route we've been traveling. I tried to phone ahead about it, but they weren't listed, and no one seemed to know about it. So, I decided just to chance it and head for the Cottonwood Ferry.

After Gizmo and I left the cabin, we wound our way through the Ozark Mountains, through the rugged hills and into some beautiful lush valleys, with lots of streams and rivers running through them. We crossed a lot of them. Never had to swim any, though. It was good to have fresh water. Easy to keep clean and to wash clothes. Easy to rub my horse down at night. The water brought mosquitos, though, which ended up being their own kind of hell. And those mosquitos got worse as we made our way down into the flatlands of eastern Arkansas and the Missouri Boot Heel.

It was mostly soybean fields out there, with small sharecroppers shacks that people were living in. A lot of 'em were only one or two rooms, and would have a family of six or seven in 'em. Mostly black folk, workin' in the fields. They'd stare at Gizmo and me as we rode past, like we were from another planet or something. One little kid asked me if I was rich, and I told him no, I wasn't. And I asked him why he thought I was rich, and he said because you must be rich to have a horse, and you got a cowboy hat, so you must be rich.

I don't know how some of those folks survive out there. The mosquitos are so thick you can scoop up a handful of 'em right out of the air. Every night I had to spray Gizmo with this insect repellent that I had. I'd spray it on a rag and wipe it in his ears to keep them out, and to keep the deer flies from biting him. Then I'd just spray it right on his body. I know it wasn't good for him, but he was so bitten up that I didn't know what else to do. Swarms of mosquitos flew in both our faces as soon as the sun went down. In some of those little towns big tanker trucks rolled through the streets fogging the whole place with insecticide. I was worried that Gizmo would get sick from eating some of the grass, but so far he hasn't.

And the mosquitos weren't the only thing. It was the dead heat of summer and the humidity must have been up in the eighties or nineties. We were both dripping wet with sweat, and I think we lost more weight just crossing those lowlands than we did crossing the desert back west. It was unbearably hot at night, and I couldn't get inside my sleeping bag to get away from the mosquitos. So I tried to sleep by laying a T-shirt over my face. I got up constantly to see to Gizmo because he would stamp and fidget and swish his tail, trying to get rid of those swarming critters. The deer flies bit him so bad his ears were bleeding. I stuffed some cotton balls in them, which helped a little, but the poor horse was at his wits' end with it all. It was hell, that's all I can say.

We spent a long time crossing those flatlands, and by the time we got to the river, we were both beat. Neither of us had slept more than an hour or so a night, and we were both covered in bites and bumps. I just wanted to quit. If I could have I probably would have, but there was nowhere else to go, so we just kept going. A lot of the land out there actually sits below the level of the Mississippi River, and when the river jumps its banks it floods hundreds of square miles of farmland. After one of those floods, when the water has drained off and the fields have started to dry up again, it brings even more mosquitos. They breed in the stagnant ponds and backwaters left by the flooding. Fogging them with insecticide doesn't seem to stop them.

A day or two's ride from the river, a man told me that yes, there was a little ferry at Cottonwood Point, but that it didn't run all the time. He didn't know what days it ran, so I figured we'd just take our chances. We finally arrived, and sure enough, the ferry was there. Or, what you might call a ferry. Actually, it was just a little raft with a motor on it. You could get three cars on it. Two of them would be parked next to each other, and a third one could be pulled up crossways behind them. The raft had no sides, just little bumpers on the edges made of four-by-fours, to keep the cars from driving into the river. I was pretty nervous about taking Gizmo on that thing, but I couldn't see any way around it. He was pretty bomb proof by then, and I figured he would take it all in stride, but I didn't want to get a half mile out into the river and have him go overboard.

The man running the ferry said he'd take us across for free, and that we'd end up about a half mile downriver from where we left. There was only one car to take across, so they pulled it onto the raft, and then I led Gizmo aboard. I had given it some thought, about what I would do if he went overboard, and I came up with an idea.

I unsaddled my horse for the crossing then borrowed a long piece of one-inch manila rope from the boat captain and draped it around Gizmo just behind his front legs and over his withers. I tied a bowline knot so it wouldn't jam, and I fed the end up between his front legs and through his halter ring. There were some cleats around the sides of the raft that they used to tie it to the dock, so I figured I'd wrap the rope around one of them if he slipped and fell into the river. That way, we could slow the raft and sort of pull him along if need be. The rope around his middle would hold

230

him up, and since it passed through his halter, it would keep his head up. Or so I thought. I crossed my fingers, and we cast off from the dock with the engine chugging along like an old locomotive.

My worries turned out to be unfounded because Gizmo saw this as a chance to catch some sleep. He paid no mind to the fact that he was floating across a mile of water on a big flat piece of wood, and he relaxed and promptly fell sound asleep. He was breathing so heavily, he was almost snoring. At one point, I was afraid he might fall over, but he locked his legs, as horses do, and just stood there with his hind leg cocked, his eyes closed, and his lower lip flapping each time he blew a breath out his nostrils. It was one of those times I wish I could have taken a picture, but my hands were full of one-inch rope.

It turned out to be a lovely ride downstream, and we landed on the eastern bank without incident. That crossing was a benchmark in the ride because I felt as if we had finally made it "back east." I know the Mississippi isn't exactly in the middle of America, but it's always seemed like it to me, as one who has always lived in the west.

Well, once we got up on shore, I thanked the boatman, and we started off down a little back road heading east toward Dyersburg. It was pretty late in the afternoon, and we'd already covered about fourteen miles, not counting the river crossing, so I wanted to find a place to spend the night. There was an abandoned shack on the side of the road, so I pulled Gizmo up behind it and unsaddled. I stashed my gear inside, but figured I'd sleep outdoors if it didn't rain because it was just too hot to stay in that old house.

Then, sure enough, as soon as the sun started to set, swarms of mosquitos appeared. I just couldn't bear the thought of facing one more night of them. The boatman had told me that once we got up into the hills near Dyersburg, they would go away. I didn't know if this was true, but I decided we would move on. I saddled Gizmo, and we headed up the road. I couldn't bring myself to ride him. He'd been through a lot, and it was bad enough that I was making him walk even farther that night.

We ended up walking all night. The mosquitos swarmed all over us, and I kept swinging the end of the lead rope in circles around my face, trying in vain to kill them or scare them off. They were in my eyes and ears. Gizmo's ears were bleeding again, and he would swish his tail at them. I never felt as sorry for an animal as I did for Gizmo then. We walked for hours, until it was almost dawn. I didn't carry a watch, so I didn't know how much time had passed, but it was a long time. We were dead tired, hot, sweaty, and I was truly afraid that Gizmo might get some sort of disease from all those bites.

Then suddenly there were no more mosquitos. We began to climb, and as the grasses of the lowlands gave way to the pine trees of the hills, we were suddenly free. We walked in swarms of them and then, in less than a quarter of a mile, they were gone. I was never so happy in my life. The boatman had been right. And it turns out that we were on the outskirts of Dyersburg, and I didn't even know it. There was no way for me to know where we were because it was pitch-dark all night (no moon), and there were no cars traveling along this back road. But we traveled over forty miles that day, and almost thirty of them had been walking that road all night.

We were both about ready to collapse, so I led Gizmo behind a building that looked like a warehouse, which turned out to be a cotton gin. I tied him to the side of a truck and unsaddled. I sat down and leaned my back against the side of the building and promptly fell asleep. We were awakened a short time later by the men who worked at the gin. They were kind enough to give me some coffee and donuts, and one of them drove off to get some hay for my horse. Before the fellow returned with it, Gizmo had used his charms and conned the men into feeding him almost all their donuts.

*********

Hub sat quietly for a while after I'd finished the story. His gaze was away from me, and when he finally spoke, it was to no one in particular.

"Like I said, that's a helluva horse. Reckon he's earned a little extra grain tonight."

The water of the Mississippi had been impressive. Crossing that river meant a lot to me, even if it meant nothing to my sleeping horse at the time. It flipped a switch on inside me that made me think, *we're really gonna make this ride.* We started from water, and we're headed for water. Life is a journey from ocean to ocean, and water marks our boundaries along the way. It separates places and brings them together at the same time. It gives life its own measure, and it takes it away.

I don't know if it makes me want to urinate, but it stirs up things inside me, just the same.

# MUSIC CITY REFUGE

There weren't many places to put a horse up for the night in the city of Nashville, at least, none that we passed as we inched our way across the southern part of town. I would be staying with my friends Bob and Sarah while we were there for a few days, but I hadn't found anything for Gizmo.

As in other cities, we camped as close as possible to the edge of town the night before, then started very early in the morning in order to make headway before the city awoke. I walked the entire way, leading my horse along the sidewalks, and we tried to remain incognito and as ordinary looking as we could. Our progress was continually interrupted by well-wishers and curiosity seekers, and twice we were stopped by television crews wanting interviews. I gave them each a quick soundbite and left. Gizmo trailed alongside me, his head down, eyes half closed, feet clipping the cracks of the sidewalk in a dragging gait that embodied his exhausted spirit.

He was wearing his fifth set of shoes, and they were paper thin. I knew I would need to replace them soon. We were both beaten down and tired from the long, hot, mosquito-infested journey through the flatlands of Arkansas and Missouri. It was much cooler here, and the biting pests had disappeared. Although we both felt a sense of relief that a great burden had been lifted, we were both trail weary and exhausted. We needed the layover badly. By mid-afternoon, we were both physically drained. I had connected with Bob and Sarah, but still had nowhere to put Gizmo. I wasn't panicked, though. I knew we could always spend the night in a graveyard then search for something the next day.

Luck was with us, however, and I met three young men who lived in a house with a large section of land next to it. They offered to let me keep Gizmo there during our layover. It was about a half acre of fenced grassland that offered good grazing for a few days. I walked around and explored to make sure there wasn't any broken glass, dangerous obstacles, or other things that could hurt Gizmo. I repaired a broken section of wire fencing, and I managed to find a small galvanized water tank and dragged it over near the house to a water faucet. I turned Gizmo out and watched as he dropped to his knees and rolled, jumped to his feet, then repeated the process three or four times. I thanked the men, told them I'd be back later to check on my horse, and then threw my gear into Bob's old Jeep and rode to his place.

A couple hours later I returned to find Gizmo reclining peacefully in the grass near the water tank. He jumped to his feet and whinnied when he saw me, then came over to nuzzle me and allow me to scratch his ears. I had managed to get a hundred-pound sack of Omelene, a feed supplement that would help Gizmo regain his strength during our stay. I fed him some, brushed him down again, and finally left for the night. I wasn't used to being separated, and I always worried about him when I was away from him at night.

I arrived the next morning to feed him and spend a little time with him. One of the men came out of the house. He was shirtless, shoeless, and drinking a beer.

"Lady next door ain't real happy about your horse", he said, "Said she's gonna call the health department."

I considered the situation for a moment then replied, "Guess I ought to go over and talk to her."

"She don't like us very much," the young man said. "Keeps callin' the cops every time we play music or party a little."

"I'll go have a word with her", I said.

I made my way around the front of the property toward her house. Gizmo followed me along the fence line. The fence turned and ran between the two properties, alongside the driveway to her home. I walked up the drive to the side of the house and knocked on the door.

A stern looking, middle-aged woman appeared at the door.

"Yes?" she said, more a statement than a question.

"Hello, ma'am. My name's John, and that's my horse, Gizmo, over there in the field next door."

Her arms were locked across the front of her in unyielding body language that looked like a fortress. "Not supposed to have horses here", she said. "Ain't zoned for 'em."

"Ma'am, he and I have traveled over three thousand miles, and we've still got a few hundred more to go. I reckon all he wants is a little rest and to be left alone. It's only for a few days, and I'm sorry if he's a bother."

Her eyes remained fixed on something in the distance and would not meet mine. She stood, unsmiling and uncompromising. "Hmmmph ..." she uttered.

"Is he making noise?" I asked. "Did he keep you up last night?"

"No, that's not the problem."

I asked what the problem was.

"Ain't supposed to be here," she replied.

"Well, I don't really know where he is supposed to be," I said. "And well, I'm just tryin' to take care of him, and ..." I paused, then continued. "Would it help if I stayed there with him?"

She made no reply, so I carried on. "I could see to it that he doesn't make too much noise or have any loud parties."

My feeble joke wasn't well received, and her frown only seemed to grow deeper.

Finally, I appealed to any love of animals that she might have. "Y'know," I said tentatively, "Gizmo likes women a whole lot more than he does men. I'm guessin' he'd enjoy your company a lot better than those rowdy guys next door."

She looked over, and her eyes met mine for the first time. It took a bit of encouragement, but I finally coaxed her down the steps and around the fence to where Gizmo was waiting. I persuaded her to walk up to him and asked her to pet him. She was reluctant, but followed me. I could see that she was afraid.

"He won't hurt you", I told her, "He loves to have his ears scratched."

She reached out tentatively to touch his nose. The first touch led to another, then another, and once she started petting him, she got into it and seemed to enjoy it, though she retained her reserved manner. Gizmo was a good sport about it and played along.

"He's very good company early in the morning," I said, "and he likes biscuits and gravy, if that makes any difference." Then I added, "He especially likes biscuits with sorghum on them."

I think that won her over.

*LOGBOOK:*
*Went with Bob and Sarah to a bluegrass music festival at Vanderbilt University today. Amazing music by the New Grass Revival, Norman Blake, Tut Taylor, Mac Wiseman, the Osborne Brothers, Jim and Jesse, and a bunch of others. There were a million beautiful women there, and I was dumbstruck. I hadn't realized how far gone from civilization I have taken myself.*

Gizmo stayed on her side of the field for the rest of our time in Nashville. I moved the water tank across the field next to her house and used her water. I stopped to check on him several times each day and usually found her there, sitting on her porch, keeping an eye on him. I left the sack of Omelene with her, with instructions on how much to feed him and a warning that too much could be harmful. She was careful to give him exactly what he needed and supplemented it with carrots, apples, and yes, biscuits with sorghum smeared on them.

On the morning that Gizmo and I mounted up to leave Nashville, she looked at me and said sternly, "You take care of that horse now, you hear?"

I could see tears in those stoic eyes of hers.

LOGBOOK:
*We've left Nashville behind us and are back out on this two lane, dodging the passing cars and trucks. Passed through Hermitage and Mt. Juliet on our way to Lebanon. A big bus pulled off the road ahead of us and Jimmy Martin "the King of Bluegrass", got out to say hello. Jimmy and the guys in his his band all stood out on the side of the two lane with Gizmo and me, talking about horses, hunting dogs, and bluegrass music. It was a pretty bizarre scene. One of those "what am I doing here?" moments.*

# HINDSIGHT

They say that the measure of a man's charity is not how much he gives, it's how much he has left over *after* he gives. That makes sense to me. The billionaire philanthropist who donates a million dollars to a cause isn't nearly as charitable as the poor man who gives his last ten dollars to a friend in need.

Now that I'm old, I can look back and see that, at twenty-four, I still had decades left ahead of me. Not anymore, though. Not unless some miracle of science comes along that will magically extend my life far into the future, and I won't be holding my breath waiting for it. No, I don't have decades ahead of me now, but I have decades behind me, and with them comes hindsight. And it occurs to me that I can measure age just like I can measure generosity. Your age isn't how many years you've lived. It's how much hindsight you've managed to acquire.

Some might say that hindsight equals experience, and in ways I suppose that's true. But I reckon that hindsight lies closer to wisdom than it does to mere experience. Somewhere in these pages I've said that wisdom is a combination of experience mixed with compassion. Hindsight seems to me to be a mixture of experience and deliberation. It's the result of looking back at your experiences and reflecting upon them. Hopefully, you learn something, but sometimes you don't. Hopefully, you'll gain a bit of wisdom, but not always.

There are two ways to view things in hindsight. One is to look back and wish you had done things differently, now that your mistakes are painfully clear. The other is to look ahead and, knowing your past mistakes, try to do better in the future. There's no reason why you can't do both at the same time, and in fact a lot of us do. We look back and wish we hadn't done something while we look ahead and try not to repeat our mistakes.

I'm not one for regrets. There are things I wish had gone differently. A failed marriage that put my daughters through things they didn't deserve. A father who left when I was young. My mother dying. I could draw up a list. We all could. But a list of your past problems is different from reflecting upon each one individually. A list becomes your burden to carry, and sometimes it becomes your prophecy. Making a list of past experiences is not the same as hindsight. I stay away from making lists. I look at my past experiences—both the good ones and the bad ones—one at a time.

And neither do I draw up lists of the positive things, but they're a lot easier to recall. The birth of each of my daughters. Raising Gizmo from a colt. Countless gigs and sessions played, the musician's I've played with, the cowboys I've made saddles for. I don't need a list for the good stuff because it naturally comes to mind for me.

I'm one of those people who learns how to use a hammer by whacking his thumb a few times, so I tend to view my life as a series of mistakes. Any wisdom I have has been achieved by learning what *not* to do. I have never learned from my successes. I'm not sure anyone learns from success. Failure is the real teacher as long as you view it in hindsight and figure out what went wrong. I would much prefer someone tell me what I did wrong than to receive patronizing praise from them. I can fix the problems they mention, and though praise feels good, it doesn't teach me anything.

Ah, but who doesn't like a little praise now and then? I certainly do. It's nice to get a few strokes here and there, to know that people appreciate you. It's healthy, and it feels good. You might not learn anything from it, but life's not only about learning. It's about giving and sharing, loving and hating, feeling bad and yes, feeling good. I felt good most of the time when people praised Gizmo and me as we traveled across the continent. But I was uncomfortable in the spotlight of television and newspapers, and I didn't seek that sort of notoriety—in fact, I mostly avoided it when I could.

It's no accident that, as a musician, I became a sideman instead of a front man. I'm a good musician, perfectly capable of fronting a band and being the one in the spotlight. But I have always preferred the anonymity that comes with being in the shadows, playing off to the side of the stage, behind the singer and out of the glare. I've never been comfortable being the center of attention. From my vantage, I can study those in the audience, and I can consider the ways in which they interact with the artist at the center of the stage. I am free to reflect upon where I am, and upon those around me. The artist in the spotlight is a prisoner, trapped by the focus of the crowd. Admiration and acclaim heaped upon the singer can feel good, and many thrive on this sort of attention. But to someone like me the price becomes the loss of freedom, the confinement that comes along with it all.

One last thing about hindsight, experience and wisdom too. None of them are worth much without a heaping helping of curiosity. Gizmo was a curious horse. Some horses are naturally curious, others not so much. Gizmo was inquisitive. He always had his ears pointed toward something. He questioned his surroundings. He questioned me. He was so naturally curious that, in hindsight, I often thought that if I had just tied myself to his tail and let him go, we would have made the journey in far less time. And the trail would have been a lot smoother. He was just a four-year-old, probably too young for a trip like that, and I seriously considered not taking him on the ride. In the end, it was his curiosity that won me over. He wanted to know things. He was alert, observant, and always had his antennae up, listening for new things.

I was always a curious person. That's true, no matter which way you read it. Curious means odd. Everyone thinks they're odd or special. I've been told that I am odd, but I view it as a compliment. And I do know I'm odd. I know this through a lifetime of comparing myself with those around me. Choosing to live with a horse for seven months on the trail is a clue. Riding freight trains and hitchhiking around the country with a guitar are other clues. Hell, being left handed and not bothering to wear socks that match… even these small things place a person outside the realm of what is considered *normal*. I know this through hindsight. Non-conformists are usually odd, and I'm nothing if not a nonconformist. I'm not trying to boast about this or make a big deal of it. In fact, I'm having to force myself to mention it here, only to make a point.

I'm curious as in odd, but mostly I'm curious as in inquisitive. And that's the important one. Because the drive to know things, to explore ideas and concepts, and to find out what the universe is made of allows you to use your hindsight to turn around and look forward, rather than to dwell in the past. Hell, it's taken me over forty years to get around to writing this book. I haven't exactly spent my life reliving the ride. I've made a point of not allowing it to define who I am. But that doesn't mean I haven't been thinking about it, because I sure have. Nearly every day I give a thought to my adventure with Gizmo. I reflect upon what we did together, what it meant back then, and what it means now. I was curious then. Curious about what was on the other side of the hill. Curious about America and the people in it. And I was curious about myself as being one of those people. I wanted to know where I fit in, and I wanted to know what it would be like to unplug myself, to have only a horse to share my life with for a while. My curiosity drove me then, and it still drives me today.

Following your curiosity is easy. Just add "I wonder" to your sentences, perhaps even those you are already sure about, so that they become questions: "I wonder what" or "I wonder about" or "I wonder if" or "I wonder when" or "I wonder how". You end up with sentences like, "I wonder about cars on the freeway" or "I wonder what dry ice feels like" or "I wonder how to make a saddle" or "I wonder if I can make it across the continent on a horse." You get the idea. I've spent my life doing this. I don't spend my time sitting down and writing those sentences, but my brain works like that. I just naturally think that way. I'm lucky that I do, and I feel a bit sorry for anyone who doesn't.

I was always a curious man. Gizmo was always a curious horse. We were brothers.

# CHICKEN TODAY, FEATHERS TOMORROW

I'm riding my sorrel companion down a two lane backroad through northeastern Tennessee. In Texas, they would call it a farm-to-market road. Sometimes it has a grass shoulder to ride on, sometimes not. The road has seen better days, but it retains its utility and manages to serve its original purpose of providing a means of driving farm vehicles (tractors, combines, cotton trucks, and others) across the local countryside without interfering with those driving on the main roads and highways. There isn't much traffic along this route, save for the occasional car or truck that passes on its way to or from town.

Gizmo trots smoothly in a gait practiced over months. The journey has covered more than three thousand miles so far, and his long pasterns, sloped at graceful angles that match his shoulders, allow for an easy and effortless pace that covers ground at roughly seven miles per hour. At this rate, we meet the our usual limit, twenty miles per day, within three or four hours, depending upon how much time I spend on the ground, walking, and leading him, or how often a motorist stops to take our picture and talk. The days are getting shorter and because of these frequent interruptions, we often stop short of our twenty-mile goal when we run out of daylight. The long-range goal—the finish line at the Atlantic Ocean in Virginia—is still a good way off, and I view the long ride less as a challenge and more as a chore now, less as something to overcome and more as simply something to be finished with.

Today follows the pattern of the past few. After several news stories on various Nashville television and radio stations, and with the publicity accumulated from local newspaper pieces back through Tennessee, Missouri, and Arkansas, it's difficult to find any time to myself. Aloneness is a thing of the past. I have once again taken to hiding in cemeteries at night—that is, when I can sneak my horse into one without being seen. People are good-hearted and well-meaning; they love to talk, and when they're finished, they wish us a safe journey and caution me against all the bad people out there who would do us harm. So far, the only evidence that those sorts of people exist is on the TV news, and I'm not so sure the news is representative of the America we have crossed. Still, I appreciate the concern for Gizmo and me.

A grey sedan slows down ahead of us and pulls off onto the grassy shoulder. The road's shoulder is invariably filled with broken glass and discarded beer cans, and I don't allow my horse to trot there. I wonder how many of the cars that pull off for us will drive away with punctured tires, but there are too many who want to talk, and I have given up trying to warn them. The driver of the grey sedan doesn't exactly climb out of his car. Rather, he seems to unfold himself as he emerges. He is enormously tall and has a thin, wiry build. It is a mystery how he managed to fit into the car at all. As the man approaches, Gizmo stops automatically, having trained himself that this is now the daily routine. When someone speaks to me, Gizmo knows he's supposed to stop.

The driver is in his fifties or sixties. He introduces himself, and I reach down to shake hands. I remain in the saddle as we chat for a while about the ride, about Tennessee, and about other things. He says he's a farmer and that his place is just up the road. He offers us a place to stay the night. I normally turn these offers down, but when he mentions feed and a stall for my horse, I'm sold. After our chat, he gives me directions, and I thank him. Then he folds himself back into the sedan and drives off.

Three hours later we arrive at the entrance to a large estate. Once again I am reminded of the irony of my mode of travel, and of my skewed worldview from the back of a horse. The man had probably driven here in less than fifteen minutes. I pull the slip of paper from my jacket pocket with the directions written on it because I think I am mistaken. The address is the right one, but this place isn't a farm—it's more like an eighteenth century plantation. The fences are rock walls, like many we have seen all through this country—made from the rocks and boulders that were removed from the land to make it tillable. The rocks were laid by hand without mortar. These fences were built long before the Civil War, most likely by slaves. They probably look much the same now as when they were made. It doesn't look so much like a plantation as it does a movie set, something you'd see in *Gone With The Wind*. I'm still not sure I have found the right place, and I check the directions on the paper again.

I had a picture in my mind of a weathered barn nestled next to an old frame farmhouse, some corrals, and maybe an outbuilding or two for tools and storage—the sorts of farms we have been riding past lately. Instead, I behold a magnificent two-story Antebellum mansion, its huge white columns supporting a covered porch that wraps around the entire second floor, a porch meant to duplicate its counterpart on the ground floor. The windows are as big as hangar doors. Those on the front of the elegant gabled dormers that perch above the second-story porch serve to define the house's roofline and suggest a third story. The structure continues to pull my eye upward until it comes to rest upon the widow's walk, augmented by a glassed cupola, which boasts a cast iron weathervane in the shape of a sailing ship.

As we make our way up the tree-lined drive toward the house, I see a large stone two-story building off to the right behind the main house. I guess (correctly) that it must be the stable area (something I have always referred to as "the barn," though that would be woefully inadequate in reference to a building such as this). It is a splendid structure—nearly as large as the house—and rests in the shade of several very large trees. The pitch of its shingled roof is drastic and does not match the gentle slope of the main house's—the first clue that this structure predates the house by many years. Its enormous windows are set well back into the walls, and yet I can see that they are closer to the outer surface than to the inner, and I realize the walls are massively thick. The second-floor windows are arranged in pairs around the building, with small porches hung beneath them. The large pair of sliding barn doors stand open at the stable's midpoint, allowing the autumn breeze to regulate both temperature and ventilation inside.

As we approach the house, with its circular drive in front, the tall man emerges from the enormous double doors that mark the residence's main entrance. With him are two black men dressed in the uniform of house staff, and an elegantly dressed woman about the same age as the man. He gives instructions to the two men, one of whom takes the reins as I step down from Gizmo. The other extends his hand—at first I don't know why—and motions that he wants to take my backpack for me. As the first man leads Gizmo toward the barn, I notice that he leaves slack in the rein and does not pull on the horse, but allows him to follow. The rein continues to hang loose as the two walk away. Because he does not pull Gizmo, I know immediately that this man knows his way around horses, and I feel better knowing this.

After the owner introduces me to his wife, I follow them into the house, where I find myself in a museum. Huge paintings, which I imagine must be hundreds of years old, cover the walls of the rooms. Through the windows, I can see what a cowboy friend used to call "nekkid art"—statues of nudes from Greece and Italy that I assume are the real thing and not fakes. Some have water fountains flowing from various strategic orifices, and some are employed as garden ornaments. Looking around the room, I see that the dining room table is enormous—twelve chairs around it. I'm told that we're not in the formal dining room, and this is not the dining room table, but only a secondary one used for informal gatherings. I later learn that the real dining room and its table are much larger.

I am shown to my room, a second-story corner bedroom with a view of the stable area from its private balcony. I can see Gizmo there. He pokes his head through the top half of a stall door, where he munches on a mouthful of hay. He retreats into the stall to grab another and returns. The loose grass drops from the sides of his mouth as he takes in his surroundings.

One of the staff members (butler, servant, help, domestic?—I don't know how to address him) knocks on my door to inform me that the family will gather downstairs in an hour, and would I like to join them? I answer that yes, I would be happy to, thank you very much. My pack has been deposited on a shelf in the walk-in closet. Miraculously, so have my saddlebags, and I have no idea how they got there so quickly. After a quick shower in the enormous bathroom, I avail myself of the cleanest clothes I have, which, embarrassingly, are not as clean as I wish they were. Later, when I return to my room, I will notice that my dirty clothes have been cleaned and pressed and laid neatly on the shelf next to my pack.

In what is referred to as the sitting room, I find the man and his wife, along with their children. The son is perhaps seventeen or eighteen, dressed in slacks and a polo shirt, his hair meticulous, his teeth white as fresh cotton. He is perfectly groomed. His speech belies the fact that the owner is his father, and the two couldn't be more different. Whereas the father's is plain, outspoken, and reveals rural country roots, the son's is eloquent, reserved, and suggests years of private school refinement. The young man is serious and somber with a severe countenance, as though a lifetime of overly zealous tutors have managed to scrub away any semblance of a sense of humor. He has taken up the mantle of maintaining appearances from his mother.

I shift my gaze across the room to the daughter—a young woman in her early twenties—who sits across from me and eyes me intently. She is silent while the parents establish a formal manner of communication and then guide the conversation toward a more informal one. I marvel at their ability to direct and control the topics of discussion and sense that this is second nature to them. When the daughter seems to feel the time is appropriate, she enters into the dialog freely, being neither shy nor inhibited. In contrast to her younger brother, she is dressed casually in jeans and flannel shirt, her long hair tied back in a haphazard fashion that speaks to functionality more than fashion. A weathered jacket is draped across the arm of her chair. I feel a bit uncomfortable looking at her because she is beautiful, because she looks at me with such intensity, and because her parents are sitting right there.

She says she has been at the stable visiting Gizmo. I can see that she has fallen in love, but I have learned my lesson well. She is in love with my horse and not with me. She overflows with this love and cannot help gushing about him. She admits that she has brushed him and given him some corn and, slightly embarrassed, says that she hopes I don't mind. I thank her, and she blushes and continues, going on and on about what kind eyes he has, how intelligent he is, and what a marvelous horse he is. She exclaims that oh, what sights he must have seen along the way. I begin to think that maybe she really is interested in me, but decide I will not fall into that trap again and resign myself to playing second fiddle to my horse.

I find myself once more sliding down a slippery slope toward a woman's charms, and even though I know in advance what the outcome will be, I find myself smitten with her. Still, I try my hardest not to let it show, and I try to include everyone in what I have to say, to avoid steering the conversation only to her. But I know I'm failing, and I know her parents know it too. I decide to keep quiet, but the family won't let me. I am a captive guest, and finally I give up and try to make the best of it.

The farm, says the father, was built by slaves. They cleared the fields and used the rocks and boulders to construct the walls and fences that surround the place as I had suspected. The stable was part of the original farmhouse that was built in 1781 but was later converted into a carriage house and stalls with slaves quarters upstairs. It too was built using these stones. Some of the house staff still live there. The house we are sitting in was built in 1821, a hundred fifty-three years ago. It is unimaginable to me to have lived in a place all my life, to have my family's history linked to the same location for so long. I stare at a large idyllic painting—it must be at least six-by-eight feet—and think that it must be worth more than the combined lifetime incomes of my entire family. I smile when I think of that.

We eventually sit down to dinner. By this time, the mother has had a few drinks (mixed drinks, but I don't know what kind) and has loosened up considerably. She begins to compare her husband to me. She says that when he was a younger man, he would not have been afraid to do the sort of thing I am doing, but that now, he has become old and scared. Her complaints become accusations that quickly escalate into a mean-spirited indictment.

I become more and more uncomfortable with this line of talk and change the subject by asking various questions of each of the family members. I ask the father how deep they have to drill for water in their wells. I ask the son what university he is planning to attend. I ask the wife questions about where she grew up. And I ask the daughter what sort of riding she does. This seems to work, and each replies in turn, and it mollifies the wife. The daughter asks if I know anything about Arabian horses, and I reply that yes, I have worked with Arabians but that I'm not exactly an expert or anything. She asks if I would like to see her horses after dinner. I look around the table for approval or disapproval and can't tell whether it would be inappropriate to accept, or whether it would be an insult to decline. Finally, I simply say, "Sure, I'd love to," and everyone seems okay with it.

The autumn evenings have been turning cool here in eastern Tennessee, and this one is no exception. After dinner, I grab my worn out denim jacket and walk with the daughter to the stable where I formally introduce her to Gizmo. I can see that he has achieved hero status with her. They say that a smile begins with the eyes, and in her case it's true. They sparkle when she looks at my horse, and I wish some of that infatuation was directed at me, but I know I will simply bear the ache of being smitten and let it go at that. She shows me two of her Arabian horses—a three-year-old chestnut mare and an older bay gelding—and talks about preparing the mare for English Pleasure competitions and riding the gelding in Park Seat show classes. Having a peripheral knowledge of these disciplines, I am content to listen quietly, watching her eyes as she expounds upon the finer points of each.

When darkness settles, we head back to the house, and she takes my arm as we walk. I don't want to reach our destination—I want this to last—but once there, we settle into one of the sitting rooms—to me, they all seem like small concert halls—with the parents. Her brother has left, so it's just the four of us.

The mother seems calm and placated now, and the discussion continues where it left off earlier, but without the tension it held then. I'm not sure why, but I sense the brother had something to do with that, and now that he is gone, things are running smoothly. I enjoy learning a bit about the history of the area, though I realize the viewpoint I am hearing is skewed toward that of members of the ruling class. I imagine its narration would be quite different if recounted by one of the staff.

The evening concludes with the man making an elegant toast to Gizmo and me. Toast making comes easily to him, I observe, and he takes pride in his ability to embellish an otherwise simple expression of goodwill into something eloquent and articulate. I thank them again for their hospitality, and everyone retires to their bedrooms.

Upon entering my room, I notice the bed has been turned down and a comforter has been laid at its foot, in case I might need it in the night. An antique porcelain wash basin and pitcher have been placed on the nightstand beside the bed, along with a small saucer of mints. A servant knocks lightly on the door and asks if I need anything, to which I reply no, thank you. I retrieve my logbook from my pack and take a seat at the desk, where I begin to write about the day's events. I hear another quiet knock at the door, and I say, "Yes? Come in." But the door does not open.

I get up to see who is there. I am somewhat taken aback to see the daughter there, although this is not entirely unwelcome. She asks to come in, and I ask if that would be wise, but she brushes past me and into the room. Not knowing what to do, I shut the door and turn to face her.

She has on a silk robe, which immediately causes me to think about what she might or might not have on beneath it, so I blush and turn to stare woodenly out the window, hoping to catch a glimpse of my horse in the moonlight and to take my mind off her. Again I mention that this might be a bad idea, to which she replies, don't you like me? I tell her that I like her very much, but that her being here in my bedroom isn't appropriate. I start to say something about her parents, and she interrupts. You have a funny way of showing it, she says.

I am now stricken with fear. As she approaches, I head to the other side of the room, to another set of windows that faces the southwest. While I pretend to be lost in thought (a very lame attempt), she comes up behind and slips her arm through mine, coming to rest beside me and leaning against me with her head against my arm. My mouth is suddenly dry, I take my breath in short gasps, and I realize I have been here before. I remember the water tank back in Arizona. I thought I had learned my lesson, but now I know I hadn't. *This time,* I think, *I won't put my arm around her.* But she turns to face me and reaches up to kiss me, and one thing leads to another.

The next morning, I am in the saddle, and I bid our farewell to the parents. The son is nowhere to be seen, but I spot the daughter through an upstairs window. I try to keep my cool when she blows me a kiss, and I reply discreetly by tipping my hat and nodding. I turn my horse down the tree-lined drive and back onto the two lane to the east.

Twenty-two miles down the road, late in the day, we are searching for a place to spend the night. We come upon a lonely tobacco shed that leans to one side in a decades-old fight against gravity and the wind. It is held upright only by the moldy stacks of decayed tobacco piled inside. On its lee side is a pen that houses several pigs. As it begins to rain lightly, I pull Gizmo inside the shed, unsaddle, and make camp that night with our new porcine neighbors. Before I fall asleep, I think about the daughter the night before, and about the pigs who are our neighbors tonight, and I smile.

# THINGS THAT GO BUMP IN THE DARK

We wandered through Knoxville today. I pushed us into town as far as I could last night, and we camped out in the veterans' cemetery. The grass had been cut pretty short, but Gizmo managed a decent meal. It's hard getting all the way through a big city like this with a horse. I don't like having to ride him on the pavement of the streets and, besides, it's dangerous. So, I end up walking most of the way and leading him. I don't mind, but it's slow going. People stop us all the time. Now, I try not to stop to talk. I look for a place on the map and tell them to meet us there in the evening, and we keep moving.

I was supposed to meet up with a fellow at the University of Tennessee to do a radio show. I had no idea the place was so big. I got lost trying to find my way around the campus, so finally I just blew it off and kept heading east. We didn't quite make it out of town, but I found a nice park down in a little hollow, nestled among the big buildings downtown. It's a bit weird because even though we're hidden here, I can still see the tall office buildings sticking up above the trees.

So here I sit, in a dugout. It's not a mud house, it's an actual dugout. First base dugout, to be precise. I'm sitting in the one that says "Home Team," and Gizmo is grazing in the infield. It's dark but he's easy to spot under the full moon out there near the third base line. The baseball field is part of a small community complex here. It's concealed down in this wooded area, a little paradise right in the middle of Knoxville. We stumbled upon it late in the day as it was getting dark. I'm really thankful for it because I thought we were going to end up walking the streets of downtown Knoxville in the middle of the night. But here we are, hidden away in this beautiful little park. The field is fenced so I don't have to stake Gizmo out. He can run free for the night. I have a roof over me, which is good because it's been sprinkling a little bit. I should be able to stay dry here.

When we got here earlier this evening, I unsaddled Gizmo, brushed him down, and turned him out into the field. Then I stowed the gear and pulled out a paperback novel (*Action at the Bitterroot* by Paul Evan Lehman) along with the remaining Fig Newtons someone had given me earlier today. The sun had set, but still a little light remained, so I settled down to read. Like I said, it's almost a full moon tonight, so I was able to read for a while. There were three Fig Newtons in the bag, and I ate them for dinner as I read.

A car drove down into park where we are and pulled into the parking lot across the way. It was soon followed by another, and then others. There is a small community building here, and the people all got out of their cars and went in. I figured they were having some sort of meeting. The occupants of one of the cars, a middle-aged couple, spotted Gizmo, and they came over to see what was going on. We spoke for a few minutes, and they told me they had seen us on the television news from Nashville. They asked if I would like some cake and coffee, which of course sounded great to me. So, I told Gizmo I'd be right back and went with them to the clubhouse.

There was a big group of people there—maybe thirty or more—and they were very friendly and all greeted me warmly. I asked about their meeting, and what sort of group they were, and one of them told me it was the local *KC* group, and that they meet every Monday evening. I had no idea what that was, so I just let it go at that. There were two big chocolate cakes sitting on a table next to a large coffee urn, along with a bunch of coffee mugs, forks, spoons, and paper plates. I was trying not to stare at the cakes, but they were huge rectangles of dark chocolate, and the idea of scarfing down a bunch of that sugar and caffeine was damned hard to resist. I was hoping they'd see my longing looks and take pity on me and offer me some, but things suddenly got a bit strange.

We were ushered into another room, where I saw a bunch of chairs arranged in a circle. The Leader Man (I never did learn his name) asked us all to take a seat, so we did. Then he said that before we began, we needed to create some vibrational healing energy and send it to someone named Mary or Martha. I didn't quite catch her name, so I'm not sure which. Then they turned out all the lights, and all of a sudden, we were sitting there in the dark. I was getting a bit uncomfortable with it all, but I didn't want to spoil my chances for cake and coffee, so I just sat quietly for the time being.

Someone turned on a slide projector, and there was a big screen and they had this big picture of a lady's face there (it was Mary or Martha or whatever her name was). The man said she was in the hospital getting a procedure done (I didn't pay attention, so I don't know what kind) and that she needed the vibrations we could send her. So we sat in the dark looking at this lady's face for about five minutes, which seemed more like an hour to me because I could smell the coffee from the other room. I was looking at her face, but all I could see was chocolate cake.

Just when I thought we were finished, Mister Leader Man flipped it to another slide and we had to do the same thing, this time for an elderly couple named Jim and Barbara (he pronounced it "*JEE-yum aind BAHR-bruh*"), who couldn't make it tonight because of Jim's phlebitis. So the leader said we should all think of Jim's swollen veins and send vibrations to help shrink them. But I couldn't keep my mind off the cake, and I thought, *I wonder if they have strawberries, or maybe some whipped cream.* And then I thought, *if I send out my energy to shrink Jim's veins, will it make mine swell?* Anyway, after a long time of looking at Jim with the swelled up veins and his wife Barbara, they finally turned the lights back on. I was ready for some cake.

But no, that wasn't happening just yet. Mister Leader Man put up another slide, though I couldn't see it too well because the lights were on. It was an old picture of a guy with glasses, and I figured it was from the 1920s or 30s. He looked like he was talking on the phone, except he didn't have a phone. He just had his hand up to his ear, like he was listening to his thumb. Maybe he was just scratching, I don't know. Anyway, it turns out that it was a picture of Edgar Cayce. I had learned about him a few years ago when I was spending the night with some psychic hippies in a hobo jungle in California. So I at least knew who he was, and I figured out that this group isn't the local KC group like I thought the guy had said. It's the local *Cayce* group, as in *Edgar*.

And it turns out they thought they had somehow manifested Gizmo and me through some kind of enlightened energy transfer, or whatever Mister Leader Man called it, and we were there to bring some sort of new age enlightenment to them. I don't know. It all sounded wacky. Most of them looked like they were lawyers or worked in bank buildings. They all drove nice cars. And I'm thinking they were mostly pretty well-to-do. It's for sure they were looking for some answers to something, but I didn't know what they might be. So I figured I'd just let them go on thinking that Gizmo and I were a couple of messiah types because, by this time, I wasn't gonna leave without a cup of coffee and some grub.

Mister Leader Man had a nice suit and tie on. In fact, once I saw how expensive his clothes looked, I noticed that everybody was well dressed. Well, everybody except me. I was glad I wasn't wearing my gun, though come to think of it, they might have seen that as another sign. So, we did what they called a *sharing circle*, which means that we sat around in a circle and shared stuff, one by one. Most of them—no, *all* of them—talked about their own problems and how they were working to overcome their fears and doubts, and how they were aligning energy and manifesting stuff, and releasing tension and conflict from other planes. Those sorts of things.

I was going over in my mind what I should talk about, but when it came around to me, I ended up saying that they could all just use Gizmo's and my arrival here as a sign that points in the direction they're heading. I made up some doubletalk nonsense on the spot as it came into my head. I don't remember what I told them, exactly, but it made a big impression on them, and I had the feeling that some of them thought I was the second coming. They acted like they wanted to kiss the hem of my garment. It made me a little uncomfortable, and it felt creepy, but at least I didn't have to talk about myself any more after that. They were convinced that Gizmo and I were making this ride just for them because we're headed for Virginia Beach and that's where Edgar Cayce was from. They called it an undeniable sign from Cayce himself. I thought about denying it, but then I thought, *what the heck, I don't know the guy, maybe they're right,* and I also thought about the cake and coffee again and didn't want to mess that up. And I was hoping for some whipped cream with it.

They talked about what sorts of reincarnations they expected, like what sorts of people they had been in past lives and what they were hoping for the next time around. One guy said he had been a scientist in Atlantis in his past life.

I thought he'd said *Atlanta,* so I said, "Yeah, it's still pretty warm down there this time of year, isn't it?"

Then Mister Leader Man read a bunch of quotes from a Cayce book, mostly about spreading light and synchronizing your dreams and the sorts of things that tend to fly right past me because I don't understand any of it. Mister Leader Man called it dream stuff. All this talk about dream stuff was making me sleepy, and by the time he finished reading I was having to pinch my leg to keep from drifting off.

I was thinking about trying to excuse myself and was going to tell them that I needed to check on my horse, but right about then the session broke up, and we all stood up and went back into the room with the cake and coffee. I didn't care about manners anymore, so I went right to the head of the line. I don't know if it was because of all the waiting, but that was the best chocolate cake I ever had. I ate a piece then snuck two more. I drank a bunch of coffee. There's something about empty calories and caffeine that seems healthy in the right circumstances. I'm pretty sure I could live on those two items alone. The thing I noticed then was that almost none of them ate any of the cake. I figure they must not have been hungry.

And here's the payoff: When everyone was leaving, a lady said there was cake left over and do you want to take it with you? So, I ended up with a whole cake and part of another one. Oh, and she gave me a plastic jug with the rest of the coffee too. I told her I'd leave the jug on the front porch in the morning.

So here I sit, in the first base dugout, watching my horse in the infield, like he's going after ground balls. I don't know if we were the answer to anyone's prayers, but those folks were sure the answer to mine. I'm full and content. Gizmo's out there eating a whole cake. He has chocolate all over his nose.

# NEWS AS ENTERTAINMENT

Being interviewed by the news media can be like being taken out to dinner at a bad Thai restaurant. You're flattered and grateful for the invitation, but by the time you finish the meal you end up feeling a bit like you've contracted a venereal disease. I think 1974 was the year I first became aware that news was only entertainment disguised as information. I'm not certain most people truly saw it like that at the time. Oh sure, there was talk about how the television news had adopted a commercial feel, with its highly paid news anchors and fancy sets, but the idea of a ubiquitous news machine that was focused entirely upon entertainment and the sale of air time was still in its infancy back then. Most still considered it a service, and a news program was supposed to simply relate what was going on in the world, without bias.

People my age witnessed the birth of *infotainment* (though it wasn't called that back then), but we didn't have a clue about what the broadcast media would eventually become. I could see that the news was packaged and sold much like it always had been, but I also saw that its commodification was accelerating (and I didn't even know what "commodification" was back then). It was plain to me because Gizmo and I became the commodity being sold.

We encountered reporters from a lot of publications—big city and small town papers and magazines—that featured stories about our ride. It didn't take long to figure out that every reporter who came to interview me had a pre-written story, ready to go. It was like a TV dinner, pre-packaged and frozen, and they merely had to pop it into the microwave and heat it up. All the reporters needed was for me to fill in the blanks for them. The selling point for microwave dinner is the picture on the box, not the food inside.

The ride was a human interest piece. It wasn't a hard hitting news story. That part was understandable, and I didn't mind. But I wanted our journey to be more than a quick diversion for readers. I had hoped it would inspire people, even if only a few. I didn't mind that the interviews focused on the "lone cowboy with the horse" angle. And since I wasn't making the ride to support a cause, and I knew the story resonated with people, I wanted them to be able to fantasize and dream the way I had and to take a little bit of

Gizmo and me into their own lives. But I wanted them to see me as more than just a cliché cowboy, a "yes ma'am, no ma'am" silent type, simple minded and strong, an actor in a B western. I wanted them to see Gizmo as more than just a horse. I wanted them to see him as an intelligent creature, one with thoughts and feelings and moods, a compatriot and friend to a man whose story was far more complex than simple tales told through sound bites.

It's true, I wasn't making the ride for others—I was doing it for myself—but if the media wanted to tell our story, I wanted it to be for the benefit of people and not for our glorification, or for the profit of media corporations. Sound a bit idealistic? Yep, that was me.

I was fascinated at how predictable the reporters seemed to be. Not all were—there were some who were original, creative, and perceptive, but they were a small minority. Most approached the story in unoriginal and often trite ways, summing it up in a single sentence by anyone seeing or reading it: "Here's a cowboy riding his horse across the country, just like in the Old West." Simple as that for most reporters.

Watergate was happening then, and it showed us how the news industry changed from the business of information to the business of entertainment. Even as it brought down a sitting president, the news media—our Fourth Estate—began to abdicate its responsibilities and to alter the definition of news, replacing information with entertainment, education with diversion, and public knowledge with uninformed opinion.

A man in a red jacket with a major media company logo on it spends a half hour preparing his hair and makeup then stands with Gizmo and me on the street corner and reads a list of questions that someone else had written for him. I try to answer them, all the while holding Gizmo so the cameraman can get a good shot of him for a soundbite on the nightly news. Sometimes I encourage the news person to stand next to Gizmo, but they almost never do because they're either afraid of horses or of getting their clothes dirty, or both. A half hour of interview time ends up as thirty seconds on the nightly news.

Gizmo took it all with good humor, as he did everything else. By the time we reached eastern Tennessee and North Carolina, I was aware of an interesting pattern to these interviews. Some of the reporters brought along treats—apples, carrots, sugar cubes—and gave them to Gizmo while we talked. The thing I noticed was, all the interviewers who brought along treats were newspaper reporters. None were television reporters. Not all newspaper writers brought them, but all the treats Gizmo received from reporters along the way were from newspaper people. I've never lost any sleep over that, but I wondered back then about the possible reason for it, and I still do.

Newspaper reporters write their own material. For human interest stories such as ours, they often have at least a day or two to get it done, so they can spend more time with it. Television requires a story to be produced within hours, and today that has shrunk to minutes. Newspaper reporters mostly worked alone. Big city papers often sent a photographer along, but most reporters took their own photographs. Television reporters worked with a crew—sometimes as many as five or six—but always with at least two or three. There was a cameraman, a sound man, and usually a producer. Sometimes, there was a grip and a driver as well. There were often makeup people and others working with the crew. Though I was talking with the reporter, I soon learned that they had very little influence upon what people actually saw and heard. They were the on-air talent, just as Gizmo and I were.

Typically, the stories written in newspapers were closer to the truth than were the televised versions. The writers had more freedom, more space, and often more time to deal with the issues of our story than those who worked in television. That doesn't mean that the print media didn't tweak the narrative to fit their own storyboard. But I found I could be assertive and influence the reporter about what to write, and that, more often than not, they would write what I had said. This didn't work so well for television because they had already written the story and just needed visuals and a very short sound bite to fill in the blanks. In both cases—print and broadcast media—I sometimes played tricks on them just to see if I could plant something in a story.

> *LOGBOOK:*
> *Doing an interview with a man from the local newspaper. He was a bit of a jerk, so I told him my name was Ed Elmer Bennett, and that my horse's name was Cosmo. I told him we had started in Nome, Alaska and were headed for Missoula, Montana. I didn't mention that if that were the case, we had already overshot Missoula by hundreds of miles. But he didn't know any better.*

I mentioned that I had seen a lot of animals killed along the side of the road, and I suggested that maybe more were killed by cars than were killed by hunters. Smelling a juicy story, the reporter jumped on it and asked me how many dead animals I saw along the roadside. When he tried to get a specific number from me, I told him I had no idea. He persisted and kept at me, insisting on getting some sort of roadkill count that could push his story to the front page. It was obvious that he thought he had some sort of scoop. I kept trying to tell him that I really had no idea of the numbers, just that there seemed to be a lot of them along the roadside. Finally, after constant badgering, I gave in and simply made up a number off the top of my head. "About eleven hundred per mile, I think," I told him. I knew it was a ridiculous number. That's one every four or five feet. But he didn't seem to want to do the math, he just penciled it in and included it in the article.

I knew the "John and Gizmo Story" wasn't the most important narrative of the day. And all these years later, it still isn't. It was important to Gizmo and me, but it wasn't truly important to anyone else. I never had bad feelings about the way we were represented in the press. In fact, I'm grateful that we were given all that coverage and notoriety. And it proves that you can't go wrong with a picture of a horse on the cover.

# SPOONS AND BONES

It was close to five o'clock in the afternoon when we made camp on the outskirts of Mountain City, Tennessee. It was a brisk afternoon under a cloudless sky. My jacket was buttoned all the way up, and I hunkered down inside the fleece collar I had sewed on to it. I had been given a pair of warm gloves back near Knoxville, and they came in handy now. In the last few days, several locals had told me to be ready for snow because it often came early to this part of the world. It was the eighth of October, and I hoped the weather would hold long enough to see us through to the end of the ride.

I managed to find a small section of fenced pasture, unused and hidden in a hollow that was off the main road. I could turn Gizmo out on the grass there. Next to the pasture was an old shed that hadn't been opened in years where I could stash my gear. I could even sleep inside if the weather didn't cooperate, though it was a likely dwelling for black widow spiders, and I was naturally wary. When I finished unsaddling and grooming Gizmo, I sorted my gear and began to address my own needs. The days were getting shorter now, and darkness would be upon us soon.

As I was rummaging through my saddlebags for my last packet of dried macaroni, a pickup truck pulled off the dirt road and stopped next to the gate. A man got out, climbed spryly through the barbed wire fence, and came over to our camp.

"Hello there," he said, and held out his hand in greeting.

His grip was strong, and I did my best to return it in kind as we sized each other up. His grey hair and weathered face bespoke a man retired from long years working outdoors.

I invited him into camp and spent some time answering the usual questions about the ride. He had seen us in the paper and allowed as how he had been on the lookout for us for several days. I offered him a seat on a weather-beaten log then lowered myself to the ground and made myself comfortable with my back resting against the nape of my saddle.

We spoke of everyday things: the cost of horse feed, the end of the Vietnam War, the falling price of tobacco for the local farmers, and the project to widen the highway near Bristol. I had the sense that he was assessing what sort of man I was, but in a friendly way. I had been through this process many times, and normally didn't give a second thought to how I measured up, but something about this man made me want to pass his scrutiny.

He had a gruffness about him. He was plainspoken and went straight to the heart of things. He talked sparingly, describing the things he knew and saw. At first glance, he didn't seem to go in for the theoretical. He didn't discuss abstract concepts, but chose instead the practical and the literal. He viewed his world in a direct way, as a simple and unpretentious container in which everything was held in its proper place within the natural order of things. He made basic observations about obvious things—the weather's turning colder; it's important to keep a good pocket knife handy; I'll take a good Ford pickup over a Chevy any day, but a GMC isn't all that bad; a good milk cow costs a lot more than it used to; driving a conventional cab truck is easier on your kidneys than a cab-over—but it gradually emerged that he did, in fact, contemplate the deeper meaning of the world around him.

He had spent his life as a truck driver, working for the county hauling gravel, asphalt, and well-drilling equipment. He had never been much farther in any direction than the Tennessee State Line. He and his wife of fifty-three years had no children, no grandchildren.

"You and your horse come all the way from California? Dang, that's somethin'." He paused in thought. "Never been to California. Been as far as Chattanooga. Been up to Roanoke, too. I reckon California must be a lot different than it is around these parts."

"Yeah, it is," I replied. "There's a great big ocean and a lot of palm trees, oranges, avocados, and things like that."

He looked at the ground while I was talking, but I could see he was paying attention.

"It's pretty crowded in some places, but there are other places there where you can go a long time without seeing anybody else."

"Never seen an avocado. They look like pears, don't they?"

"Well, maybe more like a green summer squash hangin' on a tree," I replied. "They're pretty good on toast with some salt and pepper sprinkled on."

"Well, I'll be ..." He stopped to ponder this, then remarked, "It's a big ol' world out there, isn't it?"

"Yep, it sure is," I replied.

"Like to see one o' them avocado trees sometime. That's a long way to go, but you made it all the way out here on a horse. So, I reckon I could drive it one day."

"It's a lot faster driving than it is riding," I joked.

"What sorta work you do when you're not galavantin' around the country on your horse?" he asked.

"Oh, I do a bit of this and a bit of that," I answered. "I'm a musician, mostly."

"Is that right," he said, more as a statement than a question. "Whatta y'all play?"

"Mostly string instruments.. guitar, mandolin, banjo, bass … those sorts of things," I said.

"Well, I've been known to sit in with some of the pickers around these parts," he said. "I play spoons and bones and do a little hambone too."

An hour later found us sitting on that old log playing music. I had dug my two harmonicas out of the saddlebags, and he'd retrieved his spoons and bones from his truck.

"I always keep 'em with me," he told me.

Gizmo stopped what he was doing and came over to watch.

We started out with "Swanee River" and moved on to some old folk and country songs. We played "T For Texas", by Jimmie Rodgers, and the Carter Family's "Bury Me Beneath The Willow" before playing a few modern country songs from the 1950s. We played "Why Don't You Love Me Like You Used To Do" by Hank Williams and "Waterloo" by Stonewall Jackson. I sang the lyrics to tunes that just popped into my head. "Fishin' Blues," "Jug Band Music," "You Don't Know My Mind," and others that seemed to just sort of materialize.

He was transformed from a slow-moving, weathered old man to a spry, lively and vigorous person who suddenly looked half his years. He played the bones tentatively at first, then gradually loosened up and relaxed. His hands twirled the bones in hypnotic rhythms with spellbinding twists and curls as he tapped out accompaniment to my crude singing and harmonica choruses.

He switched back and forth between the bones and a pair of old silver spoons that he kept in a rosewood box. In between playing the two percussion instruments he used his hands, performing hambone routines with double shuffles and triplets made by slapping his legs and chest and the occasional popping sounds produced when he cupped a hand over his mouth while tapping his cheek with the other. He was a wonder, and I sometimes fumbled with my own parts because I was lost in the spell he created. I looked over at Gizmo and saw that he too was spellbound, his face relaxed, and his eyes half closed, listening to the music.

With the sinking sun, the daylight began to evaporate. The old man slowly packed his bones and spoons into their container and stood to leave.

"Well, I reckon that'll do 'er", he said. "Gotta get on back to the house. There's chickens to feed."

"Enjoyed visitin' with you, and playing music," I replied.

"Well, by golly," he said, extending his hand, "always nice to make a new friend, ain't it?"

"Sure is," I answered as we shook hands.

He turned and headed back to his truck. After a few steps, he paused and turned back to me.

"Think maybe I might do a little travelin' … see if I can't find me one o' them avocado trees. You think one would grow here?" he asked.

"You never know," I replied.

# FOR WANT OF A NAIL

I stood in the corner of the stall, crouched in a farrier's posture, tucked up beneath Gizmo's hind leg. We faced in opposite directions, and I was looking back toward his tail. To support his hind foot while I was trying to nail the new shoe to it, I'd bent my knees and pressed them together, my boots pointing inward in a pigeon toed stance. I had managed to find two horseshoes, size 00 (double-ought), and two small mule shoes. I put the horseshoes on Gizmo's front feet and had to cut the mule shoes down with a large pair of bolt cutters before reshaping them and nailing them to the hind. I borrowed some farrier's tools from a farmer, who also had an old anvil in the corner of his work shed. I used the hammer end of a hatchet to shape the shoes to fit and was able to drive (clumsily) a set of horseshoe nails into his feet. I managed to do all this without hurting Gizmo or myself.

"You know what they say, bud," I told him as I tacked the shoe on, "for want of a nail, the battle was lost."

I didn't explain the logic of that lost nail, which led to losing the shoe, then losing the horse, losing the battle, and finally losing the war. He wasn't much interested, but I continued to talk anyway just to pass the time.

"There's more to it than just losin' the war though," I said.

I was thinking about how our inventions shape us and how we adapt to them. We think we create tools and gadgets to work for us, and maybe we do at first, but it ends up being mostly the other way around. I thought about the horseshoe and its impact on the world. It paralleled the invention of the stirrup. The most noticeable effects of these two inventions were that (A) the stirrup allowed a rider to ride more efficiently and (B) the horse and rider could travel much longer distances and over rougher terrain with the use of the horseshoes. But I got to thinking, there were greater effects than the obvious ones.

"Y'see, bud," I said, "The stirrup was a simple invention, but it was still profound. You have 'em hanging on both sides of your saddle, and they help to keep me from sliding all over the place. Makes life a little bit easier on you that way too."

He had his head in a bucket of oats and wasn't paying attention, but I explained to him that stirrups enabled a rider to carry weapons and other gear, and they freed his hands from having to hang onto the horse for balance. The rider could use a lance or a bow and arrow.

"You know those covered stirrups that are on your saddle? Well, they're not all that different from the very first ones that were used a few thousand years ago on some of your ancestors."

He snorted then looked around at me as I drove another nail home and clinched it.

"I'm guessin' your great-great-great-great grandfather probably had a saddle with some of those old stirrups on it."

As I reached for the rasp to file away the rough edges on the nail clinches, I explained to Gizmo that stirrups went far beyond simply helping the rider. They immediately gave an advantage to cavalry over infantry in battle. They allowed a rider to wear heavy armor. We wouldn't have knights in shining armor if we didn't have stirrups. A lord who could afford a cavalry had the advantage over those who couldn't. Of course, it took a lot of money to maintain a mounted cavalry.

"Now, how about this?" I asked him. "You wouldn't think a stirrup and an economic system would have much in common or could be linked in any way, would you? But you'd be wrong. Y'see, we adapted the economic system to the invention of the stirrup by creating what they call 'aristocratic feudalism.' That's a highfalutin name for a whole culture that allowed feudal lords to finance their armies."

By this time, Gizmo was finished with his oats and was nosing around in the manger, trying to find some sort of distraction. I paid him no mind and kept talking about stirrups and the economy.

As I finished with his hind foot and moved around him to shoe the other one I continued, "Without the invention of those stirrups, things would have been a whole lot different in the western world. Think about that, Gizmo."

He wasn't thinking about it. He didn't care, one way or the other. He turned to look at me, snorted once more, then went back to eating his oats.

I went on to relate how other simple inventions shaped the evolution of seemingly unrelated cultural notions. The clock took what was originally an unbroken stream of time and divided it into units, and then it became the dictator that rules our lives to this day. The automobile didn't only devastate the horse industry, it created a new culture centered around cars.

The word *teenager* wasn't invented until after the car became central to our culture. For the first time, it allowed young people to congregate away from their homes, away from their parents. Teenage culture still drives much of our popular culture.

"See? The car didn't just put you and your kind out of business, Gizmo. It made a whole new culture. But I reckon maybe that's a good thing for horses like you. You know why?"

He paused for a moment and seemed to consider my words, so I continued.

"Well, think about it. Who loves horses the most, nowadays? Right! Little girls! So, even though you're stuck with me, most of your relatives get to live with young girls who brush them and feed them and clean up after them and generally spoil them. You're all hobby horses now, aren't you?" I stopped to consider where we were and how we'd gotten there.

Part of my reason for attempting the ride was to discard some of the ties to the inventions that dictate how we live (although I kept the stirrups). I had no watch, no car, no specific schedule for each day, no pre-planned calendar of events, no phone or other direct communication with others on a daily basis, and no specific ties or obligations or places I had to be at any specific time. My flashlight didn't even work half the time. I wasn't exactly free, in the literal sense, because I did have obligations to myself and to Gizmo, but those were fluid and changing all the time as events unfolded and we were forced to adapt to them.

I drove the last nail in, twisted it off and clinched it. Then I dropped Gizmo's foot to let him stand on it so we could both have a rest. I tapped the clinches down, then smoothed the work over with the horseshoer's rasp. I spoke to him as I was doing this.

"It's a chicken and egg deal, Gizmo. So, whatta ya think? Did we invent these shoes so we could take a long ride?"

He turned to look back at me as I continued.

"Or, are we on this ride because these shoes allow it?"

# THE FORCE OF GRAVITY

We spend our lives doing battle with gravity. It's a mysterious force. We understand its properties. We know what it does, but we don't know how or why. Gravity fastens us to the earth. It causes friction when we try move. It wants to keep us still, to be at rest and confined to a single place, to reach equilibrium. We expend enormous amounts of energy struggling against it, and we do so from the day we are born until the day we die.

They say that walking is nothing more than controlled falling. You don't propel yourself forward. You thrust your foot out in front of you and gravity causes you to fall onto it, and when you do you're already swinging your other foot forward to repeat the process. Controlled falling.

Gizmo and I are so very tired. We have put one foot in front of the other for months in what feels like a losing battle with gravity. Our routine has become second nature, but the pain that we both feel has not. I hurt all over and I know that Gizmo does, too. His eyes no longer carry the sparkle they once had, and though I rarely get a chance to look in a mirror, I know that mine are dull and lifeless as well.

It's so much harder to get up on these cold mornings, and I want more and more to surrender to the pull of gravity and remain in my sleeping bag. I want to remain at rest. I want to reach a permanent equilibrium. Gravity is making even the act of lifting Gizmo's brush to groom him more difficult. His saddle seems to weigh twice what it used to and each morning I fight to gather the resolve to push through another day, another twenty miles. Gizmo has abandoned his habit of rising before dawn every morning to watch the sun rise in the east. Instead, he lies beside me and, like me, does not want to start the day. He is bone weary. He is Sisyphus and I am his stone.

*LOGBOOK:*
*Every day now is more tedious than the last. People and cement and traffic. Barking dogs and motorcycles. I dread each new day now, even though the country is beautiful. Just want it to be over, especially for Gizmo's sake.*

It is late in the evening and we are camped in a small hollow, away from the road and out of sight. We share some of the apples I have torn from trees as we rode through an orchard earlier in the day. Gizmo eats mechanically and takes no pleasure in trying to snatch them from me now. He waits until I offer one, then nibbles dispassionately, neither relishing the one he is eating nor nickering for another. He is going through the motions now, as am I. He wants the ride to be over. I sit leaned against my saddle and read a torn paperback novel that is missing its last pages. I will never know what happens, but I don't care. I keep reading because it is something to do, and I know that I keep riding for the same reason.

Gizmo drags himself over next to me to settle in for the night. He folds his legs beneath him and sinks to the grass. He groans and exhales a long, drawn out sigh, then closes his eyes. His head sinks slowly until his nose rests on the ground and he begins to snore. I reach over and pat his neck and it doesn't wake him. I am devastated by this terrible thing I have done to him, and I crumble beneath the weight of it and start to cry. My tears make small dark spots where they splash against the seat of my saddle.

Gravity has won again.

# THE EAST

There is good grass for Gizmo through here, and he picks up a little weight as we travel. He has learned to reach down, mid stride, and grab mouthfuls of grass as we ride along, not missing a stride. This is not considered to be good behavior for a horse, but I don't care. I allow it—even encourage it. Gizmo learns to eat new things here. Dried corn on the cob, baled peanut vines, and a type of sweet grass that makes his mouth foam and slobber. It seems I am constantly asking questions about horse feed, making sure he doesn't eat something that might make him sick. Horses can't regurgitate their food. They can't throw up. Everything they eat has to pass through. If it doesn't, it if gets stuck along the way, they'll probably die. I worry that Gizmo will eat something unfamiliar and colic, but he seems to be made of iron and the wide variety of feed he as eaten hasn't bothered him so far.

The Tennessee hills grow larger as we reach the eastern part of the state. Peaks and valleys become a bit more pronounced, the road more steep and winding, and the terrain more rugged. We are entering the Appalachian Mountains. The places have names I have heard in bluegrass songs I have played over the years. Names like Cumberland Mountain, Clinch Mountain, Harlan, and Black Mountain.

We are climbing into the Blue Ridge Mountains now, and the deciduous trees are turning shades of yellow, red, and orange. I am awestruck by their beauty, but the road is perilous and logging trucks pass us at high speeds with only inches between us and them. I don't lead Gizmo as much through here because I don't have room to walk next to him. If I walk in front, I am afraid he might wander into the path of a vehicle. We make a smaller footprint when I'm riding, so I spend most of the time in the saddle. My nerves are frazzled now, and I begin to lose my temper sometimes. There is no one to direct my anger toward, and I won't take it out on my horse. I vent by having arguments with myself as I ride. I am frustrated and exasperated and want only for the ride to be finished. As beautiful as the mountains are, I am not enjoying the narrow roads and logging trucks.

We stumble into North Carolina. It is cold now, and it threatens to snow each night. I'm hoping we will be able to make it out of the mountains before the snow hits. We happen upon the Blue Ridge Parkway, a national park highway that has a reduced speed limit and does not allow trucks. It is a lovely road with wide, grassy shoulders and very few vehicles. I feel enormous relief at this and am thankful for small favors.

However, the park ranger drives up and tells me I cannot ride a horse here. He orders us to leave. We are forced back onto a logging road, where we are nearly struck by a log truck within minutes. I turn Gizmo and head back to the Parkway, where we are again stopped by the ranger in his truck. I plead with him that it could be a death sentence if we're forced to take the logging road through the mountains. The ranger acquiesces and allows us to continue along the Parkway.

It is not a long ride through the national park, but it is peaceful and restful, and I can relax. Food is plentiful for Gizmo. We camp in historic sites, in old cabins that have been restored for tourists to visit. No one bothers us. The colors of the trees are magnificent as we cross into Virginia, and we enjoy a few days by ourselves with only an occasional visitor. On our last night in the Appalachians, just before we head down the eastern slope toward the Piedmont area of Virginia, the snow falls.

The snow follows us down the eastern slope of the Appalachians into Virginia. The Piedmont is a large, flat plain that sits between the mountains and the ocean. We are in Virginia now, and I am excited. I have never been to this place. It has been a name on a map for many years now, a destination, *our* destination. My horse has carried me all the way to Virginia, and I am proud of him. I don't mind that it is snowing, though I have to be careful that Gizmo doesn't slip on icy pavement. Because he is shod, snow gathers inside his horseshoes and interferes with his footing. I have to pick the snow out of his feet several times a day because it gets frozen and hard.

The Piedmont isn't exactly flat—not the way the Texas plains were—but it offers much easier travel than the mountains did. The logging trucks had been traveling down the western slope of the mountains, into Tennessee, so they have mostly disappeared now. The roads here have good shoulders. Many people stop to offer places to stay. We pass on most because I decline any that might take us even a mile out of our way. I want my companion to do as little work as possible.

It continues to snow, on and off, for several days. Winter has arrived, and I am glad that our journey is almost at its end. People are friendly and generous, and we are being well fed and cared for along this stretch. Just about every small town newspaper does a story about us, and the television crews drive out to meet us several times along the way.

*LOGBOOK:*
*Gizmo is enjoying the long grass through here. He rolls in it and just lays there, sighing and relaxing. He doesn't mind the snow, and in fact I think it feels good to him. He has grown a bit of coat in the last few weeks, so he's prepared for the winter. I keep watch over him, just to make sure he doesn't get cold, but he's tough and doesn't mind the snow at all.*

Gizmo and I travel through Danville and cross the site of the wreck of the Old 97, where it left the tracks and plunged into the Danville River. I stop to read the memorial plaque there, as I do at all the historical sites we pass along the way. I've happened upon countless plaques like this along the road, found in out-of-the-way places, explaining the history of the area. America's beginnings can be seen here, and I am fascinated by how much history there is and by how many people simply drive past these plaques and never read them. Many describe scenes and events from the Civil War and harken back to times of slavery and a broken Union.

Southern mansions are evidence of Danville's past prosperity, the fabulous wealth gained by the tobacco and textile magnates of bygone years. The accents of the people retain the southern drawl found in Tennessee and North Carolina, though that will disappear as we head farther east into the Tidewater area near the Atlantic Ocean.

Crops have been gathered, cattle, and sheep have been shipped. Farm activity is ending for the winter. Firewood is stacked, and wood smoke lies in the hollows, like cotton amidst the trees. People wear Mackinaw coats and rubber boots, and every morning they scrape the ice off the car's windshield. Kids gather in small groups at the bus stops, wool caps on their heads, their breath making small clouds, as they wait for the bus to take them to school. They wave as Gizmo and I ride past, and I tip my hat in acknowledgement. I enjoy seeing this, and I think Gizmo does, too. It gives the ride a sense of continuity after all these months, as if things are back to normal and life continues as usual.

Gizmo has become something of a regional hero by now, and many who approach already know his name, though few can remember mine. This is fine with me. I want him to have all the credit because he deserves it. I tend to shrink from talking about myself. I don't like blowing my own horn, and feel uncomfortable when describing myself. But I'm at ease when talking about my horse, and I often go on and on about him.

I have grown weary now, and I am a changed person just as Gizmo is a changed horse. I have gained an enormous insight into America, its land and its people, and I realize I have gained insights about myself as well. I have become trail hardened yet hypersensitive to all that is around me. I have been out of contact with friends and family from home for a long time now, and I moved completely outside of any day to day acquaintances, social gatherings, music gigs, or normal events shared with my old social circle. These things now move along with me, no longer tied to the place I live. They change from place to place, from day to day, each replacing one day's social circle with the next. Though I am often among gatherings of people here in the east, I am alone. I share no roots with anyone but my horse. I am my only constant human companion, and other than Gizmo, my only close friend out here on the trail. I talk to myself constantly, just as I talk to him.

I have experienced all of this from what I know to be a very skewed perspective, but still I realize that I have received a rare gift—an insight that no other human has been given. I know instinctively that it will always be with me and that it will take many years before it reveals itself to me fully. Wisdom cannot be rushed, and I promise myself I will allow the journey to take its time sinking in.

> *LOGBOOK:*
> *Every time I've tied Gizmo to a telephone pole or fencepost and gone inside a store to get supplies, when I come out the front door, he sees me and he whinnies like crazy. I know I'm the only constant in his life right now, but it's reassuring to know that he's glad to see me. I'm guessing maybe it's reassuring to him that I've come back after leaving him alone. I know what it's like to be deserted.*

I look at Gizmo and see a wise and mature horse in place of the green colt who set out with me seven months ago. I see an animal that has been dragged through hell and high water and has taken it all in good spirits. Like me, he will never be the same. The ride will leave its mark upon him for the rest of his life. It has transformed him into a free spirit, a drinker from the well of freedom. He has spent seven months on the trail and has never passed the same place twice. He is an inquisitive horse, and his curiosity has kept us moving forward, has kept us both alive on this journey. And each time we pass a storefront window he sees our reflection, and whinnies as if to say, "Look at us!" He knows who those two are.

Occasionally I will catch a glimpse of myself in a mirror, or in a store window. I do not recognize the gaunt, tired, leather skinned man who stares back at me with eyes that squint from long days in the sun. He is experienced, wise, sure of himself. I'm not sure if I am any of those things because I have never known what they feel like. But I know that on the inside, I'm supposed to resemble that man.

I had expected the Piedmont and Tidewater regions to be different from one another, but they blend together, and the landscape doesn't change. I learn that the Tidewater area occupies land where the waterways and lakes are directly affected by ocean tides. That is, they rise and fall with the lunar cycle because they are not divorced from the ocean by waterfalls, landmass, or obstacles. I don't notice the effect because I am seeing mostly rivers and streams, and they don't exhibit the characteristics of tidal change.

The land is still comprised of rolling hills, grassland, small forests, and is mostly agricultural. Peanut vines adjoin the tobacco fields here. The townships are now only a few miles from each other, and we pass through two or three small towns each day. I am often invited into cafes and diners for a cup of coffee, and Gizmo is given apples and carrots and other treats by well-wishers. I have a hard time refusing the coffee on these cold days, even though we are slightly behind schedule. We meet people from all walks of life, representatives of the middle-American work ethic. They are friendly and kind, and I am grateful for that.

We set our sights on the great eastern ocean.

# THE END OF THE TRAIL

The Piedmont flattened when we finally reached the coastal plain near Chesapeake and Norfolk, Virginia. It was all city now, and we struggled to make our way toward the edge of the continent. We encountered large waterways with great bridges to cross, and it was tedious going, but I caught the smell of the sea, even many miles inland. Gizmo seemed to sense it, too, and it became like a magnet to us.

October 31, was destined to be our last night on the trail. I found a semi-hidden camp in a memorial garden (a graveyard), which was as far into the city of Virginia Beach as I could manage. I had wanted to get closer to the ocean so that we wouldn't have so far to go on our last day. We had managed to make it across the Elizabeth River in Chesapeake. We had no more major obstacles in our way, except for the city streets and the traffic in Virginia Beach. Gizmo was on his seventh set of shoes, and they needed to last only one more day.

It's ironic that we spent Halloween night in a graveyard. Even more ironic was the fact that it was a full moon. I didn't realize it was Halloween, and I was a bit unprepared for all the noise and odd bits of craziness that occurred that night. Only when I sat down to make my log entry did I see that it was October 31. Fortunately, none of the revelers came near the cemetery, and Gizmo and I were left to ponder our last night on the trail alone, with only the ghosts of the city's former residents for company. And even when I realized what night it was, it didn't really dawn on me that the next day was going to be the first of November. In every single one of my projections, going back several years, I had chosen November first as the date we would finish the ride. During press interviews back in April, the day before we left Ventura, I had given November first as the date we would arrive at the Atlantic Ocean. I hadn't meant to predict it as an exact date. It was an arbitrary choice, though I'd hoped we would finish within ten days or so, either side of that mark.

But the fact is, I didn't care about that. We were tired and road weary, and we needed to stop once and for all. We had struggled through weeks of tough progress along narrow roads without shoulders, the trucks and camper vans passing so close that had I stuck my hand out, they would have hit me. My nerves were pretty well shot, my temper at times stretched to the limit. Gizmo, bless his honest heart, sucked it up and kept soldiering on. I was out of money and had been so focused upon finishing the ride that I hadn't given any thought to the return trip home.

I walked almost the entire way that final day, almost six hours leading my tired horse. It was too dangerous to ride on the city streets. The traffic was thick, and many people honked their horns at us as we made our way to the ocean. Indian Summer had suddenly come, and the weather was warm for the last few days of the ride. The first of November was warm, with the temperature in the high seventies. The sun felt good on my back as I navigated the urban obstacles in Virginia Beach and guided Gizmo to the ocean. I dismounted when we arrived and I paused to look out at it. Our destination had become anticlimactic in the scope of what we had been through in the past seven months. It seemed almost incidental, but we reached the end of the ride. I was happy.

I don't have any selfies of our arrival. I didn't think to take my camera out of the saddlebags, though I doubt I would have taken photos even if I had remembered the camera. What few pictures I have were taken by others and kindly given to me later. But I don't need a selfie to call up that picture in my mind. It's always there.

I see us arriving at the Atlantic Ocean. We make our way down Virginia Beach Boulevard, which ends at an old pier. I step down off Gizmo and coax him down a short flight of concrete stairs and out onto the sand. A crowd of people waits there—photographers and news media, well-wishers and even some that you might call fans. I step up into the stirrups for the last time and ride him down to meet the incoming tide. He wades in up to his knees, but keeps his eyes and ears pointed out toward the horizon. He thinks I want him to swim it, and he has finally had enough and starts to get a hump in his back. I don't relish the thought of getting bucked off into the ocean in front of a bunch of news cameras so I smile and turn him back to shore.

*LOGBOOK:*
*Took a long time to get to the ocean today. Lots of traffic and well wishers who wanted to stop and talk. Finished up at the end of Virginia Beach Blvd, at an old pier. Jumped Gizmo off some steps down onto the sand. A big crowd was there to cheer us on. Rode him belly deep into the Atlantic Ocean. It*

*felt like a million bucks with everyone gathered around,
congratulating us and taking pictures. Went for a long walk
alone with Gizmo and just talked to him. It's an odd feeling,
but we have nowhere to go. It's the first time that I've felt that
Gizmo and I are truly all alone.*

After the handshakes, congratulations, interviews, and picture taking are
over, Gizmo and I take a long walk down the beach by ourselves. I tell him
what a fine horse he is and what a big heart he has. I reach back into one of
the saddlebags and pull out a Snickers bar that I'd been keeping for the
occasion. I mean to break it in half and share it with him as a sort of toast
to our success. Instead, Gizmo snatches it out of my hand and eats the
whole thing. I reckon he deserves it, and I laugh out loud. As we walk alone
along the wet sand, I pat his neck and say, "Thanks, bud."

The ride is over, but our life's journey together has only just begun. I
look out to sea and whisper a thank you to Wayward and Sammy, and I see
their faces against the Atlantic sky.

We walk along the Atlantic shore. Together, my horse and I have
crossed an entire continent. I realize we have run out of trail, and we have
no place to spend the night. The ocean is in front of us, and we can only
make a sharp turn to the left or right. The fork in the trail points north or
south. I turn to Gizmo and say, "Well buddy, what the hell are we supposed
to do now?"

# THE RIDE DEFINES ME

During the ride, I never gave much thought to what might happen once it was over, or how it might affect my life in the years to come. I've always figured it was the journey that was important. The destination, not so much. So, while the goal was the Atlantic Ocean, it wasn't the real prize. I knew that before we ever started.

The real prize was this pile of memories I now have in my head. It was the experience and the wisdom gained on a whole lot of levels. Getting to Virginia Beach was an accomplishment, but it wasn't the trophy. It signaled the end of something though, just as it signaled the beginning of something else. You could say my life was split into two sections—*Before the Ride* and *After the Ride*. But that's not exactly true because I'm still on that journey. I reached one destination back in 1974, but it was just a signpost along the road, a waypoint, a bellwether that set my horse and I on a new trail.

A journey like that changes who you are. Aspects of it stick with you for the rest of your life. It changes the ways in which you see things, the things you take for granted, the things you love, and the things you think you hate. A person washes their car in the driveway, and the water pours out of the hose and down the gutter. I know now that I would lay down and drink from that gutter and be glad for it. The ride changed how I think about the world around me and how I view myself within the larger scheme of things. And the parts of it that I have clung to have sent me down my own path, whether I like it or not.

I set out to change myself somehow. I figured I could control how that change took place and what sorts of transformations I would experience. But that's not how it works. It's a bit like trying to lift yourself off the Earth by pulling on your own hair. You can leave the ground momentarily, but it won't be the pulling that does it. Something else causes it, something unseen, something you hadn't expected.

The idea of seeing my horse's hoofprints in the sand at the Atlantic Ocean was just a dream, even up to the day we finished. And when I finally saw them there, I realized I hadn't thought it out very well. It was still just a dream in my head, even as we walked along that eastern shore. The reality of what would happen next didn't settle in on me right away. It came slowly, in bits and pieces.

It sounds cliché, but it all boiled down to knowing who I really was. I thought I knew myself before I made the ride. I didn't. I was a fool who thought I knew my beliefs, my ideals, my strengths and weaknesses. But the upshot is, I had no idea how far down inside myself I would have to reach to touch the cradle of my own resolve. I thought that somehow this accomplishment would rid me of the stigma of abandonment left years before, a burden of shame left to a young boy, and that it would erase a legacy I didn't even know I owned.

I left the California coast with a view of myself as the caretaker, and Gizmo as my charge. It turns out it was the other way around. My young horse was the pilot, steadfast and faithful, trustworthy and dependable. He was my guide and my mentor, the rock I leaned on every day, and the wellspring from which I drew my faith and inspiration. In his own quiet and goofy way, he was my mirror. As I sat in camp watching him, talking to him hour after hour, day after day, month after month on the trail, I began to see my own image reflected in him. He showed me that I couldn't predict how I would behave when things turned bad. I had always thought that I knew myself well enough to know how I'd react to a given situation. I was wrong, and I learned that from seeing my own reflection in my horse.

Once the ride began I settled into the routine of daily travel. I learned what worked on the trail and what didn't. That seven month ride amounted to over 5,000 hours, and I spent most of those with no one except a four year old horse for company. It wasn't the first time I had spent long hours by myself, but it was the first time there was someone else to think of. I could have made the ride on a bicycle, and I would have been truly alone. Gizmo's presence created a dependence and the need for a shared trust.

Locking a bicycle to a post while you go into a cafe for a meal is not the same thing as tying a horse to that post and going in. You can leave the bike there without worry. The worst thing that can happen is that someone might steal it. It won't come untied and run out into traffic. It doesn't need to eat or drink, so you can leave it there for days if you like. But you have to keep an eye on your horse—*always*. He is completely dependent upon you, as you are upon him. He trusts you to care for him and to protect him. And he is *company*. He is your companion, your pal, your confidant, your best friend. You might name your bicycle, but it won't respond to you when you call its name. You can be alone with a bicycle, but you're never alone when you're with a horse.

I hadn't given any thought to following up on the ride by writing or doing interviews, or any activities tied to the journey. I hadn't considered, even for a moment, making money from the ride, or capitalizing on it in any way. To be honest, I hadn't even thought about where we were going to spend the night when we reached the Atlantic Ocean and ran out of trail. A bit of notoriety had visited us as we made our journey, but I knew this would fade quickly and soon become a thing of the past. I had done what I set out to do, and that was that. Gizmo had done more than a horse should ever have to do, and I meant for him to live out his days in a good way, not as an oddity or attraction for people to point their cameras at.

Toward the end of the ride we were invited by the American Quarter Horse Association to be guests of honor at the Quarter Horse Congress, their year-end championships in Louisville, Kentucky. Truth be told, they didn't care about me, but Gizmo was a Quarter Horse and was a star in their eyes. That was fine with me. I told them we'd be happy to attend if we could get there somehow. Luck was with us, and we managed to hitch a ride with a local Virginia couple who were taking their horse to the show and had an empty spot in their horse trailer. Once at the event, Gizmo was given a stall, along with bedding, hay and grain. I had about ten bucks in my pocket, and I didn't let on that I couldn't afford a hotel room. At night, I excused myself early from any functions or gatherings and slipped off to stay in the stall with Gizmo, and no one was the wiser. Truth be told, I was more comfortable staying in the horse barn with him.

We met a lot of celebrities and were toasted over and over for our accomplishment. We were trotted out into the main arena a few times to be introduced to enthusiastic crowds. They wanted me to saddle Gizmo and ride him into the arena, but I declined. He had been ridden enough. My family sent a bright red horse blanket that had maps of the United States embroidered on its sides with the words *Transcontinental Ride* and a crooked line that represented our journey. So I dressed him in that, and I led him into the arena. During the week we were in Louisville, I asked around and found a reining horse trainer from California who had an empty stall in his truck. I offered to help drive if he would give us a lift back home. In effect, we made the entire return trip home by hitchhiking.

It's easy now to look back in hindsight and know what I could have done when the ride was over—maybe what I should have done—and compare those things to what I ended up doing. I was still young, and so was Gizmo. I had no idea what life had in store for me, but I wasn't going to wait around to find out. I needed to survive, so over the next few months I wrote a series of articles for *Horse & Rider Magazine*. They ran for seven issues the following year, starting in April of 1975 and running parallel with the seven months we had spent on the trail in 1974. I wrote another piece for the inaugural issue of *Horse Illustrated*. As a way of giving back, I donated my time by giving speeches and presentations for environmental and trail groups and other organizations.

During the course of those writing exercises I wrote a rough draft of a book manuscript. It evolved into a large tome of episodic and mostly boring accounts of our exploits, and I knew that it wasn't worth publishing—not because the story was bad, but because I was too close to it at the time, too caught up in it still. I didn't care for what I had written but it began to gain interest by word of mouth from movie people— producers and writers and such—who saw potential in the story for film or television. I spent several months going to interviews in fancy offices at studios and in lavish Beverly Hills homes and with all sorts of Hollywood types. I must admit that it was seductive, and I got caught up in it for a little while. But as I said, I was a bit too close to it all then.

All this time Gizmo was doing what horses are meant to be doing; he was enjoying life in a huge pasture in the mountains near Santa Barbara, turned out for a year to simply graze and wander the hills and valleys with a small band of horses and mules. I drove my old Chevy pickup truck up to visit him every so often, and he always whinnied and came running when he saw me. The ride had changed him. He whinnied every time I came to see him. For years, when we lived together and I walked outside to the corrals, he would whinny whenever he saw me. It lasted for the rest of his life. My intellect tells me it was a sort of Pavlovian response mechanism, but my heart tells me he was simply glad to see me. I'll stick with my heart on this one.

It was those trips to visit Gizmo up in that pasture that ultimately saved me from myself. I was so focused upon pitching our story as a film script that I lost my way for a while. I abandoned who I had become out on that trail, and I tried to adopt the lifestyle that accompanies the movie making world. I envied those who were successful in the business, and envisioned myself as one of them.

But then, I would drive out to the ranch where Gizmo was staying and I would hike the hills until I found his horse herd. I'd call to him, and he'd whinny and come running up to me. Of course, I always had carrots or apples and a Snickers bar to feed him. And as soon as I reached to pat his neck, it was like touching a grounding rod that took me back to the trail and centered me instantly. I know that sounds a bit corny, but the truth of it is that, bit by bit, I came to realize that selling a book or a movie wasn't a dream of mine. I had no real interest in living a Hollywood life, and my journey toward it wasn't one I was enjoying.

After a time, I began to see that I could easily spend the rest of my life reliving the past. I had a horror of becoming a caricature of myself, living off the stories I told and allowing myself to be defined forever by a single event. I pictured myself telling the same stories over and over for years. I had always been one for looking ahead, and not so much for looking behind. A cowboy friend once told me, "Lookin' back don't drag much water when you're drawin' puncher's pay." I've always subscribed to that notion, and still do. So I tossed the manuscript into a box along with some other memorabilia, and I forgot about it for a very long time. The truth is, I have never read it since.

We go on with our lives and continue to experience new things. We don't have to be defined by one thing. We're pretty versatile beings. We're tough, and we're adaptable. We can reinvent ourselves almost endlessly. But we have to *want* to grow. And through that reinvention, that growth process of redefining and reclassifying, we become more human. Ultimately, it was the ride, and a four year old sorrel horse that taught me that.

There's a fork in the trail ahead, and I know I can choose either path. I can still hear Gizmo's whinny across the years, reminding me.

# AFTER THE RIDE

Once the ride was over and we were back home in California, Gizmo spent a good deal of time out to pasture, just hanging out with his equine pals. We lived in Santa Barbara for a while and made some pack trips back into wilderness areas around those parts. We moved to New Mexico a few years later, where he lived out his days under big skies and open country. He was ruined as a show horse prospect, or as a cow or reining horse, though we did help gather cattle now and then, but he was great on pack trips and trail rides.

When he was twenty two he grew ill. He lost weight, had intestinal and urinary problems, and his disposition grew cranky and erratic. Tests revealed that he had Pars Intermedia Pituitary Adenoma. That's a fancy medical term for what is known as Cushing's Disease, which is basically a benign tumor in the brain. Though benign, it causes lots of serious problems, especially in older horses, and there was no cure for Gizmo. Winter was coming on and he would have to face the cold and snow. He was twenty two years old and I didn't want him to have to go through the punishment.

I spent Gizmo's last morning alone with him, just talking and sharing some final hours together. It was a cold, bright November day. Spending the hours with him was entirely for my own sake, and I knew it wouldn't do him any real good, but I played my harmonica for him and just visited with him for a long time. He seemed relaxed and happy, listening to the music. I called the vet out and held him while the doctor gave him an injection. I eased his head down as he gently settled to the ground, and I sat there cradling him as he died. I dug his grave and buried him there, on the high desert of northern New Mexico. As I shoveled the earth over him, dark clouds rolled in overhead and it began to snow lightly. But I didn't see the coming storm as a dark sign or bad omen. The snow fell gently, in big flakes, and by the time I had finished burying him his grave was white. It was a peaceful scene. It felt like he was saying thank you.

# EPILOGUE: THE LIGHT FROM THE STARS

They say that when you're looking at the stars, you're seeing them as they were hundreds, or thousands, or millions of years ago. That the light you're seeing has traveled countless miles, over countless eons, to finally reach you. To see a star is to look into its past. You are that star's future.

The water flows under a bridge near where you are. It's a small bridge that crosses a small stream—small, at least, when there haven't been torrential storms that transform it into a formidable, raging river. And for now, it's small, but it flows surely and steadily downhill to the ocean. You know it's no accident that you are drawn here. You can't help but reflect upon all the water that's passed under the bridge. Downstream is what has passed. Upstream is what is coming. Downstream is what was, upstream is what will be.

The water passes beneath you and heads downstream to become part of the past. There is no control over it, except for how you remember it. The river affects you in some ways, even if you don't know what they are. It leaves its mark upon you, and if you've thrown something into that river, you have left your mark upon it as well. The water enters your life and leaves it just as quickly. You can see upstream for a short way—toward the future—but the river turns a corner and shifts from view.

You take your young horse and put him through an ordeal of cruel hardship for seven months, and you do the same to yourself. You've benefitted from it all, and you know that ordeal has changed your horse. You see him as being better for it all, as having become something more than he was. He is a legend now. He has grown through all the hard times and misfortunes, along with the good times and blessings. But you view him through your eyes and not through his. You cannot know how he felt about it, except that he was *alive* through it all. He was engaged and aware, curious and interested, and his inquiring mind was pushed and prodded beyond any normal life he could have lived.

Looking back across the years, you know he was happy because you *knew him*. He was your horse, and he was your best friend for two decades. He was in pain during the ride. He suffered, and so did you. You could have put an end to the suffering. He had no choice in the matter. As you look downstream through your own eyes at what has passed, you know that he was the better for it all, that it made him the horse he was.

The water flows beneath you, and you think to yourself that it's been flowing there all along. It was flowing like this back then, four decades ago when your horse carried you four thousand miles across a continent. The river changes with every moment, but it seems the same as it was all those years past. It is perpetual and continuous. It is an unbroken chain of events that carries you downstream. It *seems* constant, predictable, and knowable, because the riverbed itself is all those things. The river is capricious and ever-changing, but it runs within a predictable and stable container.

You look downstream and know that the river carries your trail dust there, to the place where your memories lie. You turn to look in the other direction, and you see the starlight that shines from around the bend in the river, upstream into the future. You find yourself in your bedroll, hunkered down for the night once more, and your young horse comes over and lies down beside you.

# ABOUT THE PHOTOGRAPHS

I took most of these photgraphs myself, using a beat up Minolta single lens reflex camera that was already six years old in 1974. It was a time long before handheld phone cameras and selfies, so I generally had to set the camera's mechanical timer, click the shutter, then run and get in the picture, all while trying to appear cool and nonchalant. What you don't see are the dozens of failed attempts. Gizmo, of course, couldn't have cared less for the camera and oftentimes wandered out of the frame at the last second. So, there were plenty of pictures taken of his feet and hindquarters as he exited the shot.

I did not have a tripod (weight issues) so I had to make do with whatever presented itself as a substitute. This generally involved using a rock or a pile of dirt to prop up the camera. Sometimes I would have to lie in the dirt, get a fix through the viewfinder, and jump up and quickly dust myself off as I ran to get in the picture. It didn't always work out. The real problem was that I never got to see any of my photos during the ride. I sent the film home and it wasn't developed and printed until I returned to California.

I used mostly black and white 35 millimeter film, ASA 400. I'm not a photographer, so I don't know all the technical details, and that's about all I remember of it. I did use some color slide film, and those photos have managed to stay in decent shape through the years, probably because I've kept all of them in a sealed box for decades.

The camera had a zoom lens that let me take long shots. If memory serves me well, it was 80-200 mm, so was a reasonably versatile lens for outdoor activities, though it didn't do too well indoors. It had no flash attachment. You photographers will know more about this stuff than I do. All I knew how to do was aim, focus and shoot, though I did get a quick lesson about apertures and shutter speeds from a friend before we hit the trail.

Many photos were sent to me by people we met along the trail, and by news photographers and passersby who stopped to take pictures. I am forever indebted to them, as the pictures of Gizmo and me riding were (for obvious reasons) not taken by me. The only videos I'm aware of would have been interviews on TV news stations across the country. Since Gizmo and I were always on the trail by the time they aired, I have never seen any of them.

Collecting pictures and memorabilia from the ride wasn't a a priority for me, though these days I'm glad that I managed to hang onto some over all these years. I'm still one for watching and experiencing an event instead of documenting and taking photos and video of it. My camera spent most of its time in its leather case, stuffed down in the bottom of one of my saddlebags. The lens had its own case, and was stuffed down into the other saddlebag on order to balance the load. As such, it became a bit of an ordeal to get to the camera in order to take a picture, and I generally didn't bother during the day while we were riding. I waited until I made camp.

A word about the treatment of the photos here: they are all sepia tone (unless you have the greyscale version of the book). They started as digital scans from negatives, slides, and photographs. These were all different shapes, sizes, and colors. There were color slides, black and white prints, and both color and black and white negatives to transfer. There was a wide variety, and because of aging and quality issues (mostly for the color photos) I rendered them in sepia. I apologize in advance to those for whom this doesn't seem authentic. And no, I'm sorry. As luck would have it, I don't have a photo of that old Minolta camera.

# THE AUTHOR

John Egenes has been a musician, a saddlemaker, a dog catcher, and a hobo, among other things. He only learns by making mistakes and he views his life through a windshield full of squashed bugs. He makes his home in New Zealand.

Visit John and Gizmo on Facebook:

www.facebook.com/johnandgizmo/

Made in United States
North Haven, CT
06 January 2022

14300274R00159